For Sophie and Tony
with all my best wishes

David Hunt.

1/11/1982

FOOTPRINTS IN CYPRUS

FOOTPRINTS IN CYPRUS

An illustrated history

edited by

Sir David Hunt

Contributors

Prof. J. N. Coldstream
Sir David Hunt
Dr Vassos Karageorghis
Dr E. J. Peltenburg
Sir Steven Runciman
Dr V. A. Tatton-Brown

TRIGRAPH — London

First published 1982 by
Trigraph Limited
21–25 Earl St., London EC2A 2HY

© Trigraph Limited 1982
(Acknowledgements for picture credits are due to each individual copyright
owner whose name is given under List of Illustrations)

British Library Cataloguing in Publication Data

Footprints in Cyprus

   1.   Cyprus — History
I. Hunt, *Sir* David
954.45   DS54.5

ISBN 0-9508026-0-3

Printed in Great Britain by
Dorriston Ltd.
Dorriston House, 21–25 Earl St.,
London EC2A 2HY

This book is dedicated
to the memory of
A. G. Leventis
a distinguished Cypriot whose
devotion to his native
island was expressed in
many generous benefactions

LIST OF CONTRIBUTORS

Dr E. J. Peltenburg

is Lecturer in Near Eastern Archaeology in the University of Edinburgh; he has excavated in Cyprus and the Middle East and contributed to the catalogue of the British Museum exhibition "Cyprus B.C."

Dr Vassos Karageorghis

is Director of Antiquities, Cyprus and has been in charge of many excavations there including those of the royal tombs of Salamis. He has published several books including 'Excavations in the Necropolis of Salamis', 'Kition' and the 'Civilisation of Prehistoric Cyprus.'

Prof. Nicholas Coldstream

is Professor of Aegean Archaeology in Bedford College, University of London and a Fellow of the British Academy; he has published books on 'Greek Geometric Pottery', 'Kythera, Excavations and Studies' (with G. L. Huxley), 'Knossos: the Sanctuary of Demeter', 'Geometric Greece'.

Dr Veronica Tatton-Brown

is an Assistant keeper in the Department of Greek and Roman Antiquities at the British Museum; she has excavated in Cyprus, South Italy and Carthage and edited and contributed to the catalogue of the British Museum exhibition "Cyprus B.C."

Sir Steven Runciman

is an Honorary Fellow of Trinity College, Cambridge and a Fellow of the British Academy; he has written numerous books on Byzantine history, his latest being 'The Byzantine Theocracy' and 'Mistra: Byzantine Capital of the Peloponnese'.

Sir David Hunt

is a former British High Commissioner in Cyprus, who before entering the Diplomatic Service was a historian and archaeologist (Fellow of Magdalen College, Oxford); he has written two autobiographical books. 'A Don at War' and 'On the Spot — an Ambassador Remembers'.

CONTENTS

PREFACE

There need be no apology for attempting a new comprehensive history of Cyprus from its origins in the neolithic age to the present day. Sir George Hill's "History of Cyprus" in four volumes, published between 1940 and 1952, and reprinted in 1972, is a work which is unlikely to be surpassed or superseded in its kind. It is a monument of British scholarship; it is also, for all its length and comprehensiveness, most enjoyable reading. Since it was written knowledge has increased, as is inevitable, both of the past and of the continuing process that we call the present. Looking back down the immensely long corridor of Cyprus history we can see fresh light breaking in at many points thanks to the discoveries of the archaeologists which have illuminated the nature of the earlier civilisations and provided *Footprints in Cyprus* with many colourful illustrations. In this respect it is fully up to date. Shortening our focus to take in the past two decades we are conscious from our daily reading during the period of the violent changes that have taken place. The most tragic was eight years ago, caused by the action of an outside power, and there are, as I write, no signs of an alleviation of the troubles of the Republic of Cyprus.

The lessons of the present situation in which the island finds itself are reflected also in its earlier history. Because it has always been more acted upon than active, a proper understanding of that history calls for a full appreciation of the changing international scene in the Eastern Mediterranean. The dominating power in the area, based on one of the three continents of Europe, Asia or Africa, has throughout the centuries found itself, by some inevitability, in possession of Cyprus; the effect of these external influences is what is meant by the title "Footprints in Cyprus". It would be quite wrong, on the other hand, to suppose that Cypriot civilisation was in consequence without any definite character of its own. At least since the arrival of the Greeks, nearly three-and-a-half millennia ago, it has developed as part of the Hellenic heritage; with variations indeed, similar to those which can be found in other Greek lands, but in essence remarkably faithful to its root in Homeric times and to the legacy of Athens and Constantinople.

That is another reason for the impulse which the modern tragedy of Cyprus·has given to the production of this book. One of the bitter consequences has been a great increase in the number of emigrants who have left their native island, often with no expectation of returning. Many English-speaking countries, and especially Great Britain, now have large Cypriot communities. There is an evident danger that their families will grow up estranged from their history and their civilisation. It is for them that this book is particularly intended. They will find a concise but adequate historical narrative illustrated with reminders of the principal material elements of their civilisation. At the same time the British public in general, who have shown affection for Cyprus not least by choosing it so often for their holidays, will be able to understand what they see when they are there and to connect it with a historical past in which they also had their share for some eight hundred years.

ACKNOWLEDGEMENTS

My first acknowledgement must be to the publishers Trigraph Limited and its directors Iro Hunt, Demetra David and Fofi Kyriakides, three public-spirited Cypriots who specially commissioned this book. Of the three I should like to thank in particular my wife Iro for making it a work of love to collect the illustrations and to plan and supervise the artistic production of this, the first illustrated history of Cyprus.

My second is to the distinguished authors who have contributed the first six and the eighth chapters: Dr E. J. Peltenburg, Dr Vassos Karageorghis, Prof. Nicholas Coldstream, Dr Veronica Tatton-Brown, Sir Steven Runciman. In addition Dr Veronica Tatton-Brown and her husband Tim Tatton-Brown have been specially helpful in other ways also over the preparation of the book.

I must acknowledge with gratitude the generous help of the British Museum and British Museum Publications Ltd. I appreciate the assistance given by members of the staff: Mr Philip Attwood, Mr D. M. Bailey, Mrs R. Bennett, Miss Susan Bird, Mrs Celia Clear, Mr B. F. Cook, Mr Stephen Pewsey, Dr M. Price and Dr Susan Walker. The Department of Antiquities of the Republic of Cyprus, under its brilliant Director Dr Vassos Karageorghis, has helped immeasurably. Between them these two institutions are responsible for a large number of the finest illustrations reproduced here. Many were also provided by the Greek publishing firm *Ekdotike Athenon S.A.* for which I am grateful to Mr John Bastias. Their publication *"Istoria tou Ellenikou Ethnous"*, in several volumes, on which we have been allowed to draw as a source, particularly of colour plates, is a monument to Greece and its history In the list of illustrations will be found full details of the museums, publishing companies and individuals to whom we acknowledge our indebtedness. Among the last category I should like to give special mention to Mr Reno Wideson and Mr Andreas Malecos.

For their invaluable help and advice I should like to thank Dr Andreas and Dr Judith Stylianou, who are second to none in their knowlege of the wall-paintings of Cypriot churches. Their book on the subject, in a much more extended and comprehensive form, is now about to be republished. To Mr A. Nicolas I am grateful for his wide knowledge of engravings and for the use of his collection of illustrations of Cypriot scenes taken from the Illustrated London News. I should like to thank Dr Homer Habibis and Mr Constantine Leventis for the use of their libraries. To those already mentioned there should be added: The Cyprus High Commissioner in London, H.E. Mr Tasos Panayides, and his Press Officer Mr S. Georgallis; the Public Information Office, Nicosia, and its Acting Director Mr K. Psyllides; the Cyprus Tourist Organisation and its London Director Mr N. Kofou; Madame Annie Caubet; Mr Remy Gorgé; Mr Aristides Coudounaris; Mr John Dickie; Mr Stathis Finopoulos; Mrs Eleni Georgopoulos; Lord Harding of Petherton; Mr George Lanitis; Mr P. Loverdos; the *Lykion ton Hellinidon*, London; Dr Antis Nicolaides; Mr W. W. Percival-Prescott; Mr H. C. Perry; Mr Martin Pick; Mr Polyvios G. Polyviou; Mr David Symons; Mr Paul Williamson.

And finally I should like to thank Mr George Dicomites, Managing Director of Dorriston Limited, printers of the book, for his personal enthusiasm and involvement and his staff for their individual efforts in its production.

9

LIST OF ILLUSTRATIONS AND PHOTOGRAPHIC ACKNOWLEDGEMENTS

The Editor and Publishers are indebted to each individual copyright owner for allowing the use of their photographs; to the Trustees of all the museums where the objects are found; and to other publishers and individuals for their co-operation. Photographs of objects in the Cyprus Museum are published by the kind permission of the Museum and the Director of Antiquities of the Republic of Cyprus. In addition to the sources mentioned below, we would like to thank British Museum Publications Limited for their co-operation with colour plates on pages 33, 34, 37, 48, 52, 58, 65, 78 and *Ekdotike Athenon S.A.* for those listed under their own name as well as those on pages 20, 21 and 57. Photographs from the British Museum are reproduced by courtesy of the Trustees.

178.	The Cathedral of St. Nicholas, Famagusta	Cyprus Tourist Organisation
179.	The Cathedral of St. Nicholas	Cyprus Tourist Organisation
180.	Stone relief from Cyprus; Victoria and Albert Museum	Victoria and Albert Museum (Photograph by Reno Wideson)
181.	"The Feast of Five Kings" — oil painting depicting the Master of the Vintners' Company of London entertaining king Peter I (original in the Royal Exchange, London) KEO (Wines and Spirits), Limassol	KEO Ltd
182.	Wall-painting of a woman donor, Panayia Phorviotissa, Asinou	Andreas Malecos
183.	"The Presentation of Christ in the Temple" — Ayios Nicolaos tis Stegis, Kakopetria	Andreas Malecos
184.	King John II — from the diary of Georg von Ehingen	A. Nicolas
185.	Sgraffiato bowl and goblet; British Museum	British Museum
186.	Buffavento Castle	Reno Wideson
187.	St. Hilarion Castle	Reno Wideson
188.	A. The harbour and castle of Kyrenia; wood engraving; Illustrated London News, 1878	A. Nicolas
188.	B. Kantara Castle; wood engraving; Illustrated London News, 1878	A. Nicolas
189.	Coats of Arms on Kolossi Castle	Director of Antiquities
190.	Kantara Castle	Ekdotike Athenon S.A.
191.	Kolossi Castle	Ekdotike Athenon S.A.
192.	1. Silver denier of Guy de Lusignan; British Museum	British Museum
192.	2. Base gold besant of Hugh I; British Museum	British Museum
192.	3. Base gold besant of Henry I; British Museum	British Museum
192.	4. Base gold besant of Henry II; British Museum	British Museum
192.	5. Silver gros of Hugh IV; British Museum	British Museum
192.	6. Silver gros of Peter I; British Museum	British Museum
192.	7. Silver gros of Peter II; British Museum	British Museum
192.	8. Silver gros of James I; British Museum	British Museum
192.	9. Silver gros of John II; British Museum	British Museum
192.	10. Silver gros of Charlotte; British Museum	British Museum
192.	11. Silver gros of James II; British Museum	British Museum
192.	12. Silver gros of Catherine; British Museum	British Museum
193.	Ten miniature compositions depicting the legend of the Discovery of the Holy Cross; church of the Holy Cross of Ayiasmati	Andreas Stylianou
194.	"The Presentation of the Virgin Mary in the Temple" Holy Cross of Ayiasmati, Platanistasa	Andreas Malecos
195.	"The Virgin Mary and the Archangels" Holy Cross of Ayiasmati (Stavros tou Ayiasmati)	Andreas Malecos
196.	"The Birth of Christ"; Holy Cross of Ayiasmati	Cyprus Tourist Organisation
196.	Silver gros of Catherine; British Museum	British Museum
197.	Catherine Cornaro by Titian, Uffizi Gallery, Florence	BBC Hulton Picture Library
198.	Catherine Cornaro, School of Bellini, Sydney University	Sydney University
199.	"St. George and St. Theodore"; Ayios Nicolaos tis Stegis, Kakopetria	Andreas Stylianou
200.	"Venice pays homage to Catherine Cornaro", by Hans Makart	BBC Hulton Picture Library
201.	The Virgin Mary *Orans*, church of the Archangel, Galata	Reno Wideson
201.	The church of Panayia Podithou, Galata	Director of Antiquities

16

I
NEOLITHIC TO LATE BRONZE AGES
7000(?)–1600 B.C.

To imagine that the fertile island of Cyprus lay deserted while there was settled village life on the intervisible coasts of Syria and Anatolia and while boats crisscrossed the Aegean to exchange precious stone from Melos seems hardly credible, yet that is precisely the situation before c. 6000 B.C. as revealed by archaeology. Most nearby populations had progressed beyond what has been called the Agricultural Revolution and were engaged in farming activities which, amongst other things, encouraged population growth. Despite these increased numbers, Cyprus remained unoccupied. Or did it? Is our evidence simply deficient on this critical point and are there hidden under the alluvium mantle of the Central Plain or buried in the limestone caves of the Kyrenia Mountains the elusive traces of Palaeolithic man? Only future investigations can decisively clarify the issue and, at present, all one can do is search the records of the earliest attested communities on the island and the general situation in the East Mediterranean basin for clues about their origins: natives, colonists, or a mixture of both?

By any standards, these communities are remarkable. In a relatively short period some developed into large, fortified centres with population estimates for the largest, Khirokitia near the south coast, of around two thousand inhabitants. This precocious centre, however, lacked many of the characteristics that accompany early large-scale population densities elsewhere such as consistently produced pottery and even nearby fields for agriculture. So there are several contradictions to the expected pattern of developments in the Near East in general and since this distinctively Cypriot phenomenon is so exciting in any study of early man, we can

Bowl of dark-grey andesite; from Khirokitia; H 10 cm, L 30.5 cm, W 27.5 cm; Neolithic period, seventh millennium B.C. Cyprus Museum, Nicosia

leave the question of origins temporarily to one side. Suffice it to say that well before 6000 B.C. there emerged in Cyprus a remarkable series of related communities which disappear from our records after only a few centuries in circumstances that are as mysterious as are their origins.

Only fourteen such communities are known at present and they are mainly strung out along the north coast or are located in the short river valleys that descend from the Troodos Mountains in the south. Despite the distances between them, they seem to possess standardised settlements in which round buildings huddle together on the tops and slopes of hills, in the latter case much as Cypriot mountain villages do today. The lower parts of these buildings are often of stone and attain massive proportions by constant additions of further skins of stones or pisé. The small interiors have hearths, presumably used for cooking and also heating in winter, benches and windows, but in many cases the area is further restricted by large and occasionally painted piers to support an upper floor beneath the beehive roof. In winter the heat would gather usefully at that higher level and smoke there would help to cure stored venison in the form of the now extinct fallow deer which seems to have been a staple part of the diet.

Except for carnelian and obsidian, a volcanic glassy rock prized for its cutting properties, there are no hints of external contact and indeed these villages are of a type not found elsewhere. Artefacts found inside them are equally unique and many exhibit a path of development that is radically separate from that of their neighbours. Thus, although Khirokitians were familiar with the properties of clay, as is clear from a few pottery fragments and a modelled head which adorned the top of a staff or the like, they laboriously produced ground stone vessels in preference to pottery ones, many no doubt in imitation of now lost wooden containers.

We can but speculate on the organisation of this assertively independent society and why some centres, like Khirokitia, grew to such a large size and others,

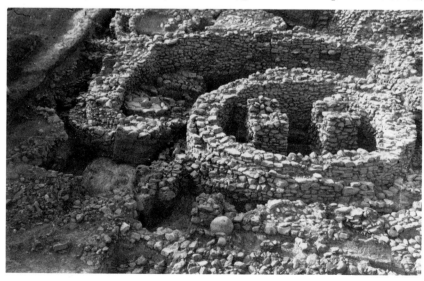

Visible remains of a house of the Khirokitia settlement

Reconstruction of part of the Neolithic settlement of Khirokitia, dating from the seventh millennium B.C. The houses, some with upper stories, had domed roofs. A street which passes through them down to the river was originally a town wall

such as the islet Petra tou Limniti, remained small. A possible insight is provided by a settlement near Kalavasos which is dominated by an exceptionally large courtyard building stained with red ochre. Surrounding it are some structures so small they may be for storage rather than for living and the whole is enclosed by a wall and ditch. Such large-scale and specialised works represent a high degree of communal authority. The earliest known culture in Cyprus therefore consists of a well-organised, complex society primarily engaged in farming, hunting and perhaps herding, rather than primitive hunter-gatherer bands that we might otherwise expect.

In all settlements the dead were buried just under floors in crouched positions but occasionally with their artificially deformed skulls raised. In some instances provision was made for offerings so presumably a form of ancestor cult existed inside households. There is also the suggestion of a higher mortality rate before the desertion of Khirokitia and so it may be that natural causes, such as diseases, to which island populations are particularly susceptible, played a part in the disappearance of this group from our records.

Like the post-Darwinian story of evolution, the documentation of early man on Cyprus is episodic and comprises a series of fully-formed cultures with little evidence for how and why they emerged or, for that matter, declined. The next recorded entity, the Sotira group, is a good case in point. Radiocarbon dates place it between 4500 and 4000 B.C. and there are only faint hints of prehistoric man on the island between its advent and the demise of the Khirokitia group some 1500 years earlier. Since it differs so much from the latter, scholars are divided on its origins, either native or intrusive, as in the case of the Khirokitia group. Once again, there are no close parallels elsewhere for this new Cypriot culture, so if people did cross to the island at its inception they underwent a radical sea-change when they pioneered their new settlements.

The Sotira group is known from some two dozen settlements on the north coast and foothills of the Kyrenia Mountains, in the Ovgos Valley to the west of Nicosia and in the Troodos Mountains foothills, particularly near the south coast where its namesake, Sotira, is located. They are small villages on promontories, hilltops and slopes. The largest, Sotira, probably had no more than fifty, mainly single-roomed, buildings at any one time, each with its own circular platform hearth and bench, often with working installations and alcoves set against walls. The free-standing, but tightly clustered buildings are comparatively thin-walled and tend to a square rather than circular plan. However, such planning was altered where circumstances dictated, as at the north coast subterranean village of Ayios Epiktitos *Vrysi*. There spacious natural or man-made hollows were deeply indented into an otherwise flat coastal promontory and wedged inside them were irregularly shaped buildings, six or more per hollow. Their roofs were well below ground level so that the whole village was concealed from the casual viewer except for the smoke rising from the promontory. Since there was an evident desire to remain below ground, the houses were not widely dispersed but in the course of time they accumulated one above the other in columnar fashion inside the hollows thus, ironically, yielding some of the best preserved prehistoric architecture on the island. This subterranean aspect of the Sotira group is also evident in a network of shafts, tunnels and chambers below the similar houses at the inland site of Philia. Its excavator has suggested that such a complex may have been used for non-utilitarian purposes, but storage cannot be precluded and indeed observers on the island in the earlier part of this century have noted the existence of deep, bell-shaped pits used as grain silos.

Despite slight differences in the plans of village buildings, their overall size and interior appointments remain quite standardised, so there should have been contact between these meagre and widespread communities. Evidence for this comes from the occurrence of beads and pendants of blue-green picrolite (like

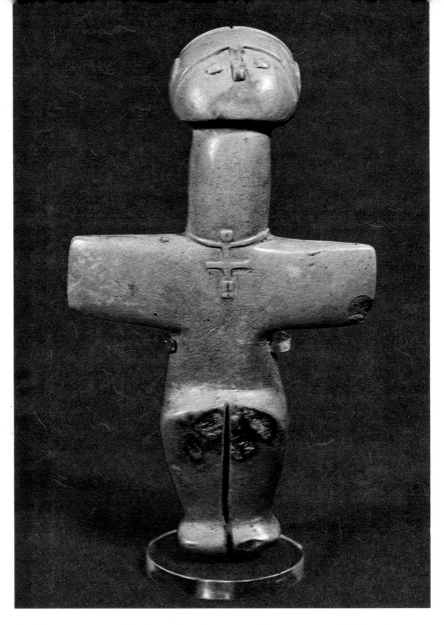

Cruciform figurine of blue-green picrolite; Yialia, Paphos District; H 15.3 cm; Chalcolithic period, c. 3000 B.C. Cyprus Museum, Nicosia

steatite or soapstone) in the north where, apart from one unverified small source, it is not to be found naturally. It occurs in and near the Troodos Mountains and was a frequently used raw material for items of adornment at Sotira. Either the northern inhabitants obtained it from the Troodos directly, which seems unlikely because there is so little of it in their villages, or they obtained it for goods in exchanges with nearby villages which, located almost as far from the sources, also possessed diminished amounts.

Pottery tells a similar story of exchange and communication. Vessels of fired and decorated clay now form a major proportion of the material remains of Cyprus and regional styles can be identified. Thus in the south a peculiar style known as combed, because of the use of multiple-toothed instruments to effect designs, was prevalent but it only trickled to the north. It too may have reached there by exchange but the clays could well be local in which case the *idea* of the idiosyncratic combing technique was somehow passed on. This pottery is handmade and because its decoration is so varied it could well be a household craft suggesting that movement of people, perhaps through inter-village marriage, could also be a unifying agent of the Sotira group.

Only one material aspect of this culture shows clear signs of development and that is the pottery. At Philia it seems to develop out of an earlier monochrome variety. This is the only clue that we have concerning the group's native emergence and so important ceramic changes are taking place in Cyprus about 4500 B.C. It would, however, be misleading to think of the Sotira group, once it had become established, as unenterprising and fossilised. Population was on the increase as can be seen from the expansion of some settlements. Decoration on pottery shows rapid changes in a lively painted tradition in the north, where Red-on-White designs include regular lattices, bold circles and festoons, accurate chevrons, filling patterns executed with a sponge and, most typical of all, dazzling ripples. Traces of decoratively entwined reeds or grasses on stones remind us of the tremendous loss in perishable arts and crafts.

It is often assumed that because a group of people are later in time they must in some way be more advanced than their predecessors, but this is difficult to confirm in a comparison of the Khirokitia and Sotira groups. The latter may have realised the potential of pottery but their villages are defended in a similar manner as before, they lack the earlier large centres which may have fostered specialists, burials are still in simple pits though outside houses, and there is no evidence for external trade. Their diet shows no great increase in variety or emphasis except for a concentration on domestic sheep and goats in the north. Yet they did successfully adapt to their Mediterranean environment, population did increase and their traditions, unlike those of the Khirokitia group, did persist. These features would seem to be the lasting contribution to Cyprus of the Sotira group.

Radiocarbon dates and pottery studies are unanimous in revealing a general population shift c. 4000 B.C. This in itself is not surprising, for unlike the early history of the adjacent mainland or on the very similar island of Crete at Knossos, there is little continuity of settlement in early Cyprus. It is as if a recurrent malaise affected its remote inhabitants and although many reasons could be deduced from later times, such as invasion, disease, famine and earthquake, these are extremely difficult to decipher from the archaeological evidence. To take the analogy of neighbouring lands where urbanisation developed one step further, it is likely that such repeated disturbances inhibited the growth of large urban centres in Cyprus. So, small-scale and shifting society remains typical of the island until well into the Bronze Age.

Symptomatic of these cycles of settled prosperity followed by apparent upheaval to return again to a new form of settled existence is our lack of knowledge concerning the intervening eras of disruption. Recent discoveries of the period shortly after 4000 B.C. have now begun to penetrate this particular Dark Age. It would seem that no outsiders are involved in ringing the changes then, but the islanders forsook established methods of building and adopted more perishable materials. They continued their underground activities as another

Bronze dagger; from Vounous; L 17.8 cm, W 3.7 cm; Early Cypriote, 2500–2000 B.C. City of Birmingham Museum and Art Gallery

Limestone conical seal;
Lemba Lakkous; L 3.1 cm,
D 2.6 cm; Chalcolithic period,
about 2500 B.C.
Cyprus Museum, Nicosia

site near Kalavasos with impressive tunnels demonstrates and they colonised the western part of the island. There, at the site of Lemba, dwellings in small hollows evolved into the substantial circular stone buildings that are the hallmark of the succeeding Erimi group of sites. In this way we can see how recourse to more temporary accommodation such as wattled huts around circular shelter pits eventually gave rise to a radically new architecture.

No doubt other cultural changes accompanied this dislocation: evidence is accumulating for a greater economic reliance on fallow deer implying increased herding and hunting for example. In the transformed society that emerges in Cyprus perhaps as early as c. 3500 B.C. there are no overt signs of immigrants, but there are several of continuity. This transition therefore seems to be an internal affair and we may better treat it as a formative stage in the evolution of prehistoric Cypriot society than as a true Dark Age.

The Erimi group takes its name from a south coast site which Porphyrios Dikaios, the pioneer of Cypriot prehistoric studies, examined briefly in the 1930's. As at Lemba, pottery associated with the early timbered buildings includes the last appearance of combed decoration and, with the later substantial buildings, a fine line style of Red-on-White. This style has many affinities with the earlier Red-on-White but a greater range of elegant shapes and larger vessels point to different uses, especially for storage. It is one which is now found widely in Cyprus and, although useful for the relative dating of sites, the suspected regional variations and time scales remain to be worked out.

If continuity and only very gradual change are to be found in pottery and buildings, innovation marks other aspects of this group. Metalwork appears for the first time on an island whose fortunes were later so closely bound up with the exploitation of its copper resources. The chisels, hooks and jewellery of this period are of relatively pure copper, but the inclusion of minuscule amounts of tin in one or two pieces has encouraged some scholars to look to a source in Anatolia where copper-working was long established. Very occasionally now obsidian, almost certainly from Anatolia, occurs in Cyprus so the possible opening of transmaritime exchange could account for this metalwork. On the other hand, some of the Cypriot objects are peculiar to the island and as their advent takes place exactly during the formative stage of the Erimi group, we can by no means rule out an indigenous role in this momentous breakthrough.

That enhanced exploitation of rocks — and native copper would be regarded as such — took place now is made clear by blue-green picrolite figurines in cruciform shape. This too is an innovation, one which became very popular in the west, closest to the picrolite veins. However, it was but a facet, albeit the most distinctive one, of an exuberant display of representational art that is one of the chief distinguishing features of the Erimi group. Most picrolite examples were meant to be worn as pendants either singly or alternating with dentalium shell spacers on necklaces and the number of figures represented can multiply so that two are depicted one above the other or three in a Legs of Man formation. Where the sex is indicated, the female is usually portrayed. Lack of wear marks and their recurrence in graves suggests that they were primarily intended for the dead. Terracotta

26

Terracotta nude female figure
with a large bowl; H 12.9 cm;
Chalcolithic I period, 3000—
2500 B.C.
Louvre

Limestone female figurine;
Lemba Lakkous; H 36 cm;
Chalcolithic period, 3000–2500
B.C.
Cyprus Museum, Nicosia

examples, fulsome and often painted, have not yet been found in graves and the explicit rendering of a seated female expressing milk from her breasts indicates another role for these types. Limestone was also favoured and the Lemba statuette epitomises contemporary sculptors' mastery of balanced forms.

These discoveries are difficult to place in terms of Cypriot society as a whole since only a few sites of this long period, c. 4000 – 2500 B.C., have been excavated. Developments of major significance are taking place in terms of the colonisation of the west, technological and artistic achievements and, at least by the end of the period, foreign contact. Important insights into the organisation of society are further gained from the introduction of the stamp seal, the advanced design of the Lemba statuette, and the differently sized buildings at Lemba which hint at property rights, specialisation and social hierarchies respectively. Since most Erimi group burials are without grave goods and in simple pits the relatively rich multiple burials in shaft graves at the Souskiou cemeteries near Old Paphos confirm the view that there is much more evidence for social differentiation than hitherto and that wealth accumulating centres existed within this little known Erimi group.

The paucity of information from the Kyrenia and West Nicosia Districts renders any reconstruction of ensuing events highly speculative since it is at least clear that it was especially in those districts that major changes took place, ones which ushered in the Bronze Age in Cyprus. The evidence to hand for this transition to what is known as the Early Cypriote, comes chiefly from very limited excavations and surveys. These indicate the presence of an Erimi population that, again as at Lemba, preferred red monochrome types of pottery late in the history of that group. This preference is a precious key if we are to understand what happens next for the whole nature of our records alters dramatically and we are faced with nothing but cemeteries for a considerable period, all with varieties of red monochrome pottery. Questions, rather than answers, abound. How quickly did these changes come about? What, if any, were the chronological overlaps between the new cemeteries and Erimi-type villages? How do we account for the changes in customs? Why did the north become so pre-eminent? Were new arrivals involved? And so on. Beginnings, however, always tend to pose more intractable problems in Cypriot prehistory as in other disciplines, but the situation which follows is little better. Owing to the way in which archaeology developed, early investigators devoted most of their energies to the excavation of well endowed cemeteries and consequently today we are left with a most one-sided picture of the whole epoch.

The older fine line style of Cypriot Red-on-White pottery is found on the adjacent mainland at Tarsus, so contacts certainly existed with an area that was soon to be in the throes of conflict surrounding the arrival of Indo-Europeans. It may be that some mainlanders found their way along known exchange routes to Cyprus and were instrumental in inaugurating widespread change. The history of many Indo-European groups is replete with examples of aristocratic minorities assuming political control of other ethnic units, so not many need be involved. At the other extreme end of a host of possible solutions is one which discounts all direct foreign participation, suggesting instead that such wealth gathering as exhi-

Clay model of an open-air sanctuary, Red Polished ware, representing a ritual around three idols wearing bull's heads and holding serpents in their hands; from Vounous; H 12 cm, D 37 cm; Early Bronze Age, c. 2600–2300 B.C.
Cyprus Museum, Nicosia

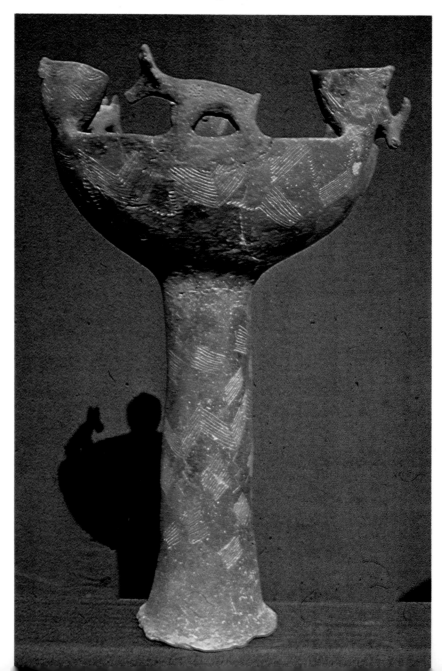

Ritual vessel, Red Polished ware, with miniature animals and cups on the rim; from Vounous; H 53 cm, D 35 cm; Early Bronze Age, 2200–2000 B.C.
Cyprus Museum, Nicosia

bited earlier at Souskiou eventually generated enough momentum, particularly through the exploitation of and trade in the rich copper resources of Cyprus, to bring about change internally. Whatever the answer, the new managers swept aside the existing props of the stage and they created a transformed Cypriot scene in the north, to a lesser extent in the south and west.

Possibly one of the earliest cemeteries, Vasilia, demonstrates the effects of new found wealth. Most tombs of Cypriot necropoleis have rather simple rock-cut chambers with blocked approach passages, *dromoi*, but here there are prestigious plaster-lined complexes up to 16m in length with niches in the walls and in at least one case a small hole connecting the burial chamber with the world above.

Kamares ware cup, imported from Crete; Karmi; H 9 cm, D 8.5 cm; Middle Bronze Age, 1900–1800 B.C. Cyprus Museum, Nicosia

Amongst the grave goods are impressively large alabaster vessels, presumably from Old Kingdom Egypt. The native pottery style is known as Philia and it is confined to the western parts of the Kyrenia and Nicosia Districts with a few outliers in the south. Other styles in the same Red Polished type of pottery may co-exist and their fragile and elaborate nature indicates that many were specifically intended as furnishings for single and multiple burials. Such burials at Vounous, one of the largest cemeteries of the period, also on the north coast but to the east of Kyrenia, were amply provisioned with slaughtered cattle, joints of meat in jars and basins, specialised cult and other drinking vessels, pottery replicas of daggers and sheaths, spindles and carding combs, decorated long copper pins to fasten robes at the shoulders and several kinds of metal tools and weapons.

Until the dating of the very localised styles of Red Polished pottery is put on a firmer basis it will be difficult to elaborate on the settlement patterns in different parts of the island and interaction between them. Nonetheless, it is likely that by the end of the period population had expanded and settlements are to be found in all areas previously occupied. Two aspects of their distribution may be noted. In the west the apparent scarcity contrasts with an earlier density so either depopulation took place here or we have still to recognise adequately human traces of the period. Elsewhere, on the "copper belt" of Cyprus stretching along the northeastern foothills of the Troodos Mountains from the Bay of Morphou to Kalavasos in the south there is a new concentration of sites that may well reflect increased interest in copper resources. Indeed, if that is their principal *raison d'etre* then considerable demand must have existed, more so than would be needed to satisfy insular requirements, and with it unprecedented technological and organisational expertise.

One of these "copper belt" settlements, Alambra, has yielded several fragments of crucibles with small amounts of copper adhering to them, so corroborating our inferences from distributional evidence. Only a small portion of it is known, but its aligned rectangular buildings and streets represent a startling break with all previous living conditions in Cyprus. Previously, villages possessed isolated and dispersed buildings, henceforth they have contiguous buildings that can expand or subdivide more readily in a pattern long familiar on the Asiatic mainland. Because of the pottery problems mentioned above, the date of Alambra is not entirely resolved, but it would appear from new excavations that this radical departure from established architectural practice was one of the innovations that mark the very beginnings of the Early Cypriot.

Other architectural evidence in the form of a terracotta model from Vounous demonstrates the concurrent persistence of the Erimi circular building traditions, perhaps for cult places only given the nature of the activities so vividly displayed in the model. The inclusion of penned bulls here and of bulls' heads as terminals for engaged pillars on other models suggests that a bull cult is an important element in Early Cypriot religious beliefs. That it is a new religious force is rendered likely by the complete absence of cattle bones in Cyprus before this period, but it would be over-simplification to identify this bull cult as the dominant component of the religion. Bulls figure prominently on similar piers and pillars earlier at Chatal Hüyük, Turkey, for example, yet in one explicit mural composition there it is shown as subservient to a female. Other figures, perhaps of religious significance, include highly stylised plank-shaped females executed in the ubiquitous Red Polished pottery.

During this period infrequent imports and what may be copies of foreign goods are found in cemeteries. To the former group may be attributed Asiatic and Minoan pottery, Minoan metalwork, Egyptian stonework and perhaps Asiatic beads of shiny blue faience, to the latter Asiatic spindle whorls and metalwork and Cycladic pottery. Contacts therefore now existed with all those areas which were to be the island's major contact partners during the remainder of the Bronze Age, and, if the actual numbers of objects are few, the quantity must be weighed in the balances of a most defective record. Much hinges on the interpretation we wish to give to these objects. They could be nothing more than random but increasing numbers of imports of little significance to social and political developments in Cyprus itself. The nature of trade in adjoining lands, however, follows another, largely non-random pattern in which Kings mount long-distance campaigns at the behest of merchants, or royal expeditions, such as that of the Egyptian King Sahure (c. 2480 B.C.) to Asia, cross the seas to cities with which there are political ties. Cyprus may have remained on the periphery of such formal and formative contacts between city states and empires, but there is tantalising, if not conclusive, evidence to indicate that such an isolated role was no longer possible by c. 2000 B.C., if not before.

Juglet with incised decoration; Phaneromeni settlement A; H 22.3 cm, D 12.5 cm; Middle/Late Bronze Age, 1650–1600 B.C. Kourion House Museum

Part of this evidence relates to the enterprising kings of Middle Kingdom Egypt (c. 2134–1786 B.C.). Inscribed objects of the royal family and other high officials of the 13th and especially the 12th Dynasties have been found in the cities of Syria, especially at Ugarit, a most important port-of-call and one close to eastern Cyprus.

Terracotta model of a
ploughing scene; from
Vounous; L 41.0 cm; Early/
Middle Bronze Age, about
1900 B.C.
Cyprus Museum, Nicosia

Terracotta sanctuary model,
Red Polished ware, from
Kotchati; W 17.7 cm,
H 19 cm; Early/Middle
Bronze Age, about 1900 B.C.
Cyprus Museum, Nicosia

Necklace of faïence beads;
from Kalavasos; Early/Middle
Bronze Age, about 1950–1850
B.C.
Cyprus Museum, Nicosia

Terracotta idol, White
Painted ware; from Ayia
Paraskevi; H 39.5 cm;
Middle Bronze Age,
1725–1625 B.C.
Cyprus Museum, Nicosia

In a colourful and convincingly accurate story of the beginning of the 12th Dynasty a high-ranking Egyptian fugitive in Syria or Palestine speaks of a flurry of Egyptian messengers suggestive of diplomatic and trading contacts. We have already seen that long distances were no barrier to direct trade links in Asia and so the appearance of Cypriot Red Polished pottery at Ugarit, although poorly dated, and North Syrian painted pottery in Cyprus indicates some kind of Cypriot integration into this complex network. The Egyptian evidence at once lends a literate dimension and chronological precision to these relations.

The second major body of evidence concerns the identification of the place names *Alasia* and *Asy* which first occur c. 1750 B.C. in such a manner that the writers would seem to be quite familiar with the place, though for how long is not possible to say. Assuming that the name *Alasia* has not experienced geographical displacement in the course of time, a known phenomenon affecting remote places and movement of people carrying with them a place name, then it is to be located by the sea with close connections to Ugarit and North Syria, Egypt and the Hittites, and it is most widely known for mining and disseminating copper. These characteristics suit Cyprus admirably, but clear corroboration from the island itself has been lacking and hence there is often reluctance to apply this historical evidence fully to an interpretation of insular developments. Here it is regarded as positive circumstantial evidence which demonstrates that Cypriot copper was reaching Mesopotamia by c.1750 B.C. and that Cypriots were living abroad, in North Syria by c.1650 B.C. It remains to be seen what, if any, the impact of this involvement was on the island. Factors that impinge on this major issue are population size, political integration and remoteness since distant regions with desirable raw materials lacking numbers and political cohesiveness such as the copper-bearing areas of Timna in Palestine and Sinai are frequently exploited and seldom turn such commodities to their own advantage.

Apparently lacking urban centres contemporary with Middle Kingdom Egypt, it is unlikely that Cyprus could have participated in the inter-state exchanges just mentioned, at least not in the same manner. At the beginning of this period the Cypriot population was still located in the older centres, especially in the north, but it is becoming clearer that the south-west was also well populated if not as rich in material goods. As it progressed settlements appear on the southern slopes of the Kyrenia Mountains overlooking the potentially rich, but perhaps well wooded Central Plain. By c.1650 B.C. there are new foundations on the south and east coasts, ones which were to become international urban emporia. There is little reason to doubt that they owe their origin to the realisation of the potentials of trade with the east and so it is striking that their inception takes place after the Middle Kingdom when Egypt lacked traditional central authority and when the largely Asiatic cities in the Nile Delta prospered. We are still woefully ignorant of the size and complexity of these cities, but at some stage during these centuries a diversified response to the situation makes its appearance, the fort.

There is unlikely to be a single all-embracing cause for fort construction since the twenty or so known examples vary considerably in type. They occur primarily along the edges of the Central Plain and in the Karpass. The best known, Nitovikla, consists of a square fortress at the edge of an enclosed plateau. Two square towers flank its gateway, which was built on massive ashlar blocks. Leading off its central court, a range of chambers may have acted as the base for a parapet walk behind the very thick walls. Nitovikla, which is placed at the base of the Karpass overlooking the Bay of Famagusta, contrasts with Dhali *Kafkallia*, an inland fort not far from classical Idalion. There, a low straggling wall encloses 12 ha. (30 acres), much of it occupied by rectangular buildings. It lacks a fortress and much of it would be difficult to defend against a determined aggressor. So novel is the concept of these enclosed sites that intruders, as in the case of renewed fort-building at the end of the Bronze Age, have been adduced to explain Nitovikla, though more inland forts are frequently interpreted as a result of localised hostilities. Yet Nitovikla has produced no foreign goods, whereas a tomb at Dhali *Kafkallia* has yielded a rare bronze belt of a type known only from the Nile Delta in Egypt and from Palestine. Clearly, the patchy nature of our information from these forts can only permit the most speculative of explanations. Their distribution, at least, confirms the decline of the importance of the north though not the area around the Bay of Morphou which was soon to become seriously involved with Minoan Crete. Their distance from the sea indicates that they are not a response to sea raiders known from slightly later historical records. It is also the case that at least one, Nitovikla, was violently destroyed and so, far from mere symbols of prestige, they do reflect a period of unrest. Mass burials under immense tumuli may also hint at such a state of affairs.

Two conflicting tendencies can thus be observed in Cyprus in the earlier part of the second millennium B.C. Developments in ceramics and metallurgy are essentially variations on themes established previously. These expressions of continuity also exist in settlement size and in burial practices which, apart from the eastern tumuli just mentioned, only become more elaborate in cultic matters. Subsistence economy too shows little change from that known in the Erimi group, but we could be better informed about the intervening period when the introduction of ox drawn ploughs probably permitted heavier soils to be cultivated. Against this picture of innate conservatism must be placed the early hints of innovation, mainly in the form of imitations and imports, for example of a type of Syro-Cilician painted pottery which at the Syrian city of Ebla was deemed important enough to include amongst the funerary gifts of a dignitary. Closer to 1650, Cypriot pottery in turn began to penetrate Levantine markets in increasing quantities where previously Cypriot copper had been dispatched to Mesopotamia. Even within the fairly uniform metalwork in Cyprus, there are anomalies such as a group of Nicosia area sophisticated shaft-hole axes which some see as the product of itinerant Asiatic metalworkers. Whether or not foreigners at any level of society are involved, and there is no question of mass invasion, it seems likely that these opposed tendencies led to stresses which precipitated the creation of forts and presumably a kind of military aristocracy that usually accompanies such works. At the moment the simplest but by no means only explanation would seem to be that the observed changes and copper exports are interdependent. The new cities that were generated by this trading have yielded developed, but thoroughly Cypriot, materials and hence the ultimate impact was not foreign exploitation but a positive Cypriot response.

Bronze axe; L 19 cm; Middle Bronze Age, 1900–1625 B.C. Cyprus Museum, Nicosia

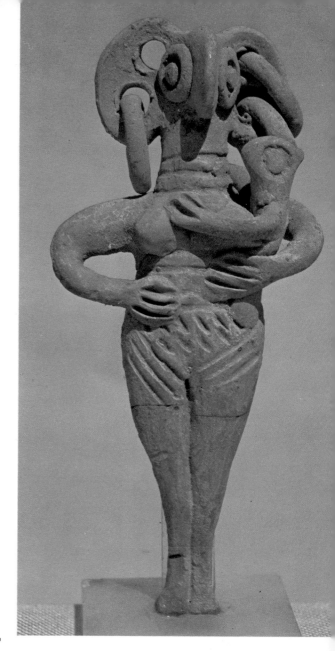

II
THE LATE BRONZE AGE
(LATE CYPRIOTE)
1600–1050 B.C.

Cyprus entered the Late Bronze Age experiencing the same atmosphere of unrest which prevailed towards the end of the Middle Bronze Age. It is difficult to determine whether this was the result of raids from external enemies such as the Hyksos or of friction between East and West, the two traditionally antagonistic parts of the island, for the control of the island's resources of copper and fertile arable land. Forts and refuges were built in various areas and mass burials are observed in tombs, mainly in the north; the latter, however, may also be explained by an epidemic.

When the Hyksos were expelled from Egypt c. 1555 B.C. and peaceful conditions were established in the Eastern Mediterranean, many causes of the unrest of the earlier half of the 16th century B.C. were removed. Peace encouraged

Terracotta figurine of a standing naked woman, with bird-like head, holding baby in left hand; provenance unknown; H 14 cm; Late Bronze Age, 1450–1225 B.C. Cyprus Museum, Nicosia

37

trade which in turn aided growth of the major urban centres, both those inland which had an agricultural economy as well as the main harbour towns. Thus the acute problems which the growth of population had created could now be solved satisfactorily. This is the time when Morphou-*Toumba tou Skourou* flourished on the north-west coast, and Enkomi on the east coast emerged as a major harbour town. Several other harbour towns such as Hala Sultan Tekké and Maroni developed along the south coast. There was free communication throughout the island, which facilitated the expansion of trade, especially the transport of copper from the mines to the 'industrial' centres and harbours, and brought about the development of a homogeneous culture. Artistic achievements, notably the pottery industry, are widespread. Two major wares make their appearance: the White Slip and Base Ring wares which were to dominate Cypriote ceramics for over three centuries and to gain great popularity in the Near East and even in the Aegean.

Pottery production was particularly lively in the Morphou region. A potter's quarter was excavated there which illustrates the extent of the industry and, judging from the vases found in adjacent tombs, the quality of the products.

Traditional trade-links with the Syro-Palestinian coast continue, but a new element is now introduced: trade with the Aegean. Though only very few Cypriote objects dating to the 16th century B.C. have been found in the Aegean region and Aegean objects uncovered in Cyprus are rare, trade is nonetheless apparent in the 16th century B.C. This is about the time when the Cypriots borrowed a linear script from the Cretans which is known as the Cypro-Minoan script. Cyprus could export raw copper and foodstuffs to the Aegean, but there is no conclusive evidence for the nature of this trade.

Several major sites dating to the Late Bronze Age have already been excavated and have revealed architectural remains of a military, religious and domestic character, mainly of the Late Bronze Age II period (1450–1200 B.C.).

Despite these peaceful conditions during the Late Bronze Age cities in Cyprus were fortified. A mudbrick city wall was built around the town of Kition on the south coast at the beginning of the 13th century B.C. It has rectangular bastions at intervals built of blocks of stone *(ashlars)* against its mudbrick facade. At Enkomi a fortress was constructed in the northern part of the town.

Religion was based on fertility, which formed the nucleus of religious beliefs of the Cypriots from the 4th millenium B.C. onwards. Sanctuaries exist in rural centres as at Ayios Iakovos near the north coast, and also in urban centres like Kition and Myrtou-*Pigadhes*. The sanctuaries of Kition, of which two have already been excavated, follow a Near Eastern plan, with an open courtyard and a holy-of-holies associated with a 'sacred garden'.

Domestic architecture is known mainly from Enkomi. Dwellings consist of a rectangular open courtyard with rooms on three sides. The courtyard was also used for burials in chamber tombs. There were no separate cemeteries.

Workshops have been found at Kition, Enkomi and Apliki for the smelting of copper. Near the workshops at Kition there was a bathroom with a cemented

Silver bowl, inlaid with gold and niello; from Enkomi; H 6 cm, D 15.7 cm; Late Bronze Age, 1400–1375 B.C. Cyprus Museum, Nicosia

floor. At Enkomi there were also lavatories and bathrooms and a well-organised drainage system. Bathtubs of clay or limestone point to the high standard of living of the inhabitants of the urban centres.

The tombs are usually chambers with a passage (dromos). The burial was accompanied by gifts: vases, jewellery, other luxury goods such as alabaster and faience vases, cylinder seals, etc. Occasionally built tombs are found, the chambers of which are either rectangular, with a flat or corbelled roof and with a stepped dromos, or 'tholoi' with a domed roof, following Near Eastern prototypes.

Trade in copper resulted in the influx of considerable wealth as is apparent from the quality and quantity of gifts which were deposited in the tombs of rich merchants at Enkomi, Kition, Hala Sultan Tekké and elsewhere.

In addition to the numerous types and fabrics of Cypriot vases from tombs and settlements of the Late Bronze Age II period there is also a profusion of Mycenaean pottery. Though pottery from the Greek Mainland and Crete made its appearance in Cyprus during the 16th and 15th centuries B.C., it was after c. 1400 B.C. that such pottery was brought to the island in quantity. There has long been controversy among scholars as to the place of manufacture of these Mycenaean vases: whether all were imported from such centres as the Argolid in the Pelo-

40

ponnese, or whether some at least were made in Cyprus by Mycenaean artists who established themselves on the island together with merchants after 1400 B.C., when the Mycenaeans expanded en masse eastwards. Whatever the solution of this problem may be, the fact remains that extraordinarily large numbers of Mycenaean vases of the 14th and 13th centuries B.C. have been found, particularly of the so-called 'pictorial' style which must have been much favoured by the local population. Such vases are decorated with purely Aegean motifs and compositions and constitute a fine expression of Mycenaean art, with occasional influences from the Near East, especially in the repertory of shapes.

Other artistic accomplishments of the 14th and 13th centuries B.C. illustrate not only the taste of the Cypriots but also the cosmopolitan character of the urban centres in which this art flourished. There is a preference for a combined style which betrays both Near Eastern and Aegean elements as is evidenced in glyptics and jewellery. The gold diadems with embossed decoration of sphinxes, flowers, etc., are cases in point. Worthy of special mention are two exceptional pieces which were found in Cyprus and date to the 14th and 13th centuries respectively. Whether they were made locally or were imported is not certain, but they indicate the artistic taste which prevailed among the island's inhabitants. The first is a hemispherical silver bowl with a wishbone handle from a 14th-century B.C. tomb at Enkomi. It is decorated with oxen heads and flowers in an inlaid technique with gold and a black substance known as *niello*. Only one other vase, found at Dendra in the Peloponnese, is comparable. The second is a conical rhyton (ritual vase) of faience from a tomb at Kition, dating to the second half of the 13th century B.C. Its surface is covered with blue enamel and it is decorated in three registers with galloping animals, a hunting scene and running spirals. The decoration is painted in yellow and black or inlaid in red enamel. The style of the motifs is characteristic of the mixed Aegeo-oriental style mentioned above.

Writing would have been a necessity in this developed and sophisticated Cypriot society during the Late Bronze Age, and even more so in a country whose economy depended largely on trade with neighbouring countries. The Cypro-Minoan script developed and became current throughout the island. Though long written documents in the form of baked clay tablets of a cushion-shaped variety like those of the Near East have been found only at Enkomi, there is evidence of the script in all parts of the island. Signs from it are engraved or painted on vases or engraved on bronzes, cylinder seals, clay balls, ivory objects, clay loomweights, etc. There are about eighty signs in the Cypro-Minoan script. Several attempts have been made to decipher the Enkomi tablets but no satisfactory results have yet been reached and the language of the documents remains unknown. Several theories have been advanced, the latest being that it is Hurrian. What is certain is that these tablets are not lists of objects or inventories, like the tablets of the Mycenaean and Minoan palaces, but continuous texts; it has been suggested that they may be poems. Some texts in the Cypro-Minoan script have also been found at Ugarit, the cosmopolitan town on the Syrian coast opposite Cyprus, with which the island maintained close commercial relations. The suggestion has been put forward that there was a commercial colony of Cypriots at Ugarit.

At this time of lively interrelations in the Eastern Mediterranean, in which

Cyprus played such an active role, it is not surprising that the island should be mentioned in Near Eastern texts. In the correspondence found in the Palace of Akhenaten at Tel el-Amarna in the Nile Delta and dating before c. 1375 B.C. between the Pharaoh and the king of Cyprus, which is called Alashiya, it is recorded that the king of Alashiya used to send copper ingots to the Pharaoh as tribute for Egypt's peace-keeping role in the Eastern Mediterranean. (Some scholars, however, still do not accept the equation of Alashiya with Cyprus.) The island was known even earlier as a copper-producing country, since it is also mentioned in the tablets from Alalakh in Syria and Mari in Mesopotamia in the 18th and 17th centuries B.C. respectively. There is valuable information concerning the internal problems of the king of Alashiya in his correspondence with the Egyptian Pharaoh. In one letter the king explains that for three years he had not been able to send the amount of copper promised to the Pharaoh because most men in his country had been killed and there was nobody to smelt it. This may have been because of the invasions of the Lukki from western Anatolia who are mentioned in the same correspondence.

Reference to Cyprus (Alashiya) is also made in the Hittite tablets. The Hittites claimed that Cyprus formed part of their empire; but archaeological evidence is lacking and therefore this may simply be a boastful assertion.

The end of the 13th century B.C. witnessed the disruption of Mycenaean society on the Greek Mainland and the destruction and abandonment of the main Mycenaean centres in the Peloponnese such as Mycenae, Tiryns and Pylos. The inhabitants of these towns left their homes and sought their fortunes by sailing eastwards. On their way to the Eastern Mediterranean, a route which they knew already from their trading ancestors, they may have passed by Anatolia where they were joined by other bands of adventurers with whom they raided coastal towns until they finally reached the Eastern Mediterranean. We propose that these were the 'Peoples of the Sea' who are mentioned in oriental documents: adventurers who caused the destruction of Cypriot cities such as Enkomi and Kition. Some of them may have settled in Cyprus and rebuilt the destroyed cities, while others may have continued eastwards to the Syro-Palestinian coast, where they seized and occupied towns belonging to their Canaanite predecessors. There must have been several groups of such adventurers and soldiers of fortune roaming around the Eastern Mediterranean. Egyptian records graphically tell how one of these groups invading Egypt was defeated by Rameses III c. 1186. There is an echo of these troubled times in the correspondence between the king of Alashiya and the King Hammurabi of Ugarit with whom Cyprus had an alliance. They exchanged information on the appearance of foreign ships near their coasts and advised each other on what measures should be taken to avert the dangers which menaced their lands.

The period which followed the destruction of the main cities of Cyprus is known as Late Cypriote III and begins c. 1200 B.C. Though it is not easy to define with certainty the chronological limits of the various phases of this period and the events which brought about the destruction and rebuilding of the coastal towns, recent archaeological discoveries have thrown light on the matter. On the promontory of Maa-*Palaeokastro* on the west coast in the Paphos District, the latest excavations have revealed a well-fortified military outpost built at a time when Mycenaean IIIB pottery was in use, about the last quarter of the 13th century B.C. This outpost was in service for less than 50 years, and since there was no previous continuity at the site it is easy to define the beginning and end of the settlement. Two distinct building periods have been observed. The first is

Mycenaean terracotta standing female figure; provenance unknown; H 13 cm; Late Bronze Age, 13th century B.C. Cyprus Museum, Nicosia

Mycenaean amphoroid krater decorated on both sides with an octopus with stylised tentacles spreading over the greater part of the surface; H 34 cm; Late Bronze Age, early 14th C. B.C. Cyprus Museum, Nicosia

associated with the construction of a formidable 'cyclopean' wall, 3.50–4.00 m. thick, to defend the settlement from the sea and from inland; there was also a building, constructed of ashlar blocks near the dog-leg city gate, which may be a sanctuary. This building was destroyed soon after its construction and other smaller rooms were built above it; these were also abandoned at a time when Mycenaean IIIC:1b pottery was in use, a few years after c. 1200 B.C. The first building period may be associated with the arrival of the Sea Peoples, and the second with other invaders from the Aegean who brought with them a new style of pottery which is known in the Peloponnese and who settled at Maa-

Palaeokastro, after having perhaps destroyed the buildings of the previous occupants. These colonists, whom we may associate with the Homeric 'Achaeans', gradually abandoned this small military outpost and moved to the nearest urban centre of Palaepaphos. A similar phenomenon may be observed at Lara, a short distance north of Maa-*Palaeokastro*, where a defensive wall has been traced along the seaward side of the promontory.

A second military outpost has recently been investigated on the plateau of a hill at Pyla-*Kokkinokremmos*, northeast of Kition. The duration of this settlement was

Mycenaean amphoroid krater, known as the 'Zeus krater', from the principal scene which apparently depicts Zeus holding the scales of battle before warriors departing for war; from Enkomi; H 37.5 cm; Late Bronze Age, 1400–1375 B.C.
Cyprus Museum, Nicosia

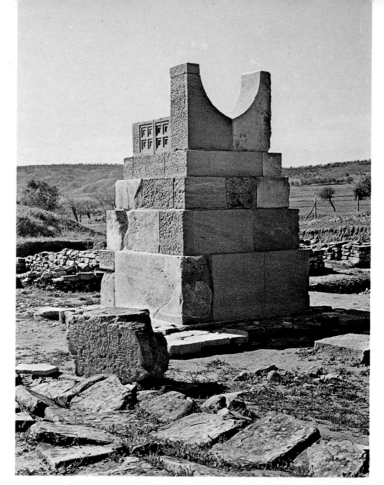

A rural shrine of the Creto-Mycenaean type (note the 'horns of consecration'), near Myrtou; Late Bronze Age

Two clay tablets from Enkomi inscribed in the Cypro-Minoan script; (left) W 9 cm, H 10 cm; (right) W 7.5 cm; H 5.5 cm; Late Bronze Age, 1220–1190 B.C.
Cyprus Museum, Nicosia

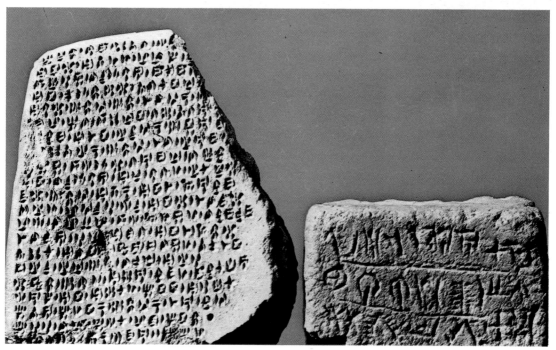

even shorter than that of Maa-*Palaeokastro*. There is only one floor in the buildings along the ridge of the plateau which were used at the same time as storerooms and guardrooms. Mycenaean IIIB and local pottery of the very end of the 13th century B.C. was found but no Mycenaean IIIC:1 wares, which would suggest that the site may be associated with the first invasion of the Sea Peoples but not with the arrival of the Achaeans who brought Mycenaean IIIC:1b pottery The settlement of the Achaean newcomers in the main urban centres which had been destroyed and rebuilt by the Sea Peoples must have been a gradual and lengthy process resulting in the hellenisation of the island. There are indications that there was a second wave of Achaean settlers who came to the island around the middle of the 12th century B.C. and even a third one following what is known as the 'Dorian' invasion of Greece.

The beginning of the 12th century B.C. heralds a new era for Cyprus. The newcomers inject a new vigour into the cultural and artistic life of the island, introducing new skills in metallurgy, building and art.

At Enkomi a 'cyclopean' wall was constructed and a new grid was established for the whole town, crossed by streets running from one end of the city wall to the other and intersecting at right angles, connecting the various city gates with one another. There was a paved 'public square' at about the middle of town. Public buildings were constructed of large hewn blocks of stone (ashlars). The sanctuary

View of Enkomi; Late Bronze Age, 14th and 13th centuries B.C.

47

of the 'Horned God' is noteworthy, consisting of a hall and two inner cult rooms. In the hall was a sacrificial altar and a table of offerings around which were found large numbers of skulls of horned animals, mainly oxen. These were probably worn as masks during ritual ceremonies; there were also many bowls for libations. The god who was worshipped in this sanctuary was a fertility god, whose bronze cult statue was found in one of the inner cult rooms. He was a god who protected cattle and shepherds. He appears as a youth wearing a kilt and a horned helmet and has been identified with 'Apollo Keraeatas' (the horned Apollo) who was worshipped on the mountains of Arcadia and who may have been introduced to Cyprus by the Achaean settlers. On one inscription of the 4th century B.C. the name of a god called Apollo Keraeatas is mentioned and on another that of Apollo Alasiotas (Apollo of Alasia, the god of Cyprus). Both these names may have been attributed to the Horned God of Enkomi whose cult was to survive in the island for at least seven centuries.

A second sanctuary uncovered at Enkomi and constructed with ashlar blocks consists of a propylaeum and a cella (main hall). In the centre of the cella there was a stone pillar, perhaps an element incorporated from Mycenaean religion in which the pillar cult is well attested. Next to the pillar base there was a large stone capital of 'Mycenaean' type and a well. A third sanctuary was constructed at Enkomi around the middle of the 12th century B.C. It comprises a rectangular courtyard with benches along the walls for the deposit of offerings, a table of offerings and an altar for sacrifices. In a small cella adjacent to the hall the bronze cult statue of a bearded god was found. He stands on a base in the form of a copper ingot and is fully armed with greaves, shield and spear. He is known as the 'Ingot God' and has been identified with the god who protects the copper mines of Cyprus. A statuette of a female divinity of Cypriot manufacture and of the same date is now in the Ashmolean Museum at Oxford. She also stands on a base in the shape of a copper ingot and is identified with a goddess symbolising the fertility of the copper mines. Dual divinities are common in the ancient world and these two, connected with metallurgy which was of primary importance to the island's economy, call to mind the Homeric association of Hephaestos, the smith-god of Greek mythology, with Aphrodite.

At Kition a 'sacred area' was uncovered at the northernmost part of the town near the city wall. I have already mentioned that a 'sacred area' with two sanctuaries and a 'sacred garden' existed there in Late Bronze Age II. During the Late Bronze Age III period one of the small sanctuaries (sanctuary 2) was replaced by a much larger one (sanctuary 1) and sanctuary 2 was remodelled. Two further sanctuaries (4 and 5) were constructed in the same area. Sanctuary 1 consists of a large rectangular open courtyard with two lateral entrances, and a narrow compartment at the west end of the hall which was the holy-of-holies and communicated with the courtyard through three openings. Parts of the 'sacred garden' of the previous period were retained in the courtyard of the new sanctuary, which was also equipped with a rectangular water pool, probably for 'sacred fishes', recalling the 'sacred lake' of Egyptian temples of the 18th and 19th dynasties. This is one of the largest sanctuaries known from the period, measuring 33.60 m. in length and 22 m. in width. It is built of large ashlar blocks, some of them

(Opposite page)
Faience rhyton; from Kition; H 26.8 cm; Late Bronze Age 1300–1225 B.C.
Cyprus Museum, Nicosia

Gold and enamel sceptre from Kourion, Kaloriziki; L 16.5 cm; Late Bronze Age 1100–1050 B.C.
Cyprus Museum, Nicosia

measuring 3.50 m. in width and 1.50 m. in height. On the south façade of the temple there are graffiti of ships, very appropriate for a harbour town from where vessels loaded with copper ingots would set sail for the Near East and the Aegean. Votive stone anchors were also offered in the sanctuaries by sailors to the Baal of sea-farers. The other three sanctuaries were constructed on Near Eastern models, comprising an open courtyard and a holy-of-holies.

In the holy-of-holies of sanctuary 4 a hoard of ivories was found, among which was a pipe for the smoking of opium. Opium-smoking was known in antiquity for medicinal purposes and in sanctuaries was perhaps used for divine revelation through dreams. There are indications that Cyprus was exporting opium to Egypt in specially made flasks. A perforated cylindrical vase, probably also intended for the inhaling of smoke, was found in the adjacent sanctuary 5. Skulls of oxen and other horned animals were revealed on the floor of sanctuary 5, as at Enkomi; they would have been worn by the priests and worshippers during ritual performances. In addition to the main sanctuaries, two large open courtyards called *temene* were excavated adjoining the sanctuaries. In both there was a table of offerings and an altar for animal sacrifices. The table of offerings is associated with stone horns of consecration, a symbol of Creto-Mycenaean religion. A monumental altar crowned by similar stone horns of consecration was found in a sanctuary at Myrtou-*Pigadhes* near the north-west court.

Necklace with gold beads in the form of figure-of-eight shields and tubular spacers of gold wire; from Enkomi; L 31.7 cm; Late Bronze Age
Cyprus Museum, Nicosia

Bronze statuette of a male
figure wearing a conical cap
with horns; known as 'The
Horned God'; from Enkomi;
H 54.2 cm; Late Bronze Age,
1200–1150 B.C.
Cyprus Museum, Nicosia

The sanctuary of Aphrodite at Palaepaphos was a major religious centre during the whole of the first millenium B.C. It was constructed during the Late Bronze Age III period with huge ashlar blocks, as at sanctuary 1 at Kition. Stone horns of consecration were found in the area of the sanctuary as well as 'Mycenaean' stone capitals.

The 'sacred area' of Kition is in the immediate vicinity of workshops for the smelting of copper. Moreover the workshops communicated directly with the sanctuaries, which would suggest a close relationship between metallurgy and religion. This phenomenon is encountered at other Late Bronze Age sanctuaries in Cyprus, for example at Athienou north of Kition, and is also known at Near Eastern sites. The idea was to place metallurgy, the basis of the economy of Cyprus, under the protection of the gods, while at the same time allowing the religious authorities to control the daily production of copper and thus its export. Storerooms for offerings and for the general use of the main sanctuary 1 were also revealed at Kition.

I have already referred to the military architecture of this period, namely the 'cyclopean' walls. They were built in their lower courses of two rows of large stone blocks, the outer row being of larger blocks, and a core of rubble. The superstructure was of sun-dried bricks. There were bastions against the walls, similar to those uncovered at Kition and Enkomi. Cyclopean walls have also been found at Maa-*Palaeokastro* (with a dog-leg gate) and at Sinda. At Pyla-*Kokkinokremmos* a 'casemate' wall was found, recalling Near Eastern prototypes. The origin of the 'cyclopean' walls as well as the technique of ashlar construction may also be Near Eastern, perhaps Anatolian, and could have been introduced to Cyprus by the Sea Peoples. Ashlar construction, however, may be of Syrian origin since it was known at Ugarit.

The Achaeans, with their advanced metallurgical techniques, made a major contribution to the artistic production of Cyprus during the 12th century B.C. The two bronze statues of the divinities of Enkomi illustrate this, as do a series of remarkable bronze four-sided stands, resting on four wheels, which are decorated with pictorial compositions in the *ajouré* (cut-out) technique and which are fine examples of Cypriot craftsmanship. They were doubtless influenced by ivory carving which also flourished on the island. There is a profusion of bronze vases and weapons in tombs. Swords of Aegean type are introduced to the island as well as a new light-framed car-chariot which replaced the old-fashioned Mycenaean chariot with a solid body. The draught box from Enkomi, now in the British Museum, is carved with hunting scenes and animal compositions on all four sides, and is truly a masterpiece betraying Aegean and Near Eastern stylistic tendencies. A plaque representing the god Bes, carved in the *ajouré* technique, was found in sanctuary 4 at Kition. Remarkable also are the ivory handles of mirrors from Enkomi and Palaepaphos which are decorated with human and animal figures in lively compositions.

Ceramic styles followed Aegean fashions. The exuberant style of the Mycenaean IIIB period is now replaced by the more austere abstract or linear motifs of the so-called Mycenaean IIIC:1b style, though pictorial motifs are not altogether lacking.

Bronze statuette of a male figure with shield and spear standing on an ingot; known as 'The Ingot God'; from Enkomi; H 35 cm; Late Bronze Age, 1200–100 B.C, Cyprus Museum, Nicosia

Ivory mirror handle; from Palaepaphos (Old Paphos); L 21.5 cm; Late Bronze Age, 1200–1125 B.C. Cyprus Museum, Nicosia

The beginning of the 11th century B.C. witnessed a renewal of contacts with the Aegean. New ceramic styles were introduced, probably by people who fled from the Aegean after the 'Dorian' invasion and finally settled on Cyprus. Some of them may have been Cretans, judging from the Sub-Minoan influence not only in ceramics but also in coroplastic art and even religious affairs. For the first time on the island the 'goddess with uplifted arms' appears who is predominant in Crete and who in Cyprus is identified with the goddess of fertility. We find her in the sanctuaries of Kition, Enkomi and elsewhere. The anthropomorphic centaur, in a form known from Crete, was also introduced. Large bicephalic centaurs were found in the sanctuary of the Ingot God at Enkomi.

Other arts flourished at this period, particularly jewellery where the introduction of the new *cloisonné* technique is evidenced. There are some superb specimens of this technique which previously was thought to have been invented much later. A gold sceptre from a royal tomb at Kourion is a case in point. The gold tubular shaft of the sceptre has a globular head topped by two falcons and is decorated in cloisonné, having inlaid enamel of different colours within small compartments separated from each other by thin walls of gold. The same technique was also applied to the bezel of gold rings from Palaepaphos.

A major change occurs in ceramics. The new style, known as Proto-White-Painted or Proto-Bichrome ware, betrays influences mainly from the Aegean and particularly from Sub-Minoan Crete, but there are also elements in both shape and decoration from the Syro-Palestinian coast. Indeed, several Near Eastern imports, mainly lentoid flasks, have been discovered in the tombs of the necropolis at Alaas, northeast of Salamis, which dates to the first half of the 11th century B.C.

In metalwork various objects such as the bronze fibula (safety-pin) are of

Aegean origin. This indicates that women's dress fashions were influenced by newcomers from the Aegean. Hitherto Cypriot women had used ordinary pins to fasten their dresses.

Important changes are also attested in funerary architecture, a phenomenon which occurs for the first time since the arrival of the Achaean colonists. Tombs now have small rectangular chambers with long narrow dromoi. Such tombs existed in Rhodes and Crete and thus indicate the route taken by the colonists before they reached Cyprus. This last wave of Achaean colonists must be those who are referred to in mythical tradition concerning the foundation of cities in Cyprus after the end of the Trojan war, for example Teucer is the traditional founder of Salamis and Agapenor of Paphos. The 11th century B.C. witnesses the establishment of new cities in succession to those of the Late Bronze Age which had been destroyed by a major catastrophe, perhaps an earthquake or a flood, shortly before the middle of the 11th century B.C. Thus Salamis succeeds Enkomi on the east coast. Enkomi was gradually abandoned after the silting up of its inner harbour but there was a period of about 25 years from c. 1075 to c. 1050 B.C. when both towns coexisted. Other towns, such as Palaepaphos and Kition, were not abandoned immediately. Kition was rebuilt and continued to be inhabited until c. 1000 B.C., when the town finally shifted towards the sea following the silting up of its harbour.

The events of the first half of the 11th century B.C. laid the foundations for the future historical and cultural development of Cyprus. The Hellenisation of the island which had started as a slow process c. 1200 B.C. was now complete. Meanwhile the Mycenaean aristocracy dominated the local population both politically and culturally while at the same time accepting influences both from the local indigenous culture and also from the Syro-Palestinian coast, with which they kept

Ivory draughts box; from Enkomi; L 29 cm; Late Bronze Age, 1200–1100 B.C. British Museum

Side view of a bronze four-sided stand. This side shows a man carrying an ingot of copper, facing a stylised tree; from Kourion; H 11 cm, D of ring 8.5 cm; Late Bronze Age, 1200–1100 B.C. British Museum

(Opposite page)
Bronze statuette of a seated male figure; from Enkomi; H 7.5 cm; Late Bronze Age, 1200–1100 B.C. Cyprus Museum, Nicosia

Bronze statuette of a nude female figure; H 9.9 cm; Late Bronze Age, 1200–1100 B.C. Ashmolean Museum, Oxford

up trade relations as their forefathers had done in the 14th and 13th centuries B.C. It was during this time that the Greek language was introduced to the island, a fact which has recently been demonstrated by the discovery of the first Greek inscription in a tomb at Palaepaphos.

The Late Bronze Age may thus be decribed as one of the most formative periods in the life of ancient Cyprus. It prescribed the island's evolution through the first millennium B.C.; indeed, in some ways, down to the present day.

III
EARLY
IRON AGE

(CYPRO-GEOMETRIC)

The Rise of the Ancient Kingdoms

c. 1100–700 B.C.

Terracotta statuette of a goddess with uplifted arms; from Morphou, *Toumba tou Skourou;* H 16 cm; Geometric period, 1050–950 B.C. Cyprus Museum, Nicosia

The eleventh century B.C. is one of the most decisive periods in the history of Cyprus. In archaeological language, the island now enters its Iron Age. Yet the substitution of iron tools and weapons for bronze is but a trivial change, when compared to the massive immigration from the Aegean world, which was now transforming Cyprus into a predominantly Greek-speaking land. Earlier, Mycenaean settlers had merged with the indigenous Cypriots at Enkomi and the other mercantile cities of the Late Bronze Age. Now, whole communities were fleeing from the final ruin of Mycenaean civilisation at home, and were founding new settlements of their own in Cypriot shores. These settlements were to grow into the capital cities of the ancient Greek kingdoms; Kourion, Paphos, Marion, Soloi, Lapithos, and Salamis which now replaced Enkomi as the leading settlement in eastern Cyprus.

Various legends place their foundations at the close of the heroic age, in the aftermath of the Trojan War. Thus Pausanias tells us how king Agapenor of Tegea in Arcadia, sailing home from Troy, was blown off course and settled at Paphos, where he built the temple of Aphrodite. Tacitus, however, records an earlier and native Cypriot founder, Kinyras; it is surely no coincidence that the site of Old Paphos (Kouklia), alone of the ancient Greek kingdoms, has a history going far back into the Bronze Age. Kourion, according to Herodotus, was founded by Argives; he receives some corroboration from the place-name Asine, brought from the ancient port of the Argolid to an ancient village in the territory of Kourion. Likewise Salamis was so named by its founder Teucer, half-brother of the great Ajax, after the island in the Saronic gulf which had been his original home.

If the foundation legends preserve at least a kernel of historical truth, the arrival of Aegean immigrants *en masse* is amply confirmed by archaeological evidence. New to Cyprus at this time are the terracotta figures of a fertility goddess rendered in the Creto-Mycenaean manner, raising her arms in benediction; given the extreme conservatism of indigenous Cypriot worship, this sudden introduction of a new type of idol must imply a new Aegean strain in religious practice. Another novelty of eleventh century Cyprus is the first appearance of the typically Mycenaean chamber tomb with a long dromos leading into a carefully cut rectangular chamber, quite distinct from the traditional Cypriot form where the chamber opens out of a small vertical shaft. Tombs of the Mycenaean type, often richly furnished and suggestive of a newly-arrived Greek aristocracy, have come to light at Kourion *Kaloriziki*, Lapithos *Kastros*, Salamis, Alaas north of Salamis, and most recently in the Paphian cemetery of Kouklia *Skales*.

The Kouklia cemetery has produced four inscribed objects of the utmost historical importance. A bronze obelos (or spit), a bronze bowl, and a stone all bear graffiti in the native Cypro-Minoan syllabic script of the Late Bronze Age, confirming its survival into the eleventh century. On another bronze obelos, however, a fourth graffito foreshadows the Cypro-Classical syllabary of later times, and yields the genitive case of a Greek personal name in a form later shared by the Arcadian and Cypriot dialects: Opheltau, i.e. "belonging to Opheltes". Here, then, we have the earliest known syllabic Greek inscription from Cyprus, contemporary with the latest in Cypro-Minoan, and establishing beyond doubt the origin of the new settlers; they had only to adapt the earlier script to the needs of their own language, thereby evolving the Greek syllabary which we know as Cypro-Classical. So these finds bring with them a long-awaited confirmation that the art of writing was never forgotten in Cyprus, at a time when it had certainly vanished from Greece. Nor is it surprising that this evidence of continuity in literacy should have come from the Paphos region, which at the end of the Bronze Age had mercifully escaped the devastation and turmoil suffered by Enkomi, Kition, and the other great cities of eastern Cyprus.

While their kinsmen in the Aegean had already been plunged into a Dark Age of poverty, isolation and illiteracy, the Greeks of Cyprus still enjoyed a modest prosperity in their new homes, and were still freely in touch with their eastern neighbours. Many tombs contain simple gold ornaments — finger rings, earrings and pendants — often of Levantine character. Lavish bronze cauldrons, representing both Aegean and eastern types, have recently come to light in the Kouklia *Skales* cemetery. But the choicest work of this age is the gold sceptre from a rich tomb at Kourion *Kaloriziki,* with an orb crowned by two hawks, elaborated with polychrome cloisonnée enamelling: a tomb gift in every way worthy of a prince.

The fine painted pottery, as one might expect, acquires a strong Aegean flavour from 1100 B.C. onwards. After the disappearance of the native Bronze Age fabrics there arises a new tradition of painted ornament on a pale ground, destined to last all through the Cypriot Iron Age. The first phase, c. 1100-1050 B.C., is called Proto-White Painted (because it foreshadows the White Painted pottery of the ensuing Cypro-Geometric period), or Proto-Bichrome if a second reddish colour is added to the usual black. This bichrome idea is of Levantine origin, as are a few of the shapes — for instance, the lentoid "pilgrim flask". Otherwise the new style is purely Aegean, derived from the Submycenaean of the Greek mainland and the Subminoan of Crete, and yet far superior to either in the quality of its fabric and in the variety of its ornament. For example there are specimens, some lavishly decorated, of the stirrup-jar, the large container of perfumed oil with deep roots in the Mycenaean past. The tall jar (or pyxis) is a shape of Cretan character; in one instance the painter has had the imagination to add to its austere rectilinear ornament an oriental lotus flower. Even figured subjects are sometimes attempted: birds, fish, agrimi (wild goats) with Cretan affinities; now and again, a crudely simplified human being.

Then follows the pottery of Cypro-Geometric I (c. 1050-950 B.C.), the first phase of the island's Iron Age. This style is largely contemporary with Greek Protogeometric, to which it is related through a common Aegean ancestry, even though direct communication with the Aegean, was now rapidly declining. The leading wares are White Painted I and Bichrome I. The vase-forms — notably amphorae, jugs, plates, cups, and kylikes or drinking bowls — continue to be robust and well-proportioned, carrying just enough decoration to define the shape. The ornament, however, is less varied than before, and more austerely abstract. A pleasant exception to this austerity is a kylix showing a charming picture of two little birds settled upon the shoots of a palm tree. Their miniature silhouette style recalls the pottery of Hama in north Syria, and this is one of many Cypriot renderings of the oriental Tree of Life flanked by a symmetrical pair of living creatures. The shape, however, is directly descended from the late Mycenaean deep bowl, with the addition of the high foot which is a common hallmark of this phase.

No fresh impulses came from foreign parts to enliven the pottery of Cypro-Geometric II (c. 950-850 B.C.), which was on the whole an uneventful, lethargic, and to us somewhat obscure period. The same wares and shapes continued, in debased form. As the descendants of the original Greek settlers merged with the indigenous Cypriots the vitality of their way of life was becoming increasingly diluted. Let us take stock of this gradual symbiosis, from the eleventh century onwards.

As yet, we know very little of any town site in the Early Iron Age, owing to lack of excavation; but, as in several earlier periods of Cypriot antiquity, the tombs and their contents come to our rescue. In some of the Greek kingdoms it seems that the native communities must have been absorbed into the new Greek towns. Thus, near Kourion, the indigenous site of Episkopi *Bamboula* was deserted by the end of the eleventh century, although without any sign of violence; Kourion, with its rich Greek cemetery at *Kaloriziki*, supplanted *Bamboula* in much the same way as Enkomi had been superseded by Greek Salamis. Again, far inland, the western acropolis of Idalion had been a stronghold and sanctuary of the indigenous Cypriots during the troubles at the end of the Bronze Age; but this site, too, was deserted in the eleventh century, when the arrival of Greeks in the area is indicated by the fine Proto-White Painted pottery from tombs in the plain below.

At Lapithos the merging of the two peoples was more gradual, and possibly more peaceful. Each had its own cemetery of chamber tombs, the native form being usual in Lapithos *Skales*, while the Mycenaean type with long dromos at first prevailed in Lapithos *Kastros*. Extra bodies in several of the latter tombs have been interpreted as the sacrifices of slaves destined to attend their masters in the next world — evidence of a somewhat savage temperament in some of the incumbents. But by the ninth century this Mycenaean type of tomb is dying out, as even the *Kastros* tombs begin to follow the traditional Cypriot form. In funerary matters, at least, the Greeks of Lapithos were themselves going native.

One indigenous community, on the south coast, was never taken over by the Greeks. This was Amathus, first settled in the eleventh century, and destined to become one of the leading states of the Cypriot Iron Age, no less powerful and prosperous than the Greek kingdoms. From its early days, Amathus was an unusually outward-looking place, trading freely with both Greeks and Levantines, and freely accepting ideas from both directions. It is a curious paradox that during Cypro-Geometric II, when Cyprus had few links with the outside world, it was

Gold plaque with female head in repoussé, probably from a head-dress; from Lapithos; L 4.3 cm; Geometric period, 850–750 B.C.
Cyprus Museum, Nicosia

Decorated rim of a krater; White Painted ware; from Chrysochou; H 59 cm, D (mouth) 36 cm; Geometric period, 870–750 B.C. Cyprus Museum, Nicosia

Amathus which received the first post-Mycenaean imports of pottery from the Greek homeland. These are three Protogeometric drinking vessels from the island of Euboea.

Some time well back in the ninth century, Cyprus was aroused from her lethargy by a new impetus from the east. Kition, whose sacred area of the Late Bronze Age had been derelict since 1000 B.C., was now resettled by colonists from Tyre, the leading city of the Phoenician homeland and the metropolis of a flourishing commercial empire. The coming of the Phoenicians to Cyprus is but one stage of a steady westward expansion which was to take them as far afield as western Sicily, Sardinia, Carthage and Spain. A Phoenician inscription on an eighth-century bronze bowl gives the name of their Cypriot outpost as Qart Hadasht ("New Town" — the same name as was given to Carthage and Cartagena) and reveals that it was then a colony in the imperial sense, ruled by a governor responsible to the king of Tyre. Its foundation may well have occurred during the reign of king Ethbaal of Tyre (887-856 B.C.), father of the ill-famed Jezebel who became queen of Israel; for Ethbaal had been the high priest of Astarte before he seized the throne as a usurper, and it was to Astarte, goddess of fertility, love and death, that the first colonists of Kition dedicated the finest temple yet found anywhere in the Phoenician world.

The Phoenician masons built this temple upon the massive ashlar ruins of the Late Bronze Age Sanctuary 1 (see Chapter II). What had once been an open courtyard now became a columned hall, with colonnades on both sides and a narrow central aisle open to the sky. At the far end a tripartite Holy-of-Holies was roofed over and approached through three doors side by side. In front of the central door are two huge square bases for free-standing pillars; we are reminded of the famous pillars Jachin and Boaz which had stood in the temple built by earlier Phoenician masons for king Solomon in Jerusalem. After an accidental fire in around 800 B.C. the temple of Astarte was rebuilt with fewer and stouter columns in the hall, and entrance to the Holy-of-Holies was now confined to the central door.

Once settled at Kition the Phoenicians made no effort as yet to extend their political control elsewhere on the island; but their impact on Cypriot art was immediate. In earlier times Astarte had been no stranger to Cyprus, being easily assimilated with the island's goddess of fertility. But now she begins to appear in Phoenician guise on gold plaques which formed part of a lady's tiara, sometimes in full frontal nudity, and sometimes — as in one of the Lapithos *Kastros* tombs — as a bust wearing a Phoenician wig. Another important art-form introduced by these Cypro-Phoenicians is the shallow metal bowl decorated inside with figured scenes. One of the earliest is a silver bowl from Idalion of c. 800 B.C. showing an oriental cult scene: a seated goddess is approached by a priestess who stands between a table of offerings and another table bearing libation vessels; then come a chain of dancing women, and behind the goddess a row of musicians.

Vase known as the "Hubbard" Amphora, depicting a seated goddess drinking through a siphon; Bichrome ware; probably from Platani; H 68 cm, D (mouth) 38.5 cm; Geometric period 850–750 B.C.
Cyprus Museum, Nicosia

Kition, Phoenician temple of Astarte, founded in c. 850 B.C. upon the ruins of a Late Bronze Age temple, and in continuous use until the fall of the Phoenician kingdom in 312 B.C.

The coming of the Phoenicians also increased the repertoire of pottery wares in the Cypro-Geometric III period (c. 850-750 B.C.). To the traditional White Painted and Bichrome they added two important fabrics of their own, Red Slip and Black-on-Red: fabrics which are especially connected with Phoenician commerce and colonisation from Cyprus to Sardinia and Spain. Although samples of both fabrics had previously come to Cyprus as imports, it was only after the foundation of Kition that they were regularly manufactured on the island. A number of Black-on-Red juglets, probably intended for precious unguents, form part of a large deposit to consecrate the rebuilding of the Kition temple after the fire of c. 800 B.C. To the shiny orange surface of the slip, lines and small circles are added in dull dark paint. Red Slip is similar, but without decoration.

In the traditional fabrics the Geometric ornament becomes much more varied, and regional styles within the island can now be distinguished. A conservative spirit prevails in the west, where small circles are especially popular. Meanwhile eastern Cyprus preferred the motifs to be organised in square panels, and on the whole rectilinear. Eastern potters were also more enterprising in trying out figured themes in which there is now a notable increase. Aesthetically the most successful theme is the isolated bird, easy to draw, and having an obvious appeal to the vase-painter's decorative sense. When more ambitious themes with humans were attempted, the painter's imagination often outran his technique, so that his intention is not always easy to fathom; but even if the scenes appear crude and maladroit to our eyes, they may nevertheless have a rare historical or religious importance. Best known is the Hubbard amphora, an eastern Bichrome III vase with a religious scene recalling that on the Idalion silver bowl. A libation is being offered to an enthroned lady. She is surely a goddess; behind her is a winged sphinx smelling a flower, and sphinxes do not usually attend mere mortals. In the

64

Syrian manner she prepares to drink through a siphon from various vessels placed on a table for her by an attendant priestess. The bull's head on the extreme left is an age-old symbol of fertility in Cyprus, recalling the shrine models of the Early Bronze Age. The scene continues on the reverse with a chain of female dancers and a male lyre-player.

More baffling are the scenes on a Bichrome III krater. On one side, two palm-trees stand outside what looks like a tripartite building of symmetrical design, into which two women have been somehow embodied. Was the painter perhaps thinking of a great oriental shrine, like the Holy-of-Holies at Kition, with its sacred trees outside the forecourt, and its "women at the window" inside the temple — the sacred courtesans who attended Astarte's worshippers? On the other side of the krater, however, the "shrine" has come apart, one woman holds a wreath, the other a comb. Possibly the central part of the supposed "shrine" is also a comb, passed by one lady to the other; but we cannot be sure. Nevertheless, some reference to the Astarte cult is implied.

Two open-work cloisonné ivory plaques from royal tomb 79, Salamis; probably originally on the arms of the throne found in the same tomb; c. 700 B.C. H 16.4 cm. Cyprus Museum, Nicosia

Restored bed of wood, covered with ivory plaques; from Salamis, royal tomb 79; L 188.5 cm, max. H 88.6 cm; about 700 B.C. Cyprus Museum, Nicosia

A good example of the White Painted III style is a krater with a chariot team and rider which comes from Chrysochou near Marion in the far west. This area had been least affected by the orientalising ideas following in the wake of the Phoenicians, and it may be no coincidence that both the shape and the theme have precedents in the Mycenaean chariot kraters. The details of the chariot group, however, are more Assyrian than Greek — especially the horse's elaborate crest, the standard behind the charioteer, the large wheel with many spokes, and the idea of lodging spears in the chariot box. This is the work of an unusually accomplished painter, who brought up to date a traditional theme with the gear of his own day.

These vase-paintings take us well into the eighth century, an age of expanding horizons and rapidly increasing prosperity. Mainland Greece was at last recovering from the isolation of her Dark Age, Phoenician merchantmen often hawked their wares in the Aegean and Greek traders from Euboea were established at a new emporium at Al Mina on the north Syrian coast. From the Phoenicians the Greeks quickly learned the art of alphabetic writing, thereby putting an end to several centuries of illiteracy. A steep rise in population caused them to found colonies in Italy and Sicily, and to order their own affairs through the evolution of the *polis* system — the network of small autonomous city-states, each with its own clearly defined republican constitution, and its own centre of public life.

The coastal cities of Cyprus must have profited greatly as staging posts for visitors from east and west, and the lively interplay of Greek and oriental influences added much to the vitality of eighth-century Cypriot art. And yet, in two important respects, Greek and native Cypriots remained aloof from these new de-

66

velopments. Having never forgotten the art of writing since the Bronze Age, they saw no reason to abandon their syllabic signs, even with the more convenient Phoenician alphabet displayed before their eyes at Kition. To the very end of Classical times one syllabary was used for the Cypriot dialect of Greek, another for the Eteocypriot (i.e. "true Cypriot") tongue spoken by the indigenous people of Amathus and elsewhere. In political matters, too, the Cypriots were rigidly conservative. No *polis* system ever took root among them; they were never to know any form of government other than absolute monarchy, inherited from Mycenaean tradition and in line with eastern despotism. So Cyprus remained a land of about ten petty kingdoms, at first wholly independent, and then still enjoying local autonomy even after their nominal submission to the Assyrian empire in 709 B.C. (see Chapter IV).

One new development, however, made a profound impression upon the Cypriot Greeks. Memories of the heroic Mycenaean past, embodied in the saga of the Trojan War, had survived orally all through the Greek Dark Age, and were now finding monumental expression in the Homeric *Iliad* and *Odyssey*. Through recitation at public festivals, these and other epics quickly became known throughout the Greek world. Thus a recollection of bygone glories came to be shared by all

Restored throne of wood covered with ivory and with cut-out plaques between the arms; from Salamis royal tomb 79; H 72 cm; about 700 B.C.
Cyprus Museum, Nicosia.

Greeks, whether they lived in the Aegean homeland, or in the western colonies, or in the Greek kingdoms of Cyprus. Indeed, the Cypriot Greeks could boast their own epic poet in Stasinos, whom they claimed to have been Homer's son-in-law; his lost poem, the *Cypria*, formed a long prelude to the *Iliad*, telling of how Aphrodite the Cyprian goddess had provoked the Trojan War through the fatal Judgment of Paris.

Against this historical background, let us now consider the royal tombs of Salamis: the tombs of a small but wealthy kingdom under a Greek monarch and ruling class. While advertising their prosperity with a fine display of oriental luxuries, the Salaminians had also become deeply interested in their Mycenaean roots, as we shall see from the manner in which they honoured their deceased princes.

These tombs, nine in all, occupy a plot of their own to the west of the settlement, but set apart from the cemetery for commoners known as the Cellarka (cf. Chapter IV). They form a series throughout the eighth and seventh centuries, and most of them were built and furnished on a scale lavish enough to be called royal. We shall concentrate our attention on tomb 79, the best preserved, and one of the richest tombs ever to be excavated in Cyprus. It received two princely burials, the first shortly before 700 B.C., the second shortly after.

Like others in the royal cemetery, this tomb is lined with fine ashlar blocks. The dromos, nearly thirteen metres wide, leads through an anteroom to a small burial chamber roofed with a huge monolith. The great width of the dromos was dictated by the special honours paid to royalty. A dead prince would be conveyed to the tomb on his hearse or chariot, which had to be wheeled round so that its back faced the chamber doorway. The team of horses was then slaughtered as though to accompany the master to the next world, and buried with the chariot in the dromos. In this tomb, however, four vehicles and the skeletons of ten horses were found, a four-wheeled hearse and a two-wheeled chariot for each prince. From the chariot with the earlier burial all the metal parts survive, and the impressions left by its wooden parts were clear enough to allow a reasonably certain reconstruction. The whole team was decked out in bronze finery. Each of the four horses wore a breastplate, a pair of massive side pendants, a front band on the head, and a pair of blinkers, all adorned with oriental figured imagery. On the yoke were four standards in the form of an oriental palmette. A bronze warrior in Assyrian armour stood beside each wheel on the lynch pin, each end of which was covered by a hub cap in the form of a sphinx's head.

The other offerings, too, were of royal magnificence. Beside the dromos wall stood two bronze cauldrons. One is of north Syrian type, decorated with twelve protomes or foreparts of living creatures: eight griffins, and four bearded sirens with faces on both sides of their heads. This is by far the most elaborate example of a class which became widely known in the west, and helped to set off an orientalising movement in Greek and Etruscan art.

In the same deposit were the remains of the royal furniture. Like the cauldrons, they went with the first burial, and had been brushed aside in a heap to make way

Bronze figurine of a
soldier; from Salamis; it
was originally attached to
a lynch pin of the chariot
found in the same tomb;
H 26.5 cm; c. 700 B.C.
Cyprus Museum, Nicosia

decorative disc

hand grip

lynch pin

hub cap

Reconstructed chariot

rein ring

yoke standards

yoke pins

Sketch showing
reconstruction and photograph
in situ of
a chariot burial from the
royal tomb No. 79 at
Salamis; c. 700 B.C.

for the second incumbent. As with the vehicles, the perished wood had left clear impressions; thus, with the help of the ivory fittings, it was possible to reconstruct three thrones, a footstool and a bed. The main decoration of the bedstead consists of three ivory friezes carved in relief, portraying kneeling Egyptian gods, interlaced palmette and lotus blooms, and confronting sphinxes; some details are picked out in blue glass inlays, and there are traces of a gold leaf covering. One of the thrones has a comfortably concave back inlaid with ivory guilloche patterns; to decorate its sides, two splendid pairs of ivory plaques have been set back to back, so that their openwork designs seem to be in the round. One design is a sacred Tree of Life based on the lotus, with palmettes trailing along the ground. The other set presents a sphinx, the guardian of royalty, wearing the crowns of Upper and Lower Egypt, and a characteristically Egyptian headdress; in the field are more lotuses and palmettes. All these ivory panels are in the Phoenician style, a suave blend of Egyptian and Asiatic elements; typically Phoenician, too, is the soft, dreamy expression on the sphinx's face.

Furniture of this quality, richly adorned with figured ivory plaques, was an essential amenity in any royal palace of the eastern Mediterranean at this time. When we read in the First Book of Kings of the "ivory house" built for Ahab king of Israel at his new capital of Samaria, this is what is meant. Indeed, the nearest parallels to the Salamis ivories are to be found at other royal seats: some at Samaria, others at the Assyrian capitals of Nimrud and Khorsabad. In each case the Phoenician style predominates in the furniture ivories; and the ruler buried in this tomb, like the kings of Assyria and Israel, must certainly have employed Phoenician craftsmen to decorate his household.

And yet, in spite of all this oriental luxury, these tombs cannot be fully understood without looking westwards, to the ancestral land of the Salaminian kings. In the next world as in this, they were expected to keep a convivial table and a hospitable hearth; so the first prince of tomb 79 was given twelve iron spits or skewers (oboloi) and a pair of iron firedogs in the form of a ship, for roasting meat over a charcoal fire. Similar sets have been found in contemporary aristocratic burials in Argos and east Crete, recalling the gear used by Achilles when he entertained visitors to his tent at Troy; in the *Iliad* even the most distinguished heroes did not disdain the role of chef. Furthermore, almost every stage of a Homeric funeral is mirrored among the burial practices of Salamis. We have already observed how the chariot horses were sacrificed in the dromos, just as Patroclus' team was slaughtered at his burial by his friend Achilles. Sheep and cattle were also sacrificed in Patroclus' honour, and his other offerings included amphorae containing honey and oil; a large cattle bone came to light in tomb 2, while an amphora from tomb 3 is inscribed *elaion*, 'olive oil', in the Cypriot syllabary. When Patroclus' body had been burnt, his pyre was quenched with wine; a pyre deposit in tomb 1 was covered with a thin muddy layer, above which were six unburnt and unbroken vessels for putting out the flames. The hero's ashes were then gathered into a golden urn and wrapped in a linen cloth; large golden vessels are the preserve of epic poetry, but tomb 1 produced a bronze cauldron containing a cremation, with traces of cloth inside. Finally a great mound of earth was raised over a Homeric hero's tomb, like the vast tumulus over tomb 3.

For each one of these practices, taken singly, contemporary parallels can be cited from different lands; but when viewed together their close correspondence with Homeric descriptions of funerals must be more than mere coincidence. One could hardly see in them a conservative adherence to the old Mycenaean practices, since cremation had been foreign to Mycenaean tradition, and no earlier chariot burials are known from Cyprus. It is more likely that the Salaminian burial customs represent a revival of interest in the great deeds of the Mycenaean past, inspired by the circulation of the Homeric and other epic poems. This was the way in which the Greek Cypriot kingdom of Salamis chose to honour its dead princes, scions of the heroes who had once ruled over the Aegean island to which the kingdom owed its origin and its name.

IV
ARCHAIC
CYPRUS
750–475 B.C.

Gold necklace with agate pendant, from the sanctuary of Aphrodite Arsos. L 33 cm, Archaic period, early sixth century B.C.
Cyprus Museum, Nicosia

The prosperity of Cyprus in the 8th century has already been illustrated by the rich grave goods from the "Royal" tombs at Salamis. In 750 B.C., the beginning of the Archaic period, Assyria began to show increasing aggression towards her neighbours. Under Tiglath-Pileser III and his successor, Sargon II, Assyria extended her influence in Palestine, Syria and Phoenicia, and Cyprus was eventually reduced to submission in 709 B.C.

Sargon II erected a stele at Kition to record this event, describing how seven Cypriot Kings paid him homage. In later Assyrian records we read of ten kingdoms and by the 5th century there were eleven, namely: Salamis (the most important), Paphos, Soloi, Kourion (Roman Curium), Kition (Roman Citium), Kerynia (or Kyrenia), Lapithos, Marion (Roman Marium), Amathus, Tamassos and Idalion. These city kingdoms were autonomous and towards the end of the 6th century struck their own coinage. The idea of coinage came from the Greek world, but by then Persia had taken full control over Cyprus. Therefore, although the designs often copied those of Greek cities, the weights and denominations were those of their Persian masters.

The population of the island continued to be mixed with the Phoenicians still in control at Kition and the indigenous Cypriot population at Amathus. This phenomenon is well illustrated by the division of language which, although certainly occurring earlier, became more apparent in the Archaic period. The Cypriot syllabic script was used to write both Greek (that is Arcado-Cypriot Greek, probably introduced at the end of the Bronze Age) and Eteo-Cypriot. The latter is still undeciphered but it appears to be a pre-Hellenic and pre-Semitic language probably related to the native Cypriot tongue surviving from the Bronze Age. Most inscriptions in this language come from Amathus and the immediate vicinity. At Kition the majority of inscriptions are in Phoenician and the script is found on both imported and locally made vessels. The Greek alphabet appeared very occasionally in the 6th century but did not come into regular use until the 4th century.

Assyrian domination lasted less than fifty years and from about 663 B.C. Cyprus enjoyed a hundred glorious years of independence during which her own civilisation and culture flourished and developed. Many of the finest Iron Age remains and artefacts date from that period.

Ordinary people were buried in simple rock-cut chamber tombs often used on more than one occasion. The "Royal" tombs at Salamis no doubt served the kings and aristocrats. Splendid tombs built of well dressed ashlar blocks with rectangular chambers with saddle or trapezoidal roofs approached by stepped *dromoi* (entrance passages) dating from the 7th and 6th centuries have been found at other city sites including Tamassos, Amathus, Kition, Idalion and Soloi and elsewhere as at Patriki and Trachonas. The finest are those at Tamassos built about 600 B.C. whose architecture in stone imitates in detail wooden construction. The roofs of the chambers are beamed. Certain elements are of Phoenician origin like the volute capitals surmounting the pilasters supporting the entrance doors and the blind windows in one tomb whose sills are decorated in relief with a version of the eastern "tree of life", a favourite ornament in several media in Archaic Cyprus.

Another tomb in the "Royal" necropolis at Tamassos was a simple rock-cut chamber tomb, but remains of horses and bronze trappings found in the *dromos* recall the Homeric practice of sacrificing chariots, horses and slaves prevalent in the "Royal" tombs at Salamis (see Chapter III). Further evidence for a cult of the

Ox-shaped flask (askos), Black-on-Red ware; from Kourion; H 19 cm; Archaic period, 700–600 B.C. British Museum

dead comes from the Cellarka cemetery at Salamis in use from about 700-300 B.C. and situated south of the "Royal" necropolis on a low ridge of hard limestone. The tombs here evidently served the ordinary population, being simple rock-cut chamber tombs, occasionally with carved entrances, often used for more than one generation, the earliest burials being pushed aside to make room for the later ones. In the *dromoi* of some tombs, or close by, pyres were discovered containing in the ashes a number of offerings, all burnt, including vases evidently smashed after a libation had been offered. The practice may have been copied from Athens, although there is no evidence for cremation in the Cellarka cemetery such as was associated with the Athenian pyres.

When the Assyrian Empire finally broke up, at the end of the 7th century, Egypt emerged as the major power. In about 569 B.C. the Pharaoh Amasis took political control of Cyprus, which he held until around 545 B.C. when the Cypriot kings transferred their allegiance to the Great King of Persia as their new overlord. Direct Egyptian influence on Cyprus during the period of domination is not always very

Jug, Bichrome ware decorated in the "freefield" style with a bull sniffing a lotus flower, from Arnadi, H 23.5 cm; Archaic period, 750–650 B.C.
Cyprus Museum, Nicosia

75

Limestone statue of a male
worshipper in the Neo-Cypriot
style; from Tamassos;
H 145.0 cm; Archaic period,
.600–550 B.C.
British Museum

Terracotta female figure
wearing a *polos* (tall
headdress) and with upraised
arms, perhaps a goddess
Painted decoration in red and
black; from Old Paphos, H 35
cm; Archaic period, 7th to 6th
century B.C.
British Museum

apparent, but to this era belongs an interesting tomb on the outskirts of the Koufo-meron cemetery at Salamis. The short *dromos* cut in the rock leads to a rec-tangular chamber built of fine limestone blocks with a vaulted roof and paved floor. The whole of the interior of the chamber is painted like the inside of an Egyptian sarcophagus: the decoration in blue and purple is applied directly to the surface of the stone; on the side walls are lotus flowers and buds on long stems and the ceiling is covered by a network-pattern with rosettes and crosses at the junctions.

Although the Cypriot kings submitted to Cyrus, the king of Persia, in about 545 B.C., paying him tribute and placing their forces at his disposal, at first they re-tained their independence. However Darius, who succeeded Cyrus as king in 521 B.C., tightened Persian control by including Cyprus in the fifth satrapy of the Persian Empire. The island therefore shared the same fate as the East Greek cities of Ionia (on the west coast of modern Turkey). Freedom of movement within the Persian Empire intensified contact between Cyprus and Ionia and from the middle of the 6th century Cypriot art became increasingly susceptible to East Greek in-fluence. When the Ionian revolt, an attempt by the East Greek cities to rid them-selves of Persian rule, broke out in 499 B.C. all the kingdoms of Cyprus except for Amathus joined in at the instigation of Onesilos, the king of Salamis, who had re-cently dispossessed his brother on the throne. The Persians sent a military force to the island and, having heavily defeated the Cypriots in the field, proceeded in 498 B.C. to lay siege to the cities which still held out against them, including Paphos

Terracotta model of a two-horse chariot with driver and two warriors; from Ovgoros; H 16.5 cm; Archaic period, 700–600 B.C.
Cyprus Museum, Nicosia

Terracotta warrior; H 17.6 cm;
Archaic period, 700–600 B.C.
Cyprus Museum, Nicosia

Greek bronze helmet of
Corinthian type; from the
Persian siege mound at
Old Paphos; H 21.5 cm;
Archaic period, c. 500 B.C.
Cyprus Museum, Nicosia

Silver stater of Evelthon, king
of Salamis (560–525 B.C.), the
first to use coinage. Ram and
inscription in Cypriot syllabic
script
Cyprus Museum, Nicosia

and Soloi.

Excavations at Old Paphos (Kouklia) have graphically revealed the story of the siege. The Persians erected a huge mound against the north-east gate of the city, composed of rubble and broken limestone statues and monuments from an open sanctuary nearby, on to which they drove up their siege engines. The inhabitants meanwhile dug long passages and tunnels underneath the wall leading into the

Some of the 2,000 terracotta figurines from a sanctuary at Ayia Irini; mainly of the Archaic period, 750–500 B.C. Cyprus Museum, Nicosia

Faience amulet, probably
Phoenician, of the Egyptian
god Bes; from Kition; H 6.6
cm; Archaic period 600–475
B.C.
Cyprus Museum, Nicosia

Terracotta statuette of a
woman with a syrinx
(pan-pipes); from Arsos;
Archaic period, c. 670/
60–600 B.C.
Cyprus Museum, Nicosia

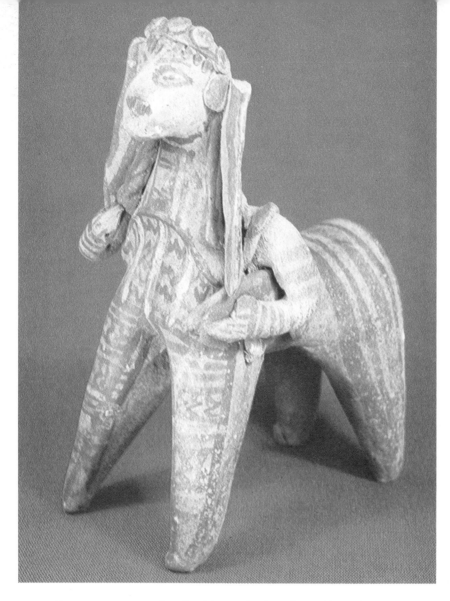

mound in an attempt to undermine it by setting it on fire and hurled stone missiles on to their attackers. All their efforts were, however, in vain and the city was taken. Soloi also surrendered after holding out for five months and all the cities in Cyprus were finally reduced.

The city kingdoms were well fortified, their walls built of mudbrick on stone foundations. At Old Paphos the wall had towers at intervals and the north-east gate developed slowly from the familiar oriental type with twin rectangular bastions projecting outwards from the city wall flanking a narrow passage. About 500 B.C., shortly before the siege, both the wall and gate were considerably strengthened, the mudbrick faces being revetted with limestone blocks and a developed system of berm, ditch and glacis was introduced.

Domestic buildings likewise were generally built of mudbrick on rubble foundations set in mud mortar. Rooms were rectangular or apsidal. Public buildings were constructed of fine ashlar masonry with mud-mortar and the ability of

Polychrome terracotta figurine of a centaur (part human, part horse) holding a quiver; decorated with red, black and white paint; unknown provenance; H 16 cm, L 11.2 cm; Archaic period, sixth century B.C. Cyprus Museum, Nicosia

Cypriot architects and masons of the period is well illustrated by the built-tombs. In the sanctuary within the walled city at Tamassos some of the structures were wooden, including a stoa; Phoenician influence is visible in the half-column capitals (evidently supported by wooden shafts) as it was in the architectural decoration of the "Royal" tombs. Phoenician influence in Cypriot architecture is also apparent in some temple plans, as we shall see, but it was particularly strong on free-standing votive monuments, pillars and pilasters dedicated in sanctuaries. To the 6th century, when Cyprus came into closer contact with the Greek world, belong a few Greek architectural fragments but the evidence for Greek temples or public buildings is very slight.

Religion played an important part in Cypriot life at all periods in antiquity. Many archaic sanctuaries containing quantities of votive offerings have been discovered. They are often situated outside the settlements to which they belong; the larger cities usually had several shrines. The typical archaic Cypriot sanctuary consisted of a *temenos* or open court enclosed by a wall with small cult buildings perhaps including a chapel and altars. Only a few large temples are known and these are situated within the city walls. At Kition the Phoenician temple of Astarte continued in use as did the two smaller temples rebuilt by the Phoenicians. The Astarte temple retained its tripartite "holy of holies" approached by a partly roofed courtyard supported by piers. Another temple-like building with a tripartite plan recalling the arrangement of Solomon's temple in Jerusalem stood within the walled area at Tamassos. It was dedicated, according to a later inscription, to Aphrodite-Astarte. A small temple on the Greek plan with *pronaos* and *cella* was built on the acropolis at Soloi and two others are known from nearby Paradisotissa. Soloi was always renowned for its pro-Greek tendencies and according to legend derived its name from the Athenian law-giver Solon, who was said to have visited the city in about 570/560 B.C.

In the Archaic period the Cypriots became acquainted with a number of Oriental, Egyptian and Greek gods. As a result several of their native cults were re-incarnated in a Greek form which is better documented by epigraphic evidence in the 5th century. The principal deity remained the Great Mother Goddess, a fertility-goddess, who was now worshipped in a number of guises, being identified with the Phoenician Astarte and Anath, the Phrygian Cybele and the Greek Athena and Aphrodite. Aphrodite became the Cypriot goddess *par excellence* described as "the Cypriot" already by Hesiod, writing about 700 B.C., as previously by Homer. The Phoenician gods Reshef, later to be identified with the Greek Apollo, and Baal-Hamman, "god of the perfumed altar" also associated with the Libyan god Ammon, were worshipped together with the hero Melqart associated with the Greek Herakles. Other male gods included the local god of music, perhaps originally the deified Kinyras, the legendary first king and priest of Aphrodite at her most famous shrine at Paphos, later also equated with Apollo, and another who was to merge later with the Greek Zeus. The Phoenicians

Gold-plated silver mountings with repoussé (relief) decoration bordered by beads of granulation, either originally forming a headdress or worn across the breast; from Yialia, Paphos district; each 2×2 cm; Archaic period, 700–600 B.C. Cyprus Museum, Nicosia

Gold earring with pomegranate pendants hung from a hollow crescent; from Soloi; L 4 cm; Archaic period, 600–475 B.C. Cyprus Museum, Nicosia

Bowl with pictorial decoration
on the inside, Bichrome ware;
from Achna; H 10.9 cm,
D 34.3 cm; Archaic period,
c. 600 B.C.
British Museum

Bowl (phiale) imported from
Chios; from Marion; D 18.5
cm; Archaic period,
6th century B.C.
Cyprus Museum, Nicosia

probably introduced the Egyptian gods such as "Bes", Ptah, Hathor and Thoeris
who often served as amulets and good-luck charms to ward off evil. They were
known before the period of Egyptian rule, during which the only evidence for
direct influence on religion is a contemporary imported bronze situla from the
sanctuary at Kourion shown by later inscriptions to belong to Apollo Hylates.
Alongside the syllabic inscription "to the god" it bears in Egyptian hieroglyphs a
dedication to the Egyptian goddess Isis whose worship is not otherwise attested
in Cyprus before the Hellenistic period.

The Cypriots believed that the god or goddess was resident in the sanctuary and
therefore participated in their religious rites, which included sacred banquets and

ritual dances accompanied by musicians playing lyres, double pipes or the syrinx (Pan-pipes) and tambourines. Worshippers offered a number of gifts appropriate to the deity, such as the dove for Aphrodite. Animals were sacrificed and incense burnt. From the sanctuary of Baal-Hamman at Meniko a lively terracotta group of the 6th century portrays two men leading a bull to sacrifice. The priests wore bull or other animal masks and the people dedicated numerous statues of lime-stone and terracotta representing themselves or the deity to act as substitutes for themselves as continuous worshippers. At Ayia Irini more than 2,000 statues and statuettes, dating mostly from the Late Bronze Age to the end of the Archaic period, were found grouped around the altar in the sanctuary. The identity of the

Terracotta group of two men and a bull; from Meniko; H of bull 28.5 cm; Archaic period, 600–500 B.C.
Cyprus Museum, Nicosia

deity, which may not be recorded epigraphically at this period, is reflected in the dedications. In the sanctuaries of male gods statuettes of horsemen and war chariots are common, while in those dedicated to the female fertility-goddess bearers of offerings, mostly women, worshippers (or the goddess herself) with raised arms, and musicians predominate. As in the Late Bronze Age the religious leaders evidently had control over the all-important copper industry at least at Kition, where a copper workshop was built close to the Astarte temple around 600 B.C. and remained in use until about 450 B.C., and at Tamassos, where copper installations within the Aphrodite-Astarte and Cybele sanctuary were in use from the third quarter of the 7th century until the Hellenistic period.

The main sanctuaries had their own terracotta workshops and terracotta figurines were also buried in tombs. A vast number were produced, illustrating aspects of both religious and daily life. The techniques vary but several are painted in bright colours of red or purple and black or brown. Figures of the 6th century from Salamis and Kazaphani wear cuirasses with pictorial decoration in the same style as contemporary vases. It was some time in the 8th century that the use of the mould for terracottas reached Cyprus from Syria and the island may have played some part in its introduction to Greece around 700 B.C. Moulded terracottas follow in style the contemporary sculpture. Fairly numerous are women votaries in elaborate costume wearing rich jewellery like the syrinx player from Arsos. Many of the small Cypriot terracottas were still entirely hand-made by the so-called "snowman" technique. Others have a trumpet-shaped body formed by hand or on a wheel and a hand-made or moulded head.

Monumental sculpture in both the local limestone and terracotta began in the early years of independence, around 670/660 B.C. Some remarkable colossal statues were produced in both media. The large terracotta statues, often over life-size, were formed of separate pieces, usually hand-made, joined together. There are a number of early examples among the Ayia Irini dedications. Figures from Tamassos look like Assyrians with their long square beards. The Cypriot sculptor in limestone was always constrained by the nature of his material. Limestone occurs in shallow beds and splits in long thin sections, resulting in a rather flat appearance. The softness of the stone precludes elaborate carving of details, although this was partly remedied by the use of paint and engraving. The earliest ("Proto-Cypriot") style was essentially a local creation, although it shows some eastern influence. The faces are usually triangular or oval with severe expressions and large protruding eyes with feathered eyebrows. Both men and women wear their hair long down the back of the neck. The men usually have long beards and wear helmets. The women are often bedecked with jewellery including necklaces, earrings and earcaps and may wear a turban or a low crown. Little attention is paid to the backs of the statues, which are usually left flat and unworked. Towards the end of the 7th century Cyprus first came into contact with Egypt and also the East Greeks through her involvement in the Greek trading post established at Naucratis in the Egyptian delta. Consequently Cypriot sculpture from the first half of the 6th century shows both Egyptian and East Greek influence. Sculptures in this "Neo-Cypriot" style usually have their hair arranged in an Egyptian *klaft* (wig), the features are softer and there is a slight Greek "Archaic smile" on the lips. The men sport long beards, sometimes square and artificially curled, like those of their

Terracotta figures wearing bull's head masks, perhaps priests; from Kourion; L 11.1 cm, W 9 cm, H 9.7 cm; Archaic period, 650–600 B.C. Cyprus Museum, Nicosia

87

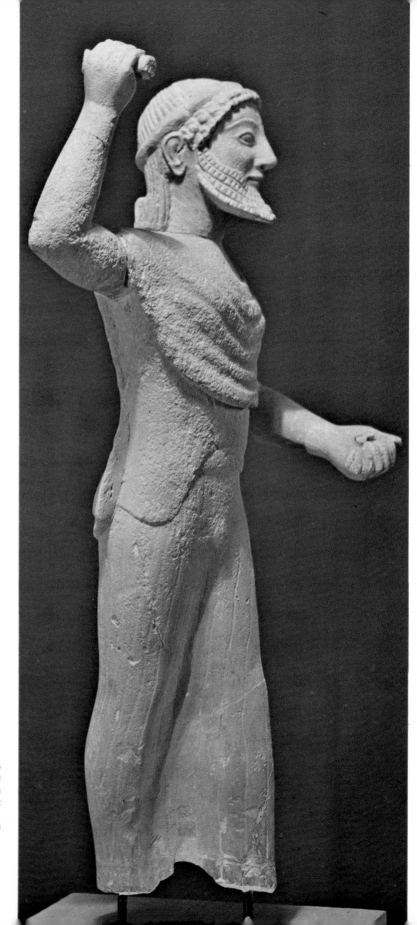

Limestone statue of Zeus
Keraunios (the thunderer)
holding a thunderbolt; from
Kition; H 56 cm; Archaic
period c. 500 B.C.
Cyprus Museum, Nicosia

earlier Assyrian rulers. They wear a variety of helmets usually derived from Near Eastern types or else Egyptian crowns. Others are dressed in "bathing trunks" often decorated with rosettes and wear headbands with similar decoration. Versions of the Egyptian kilt are worn and also common is a costume comprising a long tunic and often a mantle draped over one or both shoulders. The women continue to wear rich jewellery; their dress is usually a long plain tunic. The head is often simply covered by a veil but turbans may also be worn. The Egyptian rulers left few legacies of material culture directly attributable to the period of their rule, but to those years belong a small number of sculptures in the Cypro-Egyptian style which are faithful copies of Egyptian statues.

The intensification of contact with the East Greek world brought about by the inclusion of Cyprus in the Persian Empire had a noticeable effect on Cypriot sculptors. The Archaic Cypro-Greek style began in about 540 B.C. Statues of women show them still wearing traditional Cypriot jewellery but their features show strong Ionian influence. To the last fifty years of the Archaic period (c. 525–475 B.C.) belong some fine copies of East Greek *korai*. Likewise the men may still have long hair, now usually arranged in spiral curls, and long beards, and wear oriental helmets or Egyptian crowns, but their soft rounded features and Archaic smiles betray Greek influence. They now usually wear a *chiton* (tunic) and *himation* (cloak), typical dress of the East Greek school. There are exceptions like the statue from Kition, probably representing Zeus Keraunios (Zeus throwing the thunderbolt) whose tunic and aegis recall the costume of earlier figures. Only a few Cypriot *kouroi* (standing youths) are naked in the mainland Greek tradition. An imported example of marble dating from around 520 B.C. was found at Marion.

The vases in particular illustrate the regional differences in Archaic Cyprus. In the south and east a flourishing school was established continuing and developing the pictorial style which had its beginnings in the Geometric period and drawing its inspiration from Syrian and Phoenician textiles and metal and ivory work. The shapes were mostly developed from their precursors. The favourite fabrics were still White Painted with the ornaments in matt black on a buff or greenish-white slip (coating) and Bichrome, which adds decoration in matt red or purple. Elaborate geometric and floral motifs including the guilloche, lotus flower, open palmette and "tree of life" are combined with figures of humans, animals or mythical creatures to form compositions of a wide variety, of which the liveliest and most original belong to the years of independence. Jugs are often decorated in the "free field" style with no ground line. Birds are a favourite motif. On a jug from Arnadi a bull is sniffing a flower like the sphinx on the Hubbard amphora. Amathus again stands apart and the vessels form a particular group. Belly-shaped amphorae decorated with closely-packed ornaments were popular there. In the north and west the potters concentrated on producing elaborate compass-drawn circle designs and also preferred more intricate vessel shapes. Black-on-Red ware is more common in this region. Not all foreign influence came from the Near East. Imported Greek pottery, mostly from the East Greek area, has been found, in particular at Marion, which had close ties with the Greek world. Occasionally the style was imitated by the Cypriots themselves.

Egyptian Bronze situla with an inscription in Egyptian hieroglyphs and also an inscription in the Cypriot syllabic script which reads: "to the god" presumably Apollo in whose sanctuary it was found; from Kourion; H 11 cm; Archaic period, about 663–525 B.C. (Saite period in Egypt)
Cyprus Museum, Nicosia

Limestone head of a *kore* showing Ionian influence; from Idalion; H 34 cm, Archaic period, early 5th century B.C.

Jewellery for the most part continued the types which were by now well established in the Cypriot repertoire, but it is generally of higher quality using finer techniques. Granulation (grains of metal soldered on to a background) was a popular decoration. Statues of limestone and terracotta wear earrings, necklaces and bangles, many of which can be matched by actual finds. An example is a magnificent gold necklace from Arsos of ribbed lentoid beads with an agate pendant decorated with granulation and surmounted by a bee and two *uraei* (snakes) wearing Egyptian crowns. Earrings with tapered hoops, more elaborate versions of a type first known in the Late Bronze Age, may have pendants attached. Other earrings are boat-shaped with a hollow hoop, a type of Syrian origin known also in East Greece. Gold mountings probably originally forming a *polos*, a Near Eastern headdress, continued a tradition established in Cyprus at least from the 9th century. They are decorated in repoussé with Syrian motifs. Cyprus introduced the type to Rhodes in the 7th century.

The Archaic period was the zenith of Cypriot civilisation in the first millennium B.C. The island had three overlords in fairly quick succession but also enjoyed a century of independence during which she was able to develop art and culture in her own right. The stimulus provided by contacts with her neighbours, whether through trade or submission to their rule, led to the production of works of art with a definite Cypriot quality. In this period models were not slavishly imitated but rather adapted to suit the Cypriot taste and purpose. Cyprus also played an important role in the transmission of goods and ideas, above all to the Phoenician centres in the western Mediterranean, the East Greek cities of Ionia and the islands in the eastern Aegean. The individual city kingdoms grew powerful and able to make a stand, albeit unsuccessful, against the Great King of Persia. Their final defeat in 498 B.C. was a turning-point in Cypriot history and it was in the turmoil of Greek and Persian politics that the Classical period began in about 475 B.C.

Terracotta ram-headed god; probably from the sanctuary at Meniko; W (throne) 7.6 cm, H (total) 18.5 cm; Archaic period, 600–500 B.C.
Cyprus Museum, Nicosia

V
THE
CLASSICAL
PERIOD
475–325 B.C.

Bronze head of Apollo (the Chatsworth head) made in Athens; H 31.7 cm; Classical period, c. 460 B.C. British Museum

Participation in the Ionian revolt had brought Cyprus into the conflict between Greece and Persia and throughout the Classical period she was poised between these two major powers. Her defeat and the subjugation of her cities in 498 B.C. left Persia in control. In 480 B.C. she reluctantly contributed ships to the Persian fleet for the naval battle of Salamis off the coast of Attica which resulted in the defeat of the Persian navy. A year later the Persians withdrew from Greece while retaining their control over their Empire including Cyprus. Thereafter the Greeks made various attempts to liberate the island from Persian rule. A major expedition was launched under the Athenian commander Cimon in 450/449 B.C. By now the Cypriot kingdoms were divided in their loyalties. The pro-Persian strongholds, namely Kition and Marion with their Phoenician kings and Salamis which was held by a strong Persian garrison, were laid under siege. Marion was taken and a phil-Hellene placed on the throne. However, after the unexpected death of its commander, Cimon, the Greek and allied fleet sailed for home without completing the operations. Under the terms of the peace of Callias in 448 B.C. the Greeks agreed to give up their interests in the eastern Mediterranean and Cyprus was once again firmly under Persian control.

After the failure of the Ionian revolt, Darius, the Persian king, allowed the eleven city kingdoms to continue in existence but made sure that their kings were pro-Persian. The Phoenicians in Cyprus were generally sympathetic to the Persians, probably partly in support of their compatriots since their homeland was firmly in the Persian Empire. Therefore, in reaction to the anti-Persian feelings of the majority of the Cypriots, the Persians formed a coalition with the Phoenician settlers at Kition and succeeded in establishing a Phoenician dynasty there in the early 5th century. The kings continued to issue their own coinage inscribed with Cypriot or Phoenician letters according to the nationality of the issuing authorities. Phoenician dynasts also ruled at Lapithos and, in the first half of the 5th century, at Marion as their coins show. By the mid-5th century Phoenician Kition had brought the neighbouring kingdom of Idalion under its control, thus reducing the number of city kingdoms to ten; the number was further reduced a century later when the last king of Tamassos sold his kingdom to the king of Kition. Phoenician influence increased throughout the island, in particular after the peace of Callias. About this time a Phoenician exile even seized the throne of the most powerful kingdom, Salamis, thus effectively bringing the whole island under the control of the Persian king.

During the Classical period the despotic form of government of the city kingdoms became fully developed. All power was concentrated in the king, who was supported by "princes" and "princesses". Together they formed a supreme

Bronze statuette of a cow, perhaps a copy of Myron's statue; from Vouni, temple of Athena; L 25 cm, H 20 cm; Classical period, 475–400 B.C.
Cyprus Museum, Nicosia

court with wide responsibilities including security. At Paphos, the home of the most important shrine of the Cypriot goddess Aphrodite, and possibly also elsewhere. the king also acted as High Priest. At Idalion, before its capture by Kition, the system was slightly more democratic with the king and people on a more equal footing. The governments became more tyrannical when the Persian grip grew tighter after 448 B.C. This led to an anti-Hellenic movement and desire to ban all Greek things which lasted until the late 5th century, when Evagoras I became king of Salamis. In 411 B.C. he seized the throne from the Phoenician ruler and restored it to the Teucrid dynasty. Evagoras I was to dominate Cypriot politics for the next forty years. He was openly pro-Hellenic, welcoming both Greek imports and immigrants. The Athenians honoured him by a decree in 410 B.C. and, after their victory in the battle of Cnidus in 394 B.C. which ended Spartan domination of the sea, acknowledged the help of Evagoras by erecting a statue of him alongside one of their commander, Conon, and next to a statue of Zeus Liberator, in the Stoa Basileios in Athens. After his death he was the subject of a panegyric by the Athenian orator Isocrates. With the help of Athens and Egypt he gradually increased his control so that by 391 B.C. he ruled over practically the whole of Cyprus. However, under the peace of Antalcidas in 386 B.C. the Athenians, in return for the freedom of the East Greek cities, agreed to recognise Persian sovereignty over Cyprus and the island of Clazomenae as well as the cities of Asia. Although left with Egypt as his only ally Evagoras fought on against Persia. In about 381 B.C. Salamis was besieged and Evagoras was eventually defeated, but in 380/379 B.C. managed to negotiate a settlement whereby he lost control over the cities of Cyprus and agreed to pay an annual tribute to the Great King, but he retained the throne of Salamis. Evagoras I was murdered in about 374/373 B.C., but his successors, although weaker than himself, continued the struggle against Persia. In 351 B.C. the city kingdoms joined with Egypt and Phoenicia in another revolt from their overlord. This was suppressed and after a siege Salamis

Limestone sarcophagus decorated in low relief; one long side showing banquet scene, the deceased probably reclining on his own on the right; from Golgoi; H 95.0 cm, L 207.3 cm; Classical period, c. 475–460 B.C. Metropolitan Museum of Art, New York (Cesnola collection)

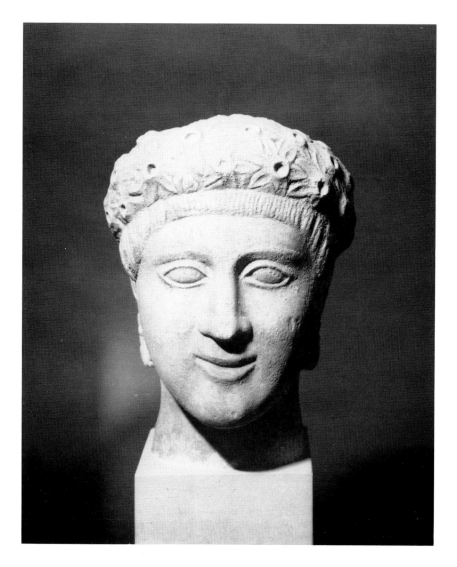

also submitted. The entire forces of Cyprus were therefore again in Persian control. Meanwhile the Greek forces under Alexander the Great, king of Macedon, were gaining considerable successes against the Persian Empire. In 333 B.C., after the defeat of the Persian forces at Issus, the Cypriot kings transferred their allegiance to Alexander. Persian domination was finally brought to an end.

Fortifications continued to be of prime importance to the Cypriot kings. At Idalion, which withstood a siege by the Kitians and Persians a generation before its final capture, the citadel wall of the early 5th century was 10.50m. thick with an inner core of small stones faced on either side by limestone blocks set in mud mortar. A tower, perhaps part of a gate, was built of fine ashlar blocks. At Old Paphos the siege-damaged fortifications were put in a state of defence again and the Persian siege mound was surrounded by a revetment wall and included in the

Limestone male head clearly following Greek models; Classical Cypro-Greek style; from Idalion; H 18.0 cm; Classical period, about 450 B.C. British Museum

95

Limestone sarcophagus decorated in high relief; one long side showing advanced guard and the two leading chariots in a procession continued on the other side; from Amathus; H 157.5 cm; L 239.4 cm; Classical period, c. 460–450 B.C. Metropolitan Museum of Art, New York (Cesnola collection)

system. The 4th-century fortifications at Golgoi, constructed as at Old Paphos of mudbrick on stone foundations, had houses built directly inside with their outer walls resting against the city wall as in the Greek city of Olynthus and, in the Hellenistic period, at Ayia Irini.

A number of important buildings or "palaces" of the Classical period are known. At Old Paphos the Persian commander, after the successful conclusion of the siege, built himself a house to the east of the gate against the inner face of the city wall leaving a gap of 0.85m. to act as a cushion against another attack. Both in plan and construction the building compares with contemporary Persian structures at Persepolis. The heavy walls were built throughout of masonry with ashlar faces and a rubble core using gypsum plaster also found in parts of the contemporary city wall. There are two storeys, the narrow rooms and long corridors of the ground floor probably used for storage while the main accommodation was evidently above. The walls of the palace at Soloi were similarly constructed with a rubble core faced by ashlar blocks. The same technique was used in part at the neighbouring palace at Vouni, although most of the walls were of mudbrick on stone foundations.

The Vouni palace occupies a magnificent position on a hill overlooking the bay of Morphou and the city of Soloi. It was built in the early 5th century by the then pro-Persian king of Marion with Persian permission to oversee phil-Hellenic Soloi. As at Old Paphos its original plan was of oriental type. The front of the palace faced south-west, where the main entrance was situated which led into the state apartments (rooms 48-56) consisting of a tripartite complex of rooms, the "liwan" type (so called from a characteristic feature of Persian architecture). From here

96

stairs descended to an open central court surrounded by columns around which the private rooms including bathrooms were arranged. Slightly later than its first construction a *sudatorium* (sweating room) was added, one of the earliest known. The phil-Hellenic king placed on the throne of Marion in the mid-5th century ingeniously changed the plan of the Vouni palace so that it conformed to the Greek *megaron* type. He transferred the entrance to the north-east (via a vestibule, room 7A) so that the state apartments were located at the rear of the central courtyard and the central part (rooms 51-53) became a hall (*megaron*). The palace was finally destroyed by the king of Soloi in about 380 B.C. Some of the walls of the Vouni palace were covered by gypsum plaster. White gypsum plaster was also used to cover the walls of public buildings at Idalion. Structures in the sanctuary of Aphrodite-Astarte and Cybele at Tamassos had doors and windows framed with wall plaster painted in red and maroon. The monumental buildings at Idalion also illustrate other construction techniques. In the earlier stage the walls were built of sandstone ashlar blocks cemented with gypsum plaster but later they were built of dry-laid limestone blocks. Roof tiles have not been found on Cypriot sites and it seems likely that the roofs and ceilings were backed with cane and, at least at Idalion, covered by gypsum plaster. Floors could be made of fine concrete.

Private houses were naturally of more modest proportions, although the plan of the town associated with the sanctuary at Ayia Irini was laid out with three principal streets running from north to south at this period. Mostly the houses were built of mudbrick on stone foundations but at Ayios Philon, a flourishing harbour town on the north of the Karpas, the architecture shows Phoenician influence. The walls of houses originally built at this period are constructed of rubble on ashlar foundations with square blocks at the angles and also acting as uprights at intervals along the walls. As in contemporary buildings on the Phoenician mainland and in the Phoenician colony at Motya in Sicily the technique is derived from timber-framed buildings.

Worship for the most part continued in the open sanctuaries as in the Archaic period and in the Phoenician temples at Kition and Tamassos. At Vouni in the mid-5th century the pro-Greek king of Marion built a temple to Athena but this bears no resemblance to Greek temples. Rather it is a more elaborate version of the typical

Bronze relief of a bull attacked by two lions; from Vouni; L 22.5 cm; Classical period, 475–400 B.C. Cyprus Museum, Nicosia

View of Vouni, with part of the north-eastern corner of the palace complex. The palace was built in the early 5th century B.C.

The courtyard of Vouni palace.

Cypriot sanctuary with its two open courtyards and the sanctuary buildings leading off the innermost. While religious rites continued as before there is now more epigraphic evidence to identify the deities by name. Aphrodite as the great fertility Mother Goddess was still supreme. Paphos remained the principal centre of her cult and she appears on coins of that city and also of Salamis in the 4th century. In Paphian inscriptions she is simply called "the queen"; in other cities she may be named "the Paphian". Athena was worshipped at Vouni, as we have seen, and also at Soloi and elsewhere; she too appears as a coin type. In the 4th century the Phoenician Reshef became identified with the Greek Apollo and in the middle of the same century the local god of the woodland, Hylates, was also equated with Apollo to become Apollo-Hylates. The principal male god in Cyprus was now identified with Zeus, the king of the Greek gods, and his head appears on coins of the 5th century. Artemis, the Greek huntress goddess, perhaps associated with the eastern "mistress of the animals", was also worshipped; a colony of Kitians established a sanctuary of their own Artemis Paralia in the Athenian port of Piraeus in 333/332 B.C.

In burial customs there were also few changes. The tradition of built tombs for the wealthy continued but the majority continued to be buried in rock-cut chamber tombs. Sarcophagi were found in the splendid built tombs at Tamassos but in general they were rare in the Archaic period. In the Classical period they became more common and simple versions, either monolithic or built of slabs fitted together, are found in the graves of ordinary people. Two splendid sarcophagi locally made in Cypriot limestone, with elaborate relief decoration in a mixed oriental and Greek style and dating from the middle years of the 5th century, must have been made for aristocrats or kings as no doubt was also the sarcophagus of imported marble probably made by a Greek resident in Cyprus about a century later. Marble sarcophagi with the lid in human form were imported from Phoenicia in the 5th and earlier 4th centuries; Phoenicians at Kition made their own versions locally. Graves may now be marked by statues or tombstones. Some of the gravestones are purely Cypriot in style but others follow Greek models; some of those made of imported marble may have been carved locally. The cult of the dead continued with evidence of libations being offered in tombs at Amathus.

The struggles between Greece and Persia for supremacy in Cyprus and the different sympathies within the island had their repercussions on Cypriot art. Contacts were now with mainland Greece and Achaemenid Persia. Attic (Athenian) pottery dominated the market particularly in the pro-Greek cities such as Marion and Salamis. The vigorous pro-Greek policy of Evagoras I and his successors led to the adoption of certain Greek forms. Influence from Classical Greece is apparent in several media, although the deliberate attempt to ban everything Greek after Cimon's death in the mid-5th century led to a certain stagnation in style.

One of a pair of gold-plated bronze hair-rings; from Amathus; L 2.9 cm, W 2.8 cm; Classical period, 475–400 B.C. British Museum

Sculpture in limestone, terracotta and bronze illustrates the different trends. There is a marked contrast between the intentional imitations of Classical Greek models and work in native styles which admitted little new outside influence.

Numerous dedications were still offered in sanctuaries. Many of the statues continued the Archaic Cypro-Greek style which gradually became stagnant and repetitive; the later pieces are very poorly carved. Some marble sculpture was imported and works like a fine marble head of the second quarter of the 5th century, probably from Lapithos, no doubt inspired sculptors to follow Attic models. A good example of this group is a limestone head from Idalion dating from the mid-5th century and therefore contemporary with works of famous Classical Greek sculptors like Phidias and Polyclitus. Among the immigrants at Salamis during the reign of Evagoras I were Greek sculptors, one of whom was probably responsible for a beautiful marble head of a goddess, perhaps Aphrodite, dating from the early 4th century B.C. It was found re-used as building material in the Roman gymnasium. Other imports which must have had an impact on Cypriot artists of the period include a magnificent bronze head of Apollo from Tamassos, known as the Chatsworth head because of its long sojourn in Chatsworth House in Derbyshire. The head was cast hollow and much of the hair was cast separately and attached; the eyes were originally inlaid. It was made in Athens in 470/460 B.C. at the time when Greek sculptors, breaking away from the rigid Archaic style, were attempting to reflect the perfect human form and give their works expression and movement. Bronze sculptures of the 5th century from the temple of Athena at Vouni are also Greek in style. Among them is a splendid cow, cast solid, which may be a copy of the well-known statue by the Greek sculptor Myron. In addition there are reliefs showing a bull attacked by two lions, exquisite, lively work. Although much limestone sculpture in the round reflected a stagnant style, some fine reliefs were carved in the later 5th and 4th centuries including gravestones following Athenian models. A number of these have been found in the pro-Greek city of Marion including an example in limestone with traces of green paint still visible dating from 420 B.C. It shows a seated woman holding a dove and an inscription in the

Silver bowl with ornaments, including an egg and dart frieze in relief; from Vouni palace; D 12.0 cm; Classical period, 450–400 B.C. Cyprus Museum, Nicosia

Greek syllabic script which reads: "I am (the stele) of Aristila from Salamis, the daughter of Onasis".

Some terracotta figures of the "snowman" type were still hand-made but the majority are now cast in moulds. The moulded terracottas in general follow Greek types; the majority of those found in Cyprus are of local manufacture but some may have been made in moulds imported from Greece.

In pottery the same fabrics continued, notably White Painted, Bichrome, Black-on-Red and Plain White (similar in fabric and slip to White Painted but without painted decoration). Bichrome Red with ornaments painted in white as well as black on a red ground became more popular. Most of the vessels are taller and slimmer versions of the earlier shapes. From the second half of the 5th century, when fine Attic pottery was imported in particular by Marion and Salamis, Cypriot potters borrowed some Greek ornaments to decorate their vases. Favourite

Marble head of a goddess, probably Aphrodite; from the gymnasium at Salamis; H 32 cm; Classical period, early fourth century B.C. Cyprus Museum, Nicosia

101

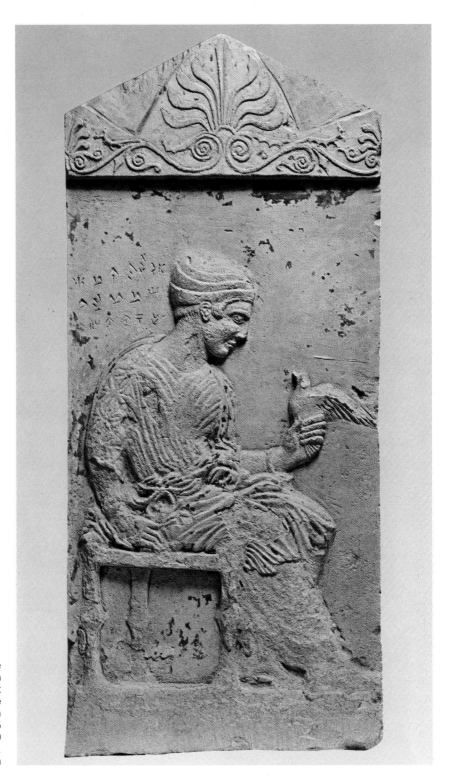

Limestone gravestone following Greek models with an inscription in the Cypriot syllabic script naming the deceased (Aristila); from Marion; H 92.5 cm, W 41.5 cm; Classical period, c. 420 B.C.
Cyprus Museum, Nicosia

vessels are pitchers with a Greek *kore* (maiden) on the neck pouring from a small jug which acts as a spout.

In the palace at Vouni a treasure of silver vessels, jewellery and coins was found deposited in a terracotta jar under a staircase leading to the upper floor, apparently hidden deliberately at the time of the final destruction by fire of the palace in 380 B.C. The finds therefore date from the 5th or very early 4th century. Among the coins are Persian gold darics and silver coins of several cities especially of Marion, Kition and Paphos. The jewellery includes open-ended bracelets of solid gold terminating in goats' or calves' heads and silver snake bracelets similar to examples probably from Marion. These are familiar in Achaemenid Persia. The gold bracelets are the oriental version of this type with a depression in the hoop; the Cypriots may have been responsible for introducing snake bracelets to Greece. Like other craftsmen Cypriot jewellers and silversmiths were now more dependent on outside models than before but they usually adapted rather than slavishly imitated them. A good example is the deep silver bowl, again from the Vouni treasure. In shape it is typically Near Eastern and similar bowls are well known in Persia; but the Cypriot artist has added a Greek egg and dart motif below the rim. It is not always easy to distinguish items of certain Cypriot manufacture from imports at this period since Classical Greek jewellery is better known from places like Cyprus outside Greece itself. The workmanship is generally of a high standard and filigree

Pair of gold-plated bronze bracelets, open-ended terminating in ram's heads; from Kourion; D 8.4 cm; Classical period, 475–400 B.C. British Museum (metal wire soldered in patterns on a background) became more popular than granulation for decoration. Enamel is used for inlay, sometimes bordered by filigree. Silver became more common than pure gold. Cypriot jewellers often worked in gold-plated bronze: animal-headed bracelets in this material, similar to the Vouni examples but copying the Greek versions of the type without a depression in the hoop, were made locally. Certain other favourite types were also evidently of Cypriot manufacture. Among them are spiral rings, probably for the hair rather than the ears, terminating in female or animal heads executed in repoussé and attached by collars with filigree ornament around the bottom sometimes bordering enamel inlays. Intricate pieces of pure gold like elaborate earrings with fine filigree decoration were probably imported from Greece. Also popular were necklaces with pendants in the form of vases or of acorns, perhaps of carnelian with a gold cup.

The political situation in the Classical period left little peacetime in which the Cypriots could develop and foster their own material culture. The island, however, as we have seen, did have an important role to play and although Classical Cypriot art is more dependent on its models some fine works were produced and the Cypriot character was maintained. The Cypriot kings changed sides to support Alexander the Great in 333 B.C. and assisted him in his naval siege of Tyre in the following year, but they did not foresee the consequences. Cyprus was to become part of the Hellenistic world and thereby lose some of her individuality.

Silver Stater of Idalion with Cypriot letters; about 425 B.C.
British Museum

Silver Stater of Lapithos with Phoenician inscription naming King Sidgmelek; about 400 B.C.
British Museum

Silver double siglos of Evagoras I of Salamis, with Cypriot letters; 411–373 B.C.
British Museum

VI
THE HELLENISTIC PERIOD

Cyprus Under the Ptolemies

325–30 B.C.

Upper part of a large terracotta statue of a woman, probably a portrait; said to be from the Paphos district; H 40 cm; Hellenistic period, early third century B.C. Pierides Collection, Larnaca

While they were under Persian control the city states had retained a certain amount of freedom, but this was lost when Alexander the Great took over in 333 B.C. He replaced the local coinage with his own imperial Macedonian coinage and also introduced Greek weights and denominations. After the death of Alexander in 323 B.C. his generals, struggling to inherit his fragmented empire, used Cyprus as a battleground and destroyed the city kingdoms of Kition, Lapithos, Marion and Kyrenia. In 310 B.C. Nicocreon, the last king of Salamis, was forced by Ptolemy I of Egypt to commit suicide. A remarkable cenotaph of this royal family has been discovered on the outskirts of the city. Subsequently in 294 B.C. Cyprus was annexed by Ptolemy I. Apart from a short period in the second century, she remained in Ptolemaic hands, usually as part of the Egyptian kingdom, although occasionally independent, for two and a half centuries. The city kingdoms ceased to exist and

Cyprus was part of the large Hellenistic state of Egypt. There was comparative peace in the island although she was subject to attacks by the Seleucid kings of Syria. In 168 B.C. Antiochus IV Epiphanes, king of Syria, conquered Cyprus but Roman envoys intervened and forced him to withdraw. Thereafter Rome, by now a major power in the eastern Mediterranean, became increasingly involved in Cypriot affairs. In about 80 B.C. the Ptolemies partly withdrew from Cyprus to appease Roman fears over the size of their empire but left a member of their family in control.

In 58 B.C. Cyprus was first annexed by Rome. The Roman tribune, P. Clodius Pulcher, a partisan of Julius Caesar, carried a law, implemented by Cato, which reduced the island to the state of a province at first attached to the province of Cilicia on the south coast of modern Turkey. During the civil wars of the Roman republic Cyprus was returned to Ptolemaic rule by Julius Caesar, who gave the island to his mistress, Cleopatra VII. In 36 B.C. this transfer was confirmed by Mark Anthony, Cleopatra's husband. Six years later Octavian, later to be Augustus, the first Roman emperor, took the Egyptian capital, Alexandria. Cleopatra committed suicide and Cyprus reverted to Rome, becoming a Senatorial Province in 22 B.C.

The Ptolemies' chief interest in Cyprus was as a source of supply of copper, corn and timber and as a shipbuilding centre. By the early 2nd century the capital had been transferred from Salamis to New Paphos. This was an ideal capital for the Ptolemies: its location on the south-west coast makes it very accessible to Egypt; the area was richly forested and had a fine harbour (the one at Salamis had by now silted up) and it was therefore an excellent site for shipbuilding. Cyprus's continued role in international trade is illustrated by a Greek ship which sank off the coast at Kyrenia at the end of the 4th century. Its cargo included Rhodian wine amphorae, millstones from the island of Nisyros and 10,000 almonds which had probably just been collected from Cyprus.

The last quarter of the 4th century saw the end of the political organisation of Cyprus into autonomous city kingdoms. Under the Ptolemies it was organised as a military command under the overall control of a *strategos* (governor-general) who was responsible to the King of Egypt, except when the island was an independent kingdom. From the time of Ptolemy V Epiphanes in the early 2nd century the *strategos* also received the title of High Priest, which enabled him to enrich the royal treasury with revenues from all the sanctuaries on the island. During the reign of Ptolemy VII Euergetes II as sole king (146–116 B.C.) the *strategos* also became admiral. All the *strategoi* were of the highest rank in the Egyptian court and were described as "kinsmen" of the king. Under the *strategos* there was a commander-in-chief of all the forces and the individual regiments had their own commanders. The important towns housed their own garrisons and the population was swelled by a large mercenary force stationed in Cyprus.

Although the Ptolemies abolished the city kingdoms some forms of liberty were preserved and certain democratic forms of internal administration were introduced. In the first three-quarters of the 3rd century minor Phoenician dynasts were tolerated at least at Lapithos in the north; but for the most part the cities were governed by city commandants who, like the *strategoi*, were always foreigners and members of the Ptolemaic court. As in Hellenistic cities elsewhere public education was in the hands of the gymnasiarchs and the gymnasium was the focus of loyalty to the regime. The coinage of Cyprus was under the control of the *strategos* and incorporated in the Ptolemaic coinage. The island's silver mines were exploited for the very active mints at Paphos, Kition, Salamis and, in the late 3rd to 2nd century, at Amathus.

In the late 4th century Nikokles, the last king of Paphos, promoted the cults of the Greek deities or of local deities assimilated with Greek gods. Under the Ptolemies, themselves of Greek origin, the Greek cults continued to flourish and the gods are portrayed and mentioned in inscriptions. Aphrodite remained the most important and the Great Mother Goddess continued also to be worshipped as Astarte. At her most famous shrine at Old Paphos the two goddesses were equated. Other Greek deities worshipped included Artemis, Zeus, Pan or Melanthios, Apollo and Dionysus. Cyprus's religious institutions were inevitably affected by Ptolemaic rule. The dynastic cult was of prime importance. Arsinoe Philadelphus, the wife of Ptolemy II Philadelphus (285–245 B.C.) was deified on her death in 270 B.C. Her cult enjoyed great popularity in Cyprus, probably beginning during her lifetime, and she was frequently identified with Aphrodite. Cities were founded in her name, including that on the old site of Marion destroyed by Ptolemy I in 312 B.C. An Arsinoeion was built at Idalion, one of the centres for the worship of Aphrodite. This is the only actual shrine dedicated to the deified queen known for certain outside Egypt, although dedications on statue bases are very common. Other Egyptian gods like Serapis and Isis were also introduced and some were equated with Greek deities as the Libyan god Ammon with Zeus, represented on coins and by a miniature bronze head from Soloi whose eyeballs are inlaid with silver.

Bull's head capital of Pentelic marble, probably the plinth of a statue; from Salamis; H 96.0 cm; Hellenistic period, third century B.C. British Museum

Dedications continued in many of the open sanctuaries but under the Ptolemies more temples were constructed. These may consist of a roofed main room (cella) leading on to one or more courtyards sometimes surrounded by porticoes like the three temples dedicated to Aphrodite, Serapis and Isis on the Cholades hill at Soloi whose plans are developed from the Classical Athena temple at Vouni. The sacred precinct within the walled area at Tamassos was entirely rebuilt in a magnificent style after its destruction by Ptolemy I in the late 4th century but excavations are still in progress and few details of this period are known as yet. At Amathus a temple of well-jointed ashlar blocks was constructed within the Aphrodite sanctuary. The temple of Zeus at Salamis was originally built in the 2nd century.

Many of the public and domestic buildings of Hellenistic Cyprus have been obliterated by later Roman constructions and by the earthquakes of 15 B.C. and A.D.

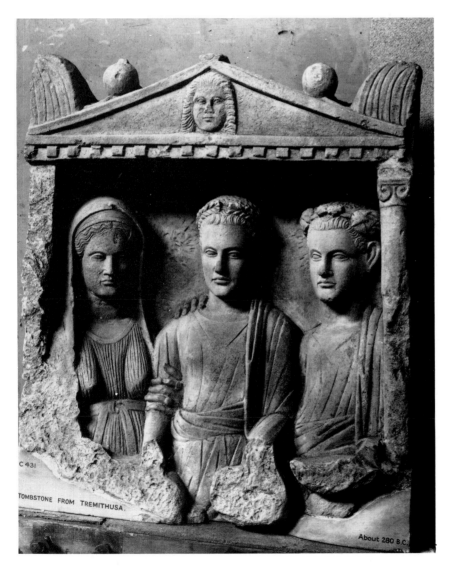

C 431

TOMBSTONE FROM TREMITHUSA.

About 280 B.C.

Limestone gravestone showing in relief a young man in the centre, probably deceased, with his parents; from Tremithusa; H 51.0 cm; Hellenistic period, c. 300–250 B.C.
British Museum

109

76/77, but epigraphic evidence records gymnasia at Salamis (predecessor of the splendid Roman one), Kition and Kourion. At Kourion the theatre was originally built in the 2nd century B.C. on a Greek plan very similar to the theatre at Priene in Ionia with a circular orchestra and high proskenion (stage) supported by half columns. These public buildings, as shown by the remains at Idalion, were sometimes constructed of fine ashlar masonry. Others, perhaps of two storeys, had a superstructure of mudbrick supported on thick foundation walls with an outer face of ashlar blocks revetting a mud backing and an inner face of rubble. Roofs were supported by columns. Occasionally buildings had pebble mosaic floors. A fine example was discovered at New Paphos dating from the time of its foundation in the late 4th century and another at Kourion perhaps from the heroon of Pnytagoras the last king of the city, whose ship was sunk while taking part in Alexander's siege of Tyre in 332 B.C. The Paphos mosaic, composed of small black and white pebbles, shows the legendary Skylla as a fish-like monster with the bust of a female figure and the forepart of three dogs springing from her waist depicted in white with reddish hair on a black background; before the monster are two dolphins and in the foreground is a fish; the panel is bordered by a meander. The Kourion mosaic is more fragmentary but it too is composed of black and white pebbles and the main preserved section is a panel bordered by a geometric pattern in which are portrayed a vessel, a dolphin and a fish in black on a white ground. Private houses were generally rather small with rectangular rooms; at

Limestone statue of a worshipper wearing typical Greek costume; from Idalion; H 116.0 cm; Hellenistic period, early 3rd century B.C. British Museum

Limestone statuette of a "temple boy"; from Idalion; H 41.0 cm; Hellenistic period, late 4th century B.C. British Museum

Idalion a two-roomed dwelling was reduced to one in the later Hellenistic period. In the settlement at Ayia Irini the architecture, as at Ayios Philon in the Classical period, was derived from timber-framed buildings. Here the houses were larger and provided with bathrooms and little workshops.

While ordinary people continued to be buried in irregular rock-cut chamber tombs there were now more elaborate versions where the chambers had niches or radiating extensions (*loculi*). Some of the dead were also buried in simple shafts or pits. Sarcophagi and tombstones are quite common. In the capital, New Paphos, impressive rock-cut subterranean tombs, versions of those found in the Hellenistic city of Alexandria, probably served the local aristocracy. Some more elaborate examples have a central peristyle (columned) court in the Doric order with rooms grouped around it; the court is approached by a flight of steps and carved in the rock face are Doric columns with an entablature of triglyphs and metopes. Recent excavations have revealed more "tombs of the Kings" in the same area with different styles of architecture.

As part of the Hellenistic kingdom of Egypt Cyprus became artistically oriented towards the Hellenistic world and her products generally conform to the cosmopolitan tendencies of the period. Much of Cypriot sculpture, however, retained its native quality. This was the result of the continued use of the local limestone and

Limestone portrait head; probably a worshipper of Aphrodite; from Idalion; H 35.0 cm; Hellenistic period, c. 270–200 B.C. British Museum

Limestone votive statue of a lyre player; from Idalion; H 55.5 cm; Hellenistic period, early third century B.C. British Museum of the purpose of the majority of the statues. Unlike the fine marble products of the Hellenistic world in general the majority were not made as memorials or for the decoration of public buildings, but continued as before to be dedicated in sanctuaries. Marble was imported for expensive commissions and is often used either in pieces or in combination with other materials, a practice that continued until the early years of the Roman Empire. The Cypriot sculptors in part respected the current fashions, producing copies in limestone of many deities. Among them their Great Mother Goddess as Aphrodite was naturally predominant. Portraits of Arsinoe often resembled Aphrodite, to whom she was likened. Fine works of imported marble such as the Aphrodite of the 1st century B.C. from Soloi sometimes served as models. Other sculptures of imported marble were probably carved locally since they exhibit individual features. They include a frieze from an Ionic temple at Soloi dating from the late 4th century showing an amazonomachy close in style to the decorated marble sarcophagus found in Cyprus now in Vienna. Another example is a bulls' head "capital" of Pentelic marble found at Salamis but not associated with any building and evidently therefore from a votive monument. Probably dating from the 3rd century B.C., with parallels for the type in Persia in the mid-4th century and Delos in the mid-3rd, it now seems likely that, unlike the others, it served as the plinth for a statue rather than the capital of a column. Expressive heads of unbaked clay from the cenotaph of Nicocreon, last king of Salamis, are local work in the style of the 4th-century Attic sculptor, Lysippos. Not more than a generation later is a limestone female head from the sanctuary at

Part of the "Tombs of the Kings" at Paphos. These underground, rock-cut tomb chambers date from the 3rd century B.C. and were made for prominent families of Paphos

Arsos, an impressive attempt by the sculptor to illustrate in his local material the individual and dramatic style of early Hellenistic art.

Portraits became more fashionable in Cyprus under the Ptolemies as they did elsewhere. The Ptolemies themselves affected the pose of gods and acquired attributes such as the club of Herakles and aegis of Zeus. Many, like the worshipper of Aphrodite from the sanctuary of Apollo and Aphrodite at Idalion made about 270–200 B.C., chose to have themselves portrayed in the Ptolemaic style. Among these votive statues female lyre players and male offering bearers usually wreathed and wearing the typical Greek costume of *chiton* (tunic) and *himation* (cloak) are common in the 3rd and 2nd centuries. Distinctive are statues of small boys found in sanctuaries of Apollo and Aphrodite in particularly large numbers in the Hellenistic period, although the type was known earlier. Known as "temple boys" they are portrayed kneeling and holding an offering; they wear tunics and usually some jewellery. Their purpose is unclear: they perhaps represent temple servants or prostitutes or they may simply have been dedicated to commemorate the first offering at the shrine. Greek gravestones were copied, sometimes rather poorly, but there are some finer versions whose figures often compare closely with known types of votive statues.

Large-sized terracottas also maintained their Cypriot character but these are rare and generally rather stiff and stylised versions of Classical types apart from a few following Attic models like the examples from Salamis already mentioned. Minor terracottas for the most part conform precisely to types found throughout the

Terracotta figure of a girl in the "Tanagra" style; from Amathus; H 21.0 cm; Hellenistic period, third century B.C.
British Museum

Terracotta figure of Athena; from Salamis; H 20.3 cm; Hellenistic period, second or first century B.C.
British Museum

Limestone female head; from
the sanctuary of Aphrodite at
Arsos; H 27 cm; Hellenistic
period, early 3rd century B.C.
Cyprus Museum, Nicosia

Hellenistic world. Generally established Cypriot traditions are ignored except for the horsemen who keep the handmade body although their moulded heads conform to Hellenistic fashions. Apart from these, the terracotta figurines are entirely cast in moulds and hollow. They were usually painted but as the decoration was often applied over a thick lime coat after firing it has usually now disappeared. Deities such as Aphrodite, Eros and Herakles are represented always in their Greek guises. Particularly common among the votaries are standing female figures wearing tight drapery with the cloak sometimes enveloping the head, local versions of the popular Greek "Tanagra" style.

In pottery also the local types were mostly replaced by imitations of forms from other parts of the Greek world, although some fabrics survive, such as White Painted and Plain White. Typical products of the Greek world like Black Glaze whose red clay is covered by a brilliant black slip and the version with painted decoration known as "West Slope" ware were imported and imitated locally Shapes including unguentaria (tubular flasks) and lagynoi (squat wine jugs with tall necks) were introduced probably from the eastern Mediterranean, although certain types of amphorae and jugs developed from earlier Cypriot varieties. In the later Hellenistic period after 150 B.C. imports from the Greek mainland became rare although local imitations are still found made either in Cyprus itself or some other Hellenistic state. Red wares now made their appearance and are

Idealised female head of unbaked clay from the cenotaph of Nicocreon at Salamis; H 25.7 cm; Hellenistic period, end of 4th century B.C. Cyprus Museum, Nicosia

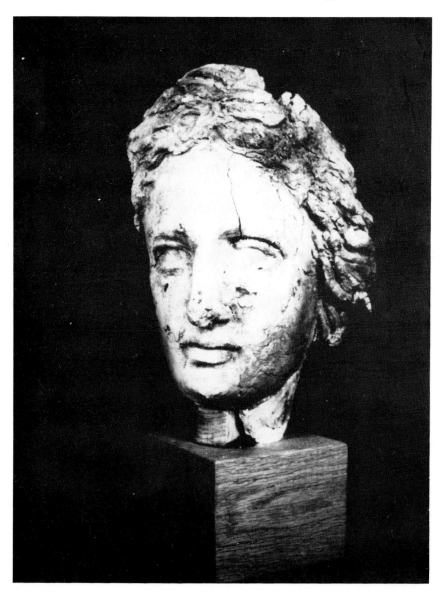

indistinguishable from those found elsewhere in the eastern Mediterranean and Asia Minor, some being clearly imitations of metal vessels. Lamps were mass produced in moulds in Cypriot workshops but again conform to general Hellenistic types.

Other arts and crafts tell a similar story. Some fine glasses were imported from Syrian workshops, but of local manufacture were glass finger rings cast in moulds and amphoriskoi (small amphorae) with S-shaped handles made of coloured glass around a removable core. A large amount of jewellery is found in Cypriot tombs of the period witnessing to the fact that after Alexander's conquest of the Persian Empire a great deal of gold became available in the eastern Mediterranean. How-

Marble statue of Aphrodite;
from Soloi; H 81 cm;
Hellenistic period, first century
B.C.
Cyprus Museum, Nicosia

ever, it is not always easy to distinguish articles of local manufacture. Techniques were simpler and both granulation and filigree are rare. An innovation was the practice of inlaying with coloured glass and stone which produced a polychrome effect and a new motif, the "Herakles" (reef) knot, was adopted by jewellers throughout the Hellenistic world from Egypt. Particularly popular in Cyprus and probably of local manufacture were earrings of twisted wire threaded with multi-coloured beads and terminating in animal or human heads. Also common is another well known type of Hellenistic earring decorated with pendants; Eros was a popular motif. Finger rings became mounts for engraved or precious stones or glass set in large round bezels. Other jewellery found in Cyprus like chain necklaces terminating in animal heads or the "Herakles" knot and snake finger rings are also common elsewhere.

In the Hellenistic period Cyprus lost her independence and consequently her culture became more cosmopolitan. However, as we have seen, the Cypriot character was not entirely suppressed. The ruling Ptolemies exploited the island's natural resources and exerted strong influence on the political and religious institutions, but the Great Mother Goddess remained supreme and dedications continued in the sanctuaries. One figure of importance of Cypriot birth was Zeno of Kition, founder of the Stoic school of philosophy, who died about 264 B.C., but his work was done in Athens not Cyprus. Names of certain other Cypriot philosophers and of historians, writers and poets are also known, but intellectual life in the island was for the most part mediocre. Cyprus finally became part of the Roman Empire in 30 B.C. but even thereafter some of her own traditions survived.

Silver tetradrachm of Ptolemy VI Philometor (180–145 B.C.) minted at Kition
British Museum

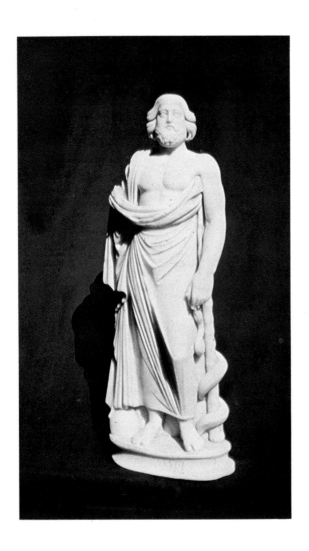

VII
THE
ROMAN
PERIOD

30 B.C. – A.D. 330

Marble statue of Asclepios, God of Medicine; from Salamis; Roman period, 2nd century A.D. Cyprus Museum, Nicosia

When the Roman civil wars were declared officially at an end in 30 B.C. the heir of Julius Caesar, soon to receive the formal title of Augustus, was left as the sole ruler of the world from the Channel to the Euphrates. His power rested on his command of nearly seventy legions and on his supreme political authority. He incorporated Cyprus, together with Cilicia, with which it had been combined under the Republic, in the province of Syria, an important military command. Its first governor was Marcus Valerius Messala, a strong partisan of the winning side, followed in 29 B.C. by Marcus Tullius Cicero, the dissolute and irascible son of the great orator. This arrangement survived the first constitutional settlement of 27 B.C. whereby Augustus in theory restricted his direct area of control to the provinces of Spain, Gaul and Syria. In 23 B.C., as part of a new and more lasting settlement, he detached Cyprus from Syria and made it one of the "public" or "senatorial" provinces which came directly under the Senate's authority. In future the governors would be nominated by the Senate, theoretically with complete freedom of choice, and would be called by the old Republican title of proconsuls. The first was appointed in 22 B.C. That the Senate's choice was subject to guidance when necessary is shown by the case of Publius Paquius Scaeva in 16 B.C.; he was nominated by Augustus and merely confirmed by Senatorial decree.

The reason why Augustus was able to allow this appearance of the free play of Republican institutions was that the "senatorial" provinces were those which contained no large military garrisons and were likely to remain peaceful. Peace and prosperity are indeed the characteristic features of Cypriot history during the early Empire. It seems to be generally agreed that the population increased in numbers, although there are no convincing estimates of the total. Cypriot manufactures were widely exported and there is evidence that Cyprus benefited, as an entrepot station, from the much expanded trade with eastern countries through the Levant. Agriculture flourished. The elder Pliny praised Cyprus wine above all others, which is evidence that it was exported since Pliny was never in the island. Timber was also in demand. The tradition of Cypriot shipbuilding was maintained.

The copper mines were actively worked. Having been royal property under the Ptolemies they now became imperial property. Their working was farmed out to contractors under the supervision of an imperial procurator. In 12 B.C. half the production of the Soloi mines was leased to Herod the Great of Judaea. The direct benefit therefore went to Rome, not to Cyprus, but the economy of the country no

Marble statue of sleeping Eros; from Paphos; H 26.5 cm; Roman period, first century B.C.
Cyprus Museum, Nicosia

doubt gained from the incidental advantages derived from the presence of this large-scale industrial enterprise.

The capital remained Paphos, which was the residence of the proconsuls. The island was divided for the purposes of local government and the administration of justice into four districts, Salamis in the East, Lapithos in the North, Paphos in the West and Amathus in the South, which also included the central mountainous area. Taxation was uniform and comparatively light. The cities appear to have been much more autonomous in their internal affairs than under the Ptolemies. This was a period when, in Cyprus as in other Greek areas under Roman rule, local patriotism was strongly encouraged. The traditional ruling classes in the cities, who had gained immensely from the stability that the absence of wars had brought, were anxious to demonstrate their affluence and public spirit. Salamis, Soloi and Curium can show large theatres. The last, in a spectacular position on the edge of a cliff, is used today for plays. The civic buildings at Salamis, including the

'The Blinding of Elymas' by Raphael

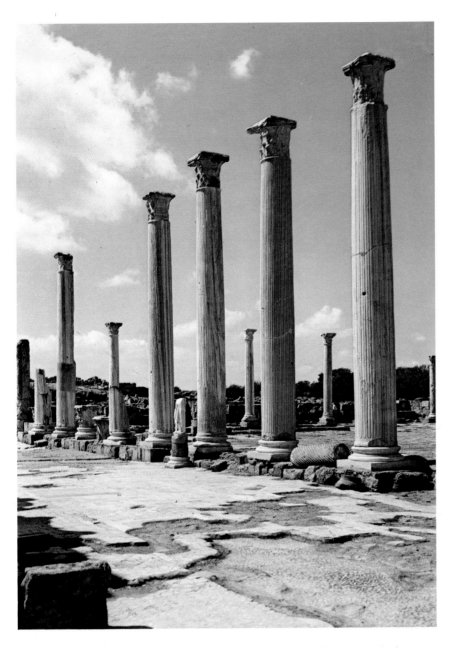

forum, a gymnasium and another large theatre restored for contemporary use, provide some of the most striking ruins in the island.

Following their usual practice the Romans devoted great efforts to the construction of a road system. The evidence for this comes partly from a late copy of a map of the Empire dating from some time between the second and fourth centuries A.D. and partly from the discovery of numerous mile-stones. From these it appears that there was a road running all round the island keeping generally close to

Columns of the gymnasium at Salamis. The majority date from the Byzantine reconstruction and came from the theatre which stood in the vicinity

General view of the excavations at Salamis; from left to right the gymnasium, the palaestra and the theatre

the coast but avoiding peninsulas. There was probably a central road from Salamis to Soloi with side roads joining it to the south coast at Kition and Amathus and another serving the Karpathos peninsula. The inscriptions show that maintenance work went on at least until the fourth century.

As with other Roman provinces there was in addition to the cities a central organisation, principally designed to further the religious cult of the Emperors. Divine worship offered to rulers was wide-spread in Greek communities, gathering in strength from the time of Alexander the Great onwards. It was almost entirely political in intention — no-one ever prayed to the Emperor when in distress — and it was encouraged by Augustus, in Cyprus as in Gaul, as a means whereby the provinces could show their political loyalty. The organisation was known as the Community (Koinon) of the Cypriots. Its main function was to arrange religious festivities and to pass honorary decrees in recognition of public benefactions but it also authorised the striking of copper money to serve as small change for the imperial coinage.

The peace of Roman Cyprus was interrupted in A.D. 116 by a Jewish insurrection, following on the risings in Cyrenaica. There were also disturbances in Egypt and Palestine but the damage seems to have been greatest in Cyprus, no

124

doubt because there were no troops in the island at all. It was led there by a member of the Jewish community who like many of his co-religionists at the time had a Greek name, Artemion. Salamis suffered worst. All the non-Jewish inhabitants of the city are said to have been massacred and the total number of deaths in the island is put at 200,000; a good deal of exaggeration must be assumed. Whatever the truth, it is certain that the situation called for vigorous action by the imperial government. An expeditionary force was sent to the island under the enterprising Moorish cavalry General, Lusius Quietus, who had held high commands under Trajan in the Parthian war. After he had stamped out the rising all Jews were expelled and none were allowed to return.

The only other episode of violence recorded from these centuries is a raid on a small scale by Goths in the year A.D. 269. They appear to have been defeated more by sickness than by force of arms and the damage done was only slight.

Natural disasters on the other hand were frequent and serious. Earthquakes are recorded in the east of the island in 18, 17 and 15 B.C. The last is said to have destroyed almost the whole city of Paphos. Augustus made a special grant for the rebuilding and authorised it to adopt the name Augusta. In A.D. 16/17 another earthquake caused damage throughout the island. Three cities are said to have been af-

Over-lifesize bronze statue of
the Emperor Septimius
Severus (A.D. 193–211) found
at Kythrea; H 2.08 m
Roman period
Cyprus Museum, Nicosia

126

The theatre of Soloi; Roman period, 2nd century A.D. (restored)

Bronze coin of the Emperor Vespasian (A.D. 69–79) issued by the Community (Koinon) of the Cypriots figuring on the reverse the statue of Zeus Salaminios
British Museum

Bronze coin of the Emperor
Caracalla (A.D. 198–217)
issued by the Community
(Koinon) of the Cypriots
showing the temple of
Aphrodite at Paphos
British Museum

Part of the Sanctuary of
Apollo Hylates at Curium
erected c. A.D. 100

fected: Paphos and Salamis are named and the third is probably Kition. In A.D. 164 Cyprus suffered badly from the plague which ravaged the whole of the Roman East, apparently brought back from Parthia by the soldiers of Lucius Verus.

Undoubtedly the most important event in the Roman period, one which fundamentally altered the whole subsequent history of Cyprus, was the introduction of Christianity. St. Paul, setting out on his first missionary journey in A.D. 45, came straight from Antioch to Salamis. He was accompanied by St. Barnabas, a member of the Cypriot Jewish community. St. Barnabas had been for some time active in preaching Christianity in Antioch and may be supposed to have suggested this first stage in the wider dissemination of the Gospel. After preaching in the synagogue at Salamis, without any success being mentioned, the two went to Paphos and had apparently no difficulty in obtaining access to the proconsul Sergius Paulus. In the Acts of the Apostles it is recorded that as a result of the miraculous blinding of a Jewish opponent, Elymas Bar-Jesus, Sergius Paulus "believed, being astonished at the doctrine of the Lord." Shortly afterwards St. Paul and St. Barnabas left Cyprus for the opposite coast of Pamphylia. The Cypriots have ever since been proud to claim that theirs was the first country in the world to have a Christian governor. The conversion of the island took time. The first Bishop consecrated was

Detail from the mosaic floor at the House of Dionysus, Paphos (the oxen of Icarius, first man to make wine;) third century A.D.

129

Floor mosaic representing the triumph of Dionysus, from the House of Dionysus, Paphos; third century A.D.

St. Heraclides or Heraclidios of Tamassos, who converted many of the mine-workers there. The people of Larnaca are particularly attached to the tradition that St. Barnabas, when he visited Cyprus for the second time in A.D. 49 in company with St. Mark, consecrated Lazarus, the brother of Mary and Martha of Bethany, as Bishop of Kition. There is little evidence for the early centuries of Cypriot Christianity, apart from some martyrologies, but it is plain that by the time of Constantine the Christians were numerous and influential and may have constituted a majority.

The architectural remains that have survived from the Roman period are the most prominent of all the monuments of antiquity to be found in Cyprus today. Apart from the civic architecture of Salamis, Soloi and Curium, already referred to, two recent discoveries at Paphos call for special mention. In 1962 excavations began on the site of a large Roman villa of the third century A.D. It had twenty-two rooms disposed around a pillared courtyard; the walls had all been shattered, no doubt by an earthquake, but in fourteen of the rooms the floors are decorated with mosaics in a remarkable state of preservation. They present mainly mythological scenes such as Pyramus and Thisbe and Apollo and Daphne; another, inscribed "the first men to drink wine" has been used with enthusiasm by the modern trade to celebrate, now as then, the excellence of Cyprus wine. Some of the mosaics suffered from Turkish bombing but have been repaired. A short distance away another villa has been excavated, thought to have been the official residence of a Roman proconsul. The mosaics here, in a slightly earlier style, are particularly fine; one represents Theseus, another Achilles.

Cyprus was a contented and loyal province under the Romans. A testimony to its loyalty is the statue of the Emperor Septimius Severus in bronze and over-lifesize which dominates one room of the Cyprus Museum in Nicosia. It may excite surprise that the grim soldier-Emperor who spent most of his life fighting on his endangered frontiers (and died in York) should be honoured in the form of a naked athlete poised for a race; but the strong line of the jaw and the imperious glare of the inlaid eyes is a reminder of the will-power that supported the Pax Romana from which Cyprus benefited for so many centuries.

Leda and the swan, floor mosaic from the House of Dionysus, Paphos; 3rd century A.D.

ΘICBH

ΠΥΡΑΜΟC

Floor mosaic representing
the legend of Pyramus
and Thisbe, from the
House of Dionysus ; 3rd
century A.D.

Floor mosaic of Ganymede
being carried off by the
eagle of Zeus; from the
House of Dionysus at
Paphos; third century A.D.

Floor mosaic from the villa of
Theseus at Paphos
showing Theseus with
Ariadne, the Minotaur and a
personified Labyrinth; third
century A.D.

VIII
THE
BYZANTINE
PERIOD
A.D. 330 – 1191

It was with the reign of Constantine the Great that the Byzantine period can be said to have begun. Not only did he found a new capital for the Empire on the site of the ancient city of Byzantium, but he also allowed the Christians freedom of worship and increasingly gave them his own personal patronage. Within half a century of his death Christianity had become the official religion of the Empire.

The new capital was inaugurated on 11th May, 330. Constantine christened it New Rome; but it was generally known, after his name, as Constantinople: though its inhabitants simply called it the *Polis*, the City: which in the form *'s tin polin,* 'to the City', survives in the Turkish name, Istanbul. It was not until the division of the Empire in 396 between the sons of Theodosius the Great that Constantinople became the fixed residence of the Emperors of the East; but already the administration of the Eastern provinces, including Cyprus, was seated there. For the Cypriots themselves the change made little difference, except that henceforward the administrators of the island tended to be drawn from the Greek-speaking world, and were more in sympathy with their subjects than their Latin-speaking predecessors.

The triumph of Christianity, however, made a vast difference in the life of the island. The Christian community seems already to have been large, though nothing is known of its organisation. But, as at least three Cypriot bishops attended the Oecumenical Council of Nicaea in 325, only 13 years after the Edict of Milan had legitimised the Church, it is likely that their sees of Paphos, Salamis and Tremithus were already organised. Twelve Cypriot bishops were signatories to the decrees of the Council of Sardica in 344. By 400 fifteen were mentioned in the letter written by Theophilus, Patriarch of Alexandria, to the Church of Cyprus; and the Metropolitan see by now was fixed at Constantia, that is to say, Salamis.

The double-eagle device of the Byzantine Empire

Traditionally the Church of Cyprus had been founded by St. Barnabas, the twelfth apostle who replaced Iscariot. We are told in the *Acts of the Apostles* of two visits that St. Barnabas paid to the island, one with St. Paul and the other, after he had quarrelled with St. Paul, with St. Mark. The tradition can therefore be accepted. He was supposed to have been born at Salamis and to have been put to death there by fellow-Jews. The early Cypriot saints, such as St. Heraclides, are shadowy figures. But the fourth century produced three historic figures who had an undoubted influence on the spread of Christianity in the island. The first was St. Spyridon, who had been tortured during the Galerian persecution early in the century but survived to become Bishop of Tremithus and to attend the Council of Nicaea. He was sufficiently revered for his body to be removed for safety to Constantinople at the time of the Muslim invasions and thence, on the eve of the capture of the City by the Turks in 1453, to Corfu, where he became that island's patron saint. Next was St. Hilarion, a hermit saint whose life was written by St. Jerome. He came to Cyprus from Palestine some time in the 330's and settled near Paphos. His body too was not allowed to rest in peace but was taken by pious thieves to Palestine soon after his death. Finally there was St. Epiphanius. He also was of Palestinian origin and came as a young man to Cyprus; he was elected Bishop of Constantia-Salamis in 368. He dominated the Cypriot Church till his

Stavrovouni Monastery ('mountain of the Cross') west of Larnaca; traditionally founded by St. Helena c. 327 The existing monastery was almost entirely rebuilt during the nineteenth century

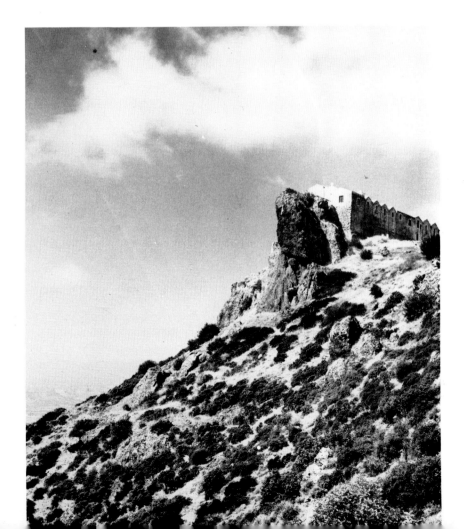

death in 403, when he was nearly ninety. He was a man of great erudition but cantankerous and obstinate. His main achievement was to hold a Council in Salamis in 401 at which Origenist doctrines were finally condemned.

These saints added to the prestige of the Cypriot Church; but perhaps more influential at a popular level was a visit to the island from that holy archaeologist, St. Helena, on her return from discovering the site and the relics of Our Lord's Passion in Jerusalem. According to the accepted story, Cyprus had been suffering from a terrible drought and consequent famine for thirty-six years, which promptly ended when the Empress arrived with some of her relics. Obedient to a divinely inspired dream she deposited the cross of the Penitent Thief in a monastery that she founded at Stavrovouni and a fragment of the True Cross at the church of Tokhni, close to her landing-place. This fragment was to prove its authenticity by triumphantly surviving an ordeal by fire in the reign of King Hugh IV. It is not possible to decide now between historic truth and legend; but it seems probable that St. Helena did in fact visit the island and that the famine, for which there is historic

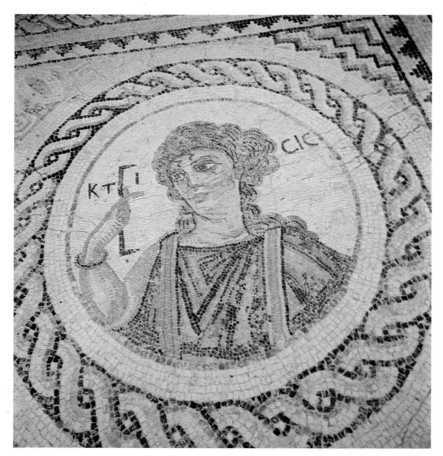

evidence, did cease about the same time; though it had probably been of lesser duration. At any rate, Cyprus was held henceforward to possess Christian relics of the greatest importance.

The establishment of Christianity undoubtedly eased the life of the population. Harsher Roman laws were repealed. The death-penalty became rare. Concubinage was abolished, as was the *patria potestas*, the right of life and death that a father had over his children. Gladiatorial sports were abandoned for the less bloodthirsty sport of chariot-racing. Above all, the Church in Cyprus was always in close touch with the people and was always ready to champion popular rights against overbearing officials. But the new religion did not ameliorate the stern laws which tied labourers to the land on which they were born. Indeed, Constantine, in his anxiety to maintain agriculture, tightened them; and a little later the Emperor Valens imposed heavy punishment on any peasant who left his district. But the Imperial control over officials was tightened. They could no longer enrich themselves at the expense of the populace. Measures were taken to see that the taxes, which were heavy, were received in full by the government.

In addition to the drought, for which there is other evidence, though it probably did not last as long as the thirty-six years of the legend, Cyprus suffered in the

Floor mosaic in the Annexe of Eustolios at Curium. It represents Creation (*Ktisis*) personified as a woman holding a measuring rod. 5th century A.D.

137

fourth century from devastating earthquakes. In 332 Paphos was badly hit. When St. Hilarion arrived there soon afterwards his biographer, St. Jerome, tells us that 'it has now only its ruins to show what once it was then.' Salamis was also damaged; and ten years later almost the whole city was destroyed by a still more severe shock, followed by a tidal wave. The Emperor Constantius II relieved its surviving citizens from taxation for four years and organised the rebuilding of the city, on a slightly smaller scale, rechristening it Constantia, though the old name continued in use.

Of the political history of Cyprus in the fourth century little is known. In about 330 Constantine sent an official called Calocaerus to govern the island. Legend relates that he found it infested with snakes, as a result of the drought. He therefore introduced the special breed of cats, which were cared for by the monastery of St. Nicholas, near Akrotiri and close to the cape called Gata after them. These cats are mentioned by many medieval travellers to the island. Encouraged, perhaps, by the success of his enterprise, Calocaerus rebelled against the Emperor in 333. Constantine sent his nephew Delmatius to deal with the rebel, who was captured and put to death at Tarsus. The island seems to have passed the remaining years of the century in tranquillity.

This political tranquillity seems to have lasted throughout the fifth century, during which the Cypriots' main attention was devoted to the establishment of the independence of their Church. The Patriarch Alexander of Antioch wrote in about 410 to Pope Innocent I to complain that the Cypriots were now ordaining their own bishops, contrary to a canon of the Council of Nicaea, which declared that the Patriarch had the right to appoint the Archbishop of Cyprus. Only if winter weather made communications impossible could the Cypriot bishops elect their chief. This canon was undoubtedly forged. The relevant canon, the 6th, merely confirmed the rights of the Church of Antioch "and of other eparchies", of which Cyprus presumably was one. The Pope ordered the Cypriots to return to their obedience. He received no answer from them. But Antioch was not prepared to let the matter rest. The summoning of an Oecumenical Council to Ephesus to discuss the Nestorian question provided an opportunity. The Metropolitan of Cyprus, Theodore of Constantia-Salamis, who had been a firm defender of Cypriot independence and who had once, when visiting Antioch, been struck on the face by a minion of the Patriarch's, had recently died. The Patriarch John of Antioch induced an old friend of his, Flavius Dionysius, who was now Count of the Orient, to send instructions to the Consular (or Governor) of Cyprus, that he was to insist that if the Cypriot bishops elected a new metropolitan, he and his suffragans must attend the Council to justify their insubordination. Heavy penalties would be imposed were they to disobey the summons.

On receipt of these orders the Cypriot bishops firmly elected a new archbishop, Rheginus, and he, with three bishops and a protopappas, set out for Ephesus. It was on the whole a successful journey. John of Antioch, who supported Nestorius, proved to be on the losing side at the Council; and the Bishops of Curium and Soloi — their colleague of Paphos having died soon after his arrival at Ephesus — gave a spirited defence of the autonomous tradition of the Cypriot Church.

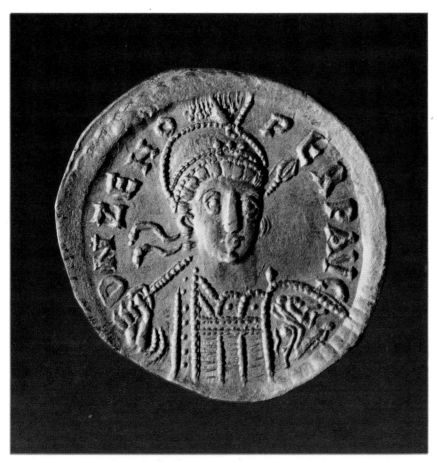

But the Fathers of the Council were guarded in their verdict. The 8th canon of the Council pronounced that if, as the Cypriots claimed, it was against the ancient tradition for the Bishop of Antioch to consecrate bishops in Cyprus, then the church authorities in Cyprus should have the free right to consecrate their bishops themselves, according to the canons and the established customs.

At the time this canon seems to have been accepted as endorsing Cypriot ecclesiastical autonomy. But Antioch had not given up the struggle. Within half a century, probably in 488, the Patriarch Peter the Fuller wrote to the Emperor Zeno, who was an old friend of his, to point out that as the Church in Cyprus had undoubtedly been founded from Antioch and as Antioch was undoubtedly an apostolic foundation, Cyprus should be under its authority. Zeno might well have accepted the argument, despite the established Cypriot claim that St. Barnabas was the founder of the island Church. Fortunately the Cypriot Archbishop, Anthemius, warned of the attack, had an opportune dream in which St. Barnabas showed him where he had been buried. As soon as possible Anthemius went in procession to the spot, where, under a tree shown in the vision, his workmen opened up a cave, in which the saint's body was found lying in a coffin; and on his breast was a copy of the Gospel of St. Matthew. There was a tradition, confirmed

Aureus of the Emperor Zeno, A.D. 474–491, who confirmed the autocephaly of the Church of Cyprus
Athens, Numismatic Museum

by the apocryphal Acts of St. Barnabas, that the saint had always carried about with him a copy of the Gospel written in his own hand, and that his devoted disciple, St. Mark, had placed the book on his dead body. Armed with the relics Anthemius hastened to Constantinople to show them to the Emperor, to whom he presented the Gospel. Zeno was deeply impressed and delighted with the gift. In return he summoned a synod which confirmed the autocephaly of the Cypriot Church; and he gave to its archbishop in perpetuity the extraordinary privilege of carrying a sceptre instead of a pastoral staff and of signing his name in purple ink, as only an Emperor might do. These symbols could be held to mean that the archbishop had temporal authority over the island; but it is doubtful whether this was what Zeno intended. Civil governors were still sent to administer it.

Antioch retained the right to provide the chrism used for the consecration of bishops, as it was now held that such chrism had to be blessed by a Patriarch. This practice lasted till 1860. From 1864 onward the chrism has been obtained from Constantinople. But neither Patriarchate could thereby claim authority over the island Church.

The Church of Antioch accepted the decision. Indeed, a later Patriarch, Severus, recorded that when he visited Constantinople in his younger days, in about 500, he saw and greatly admired the copy of St. Matthew's Gospel. The other relics of St.

Barnabas were returned to Cyprus, to a church that was built over the saint's burial-place.

Of the secular history of the island during the later fifth and the sixth centuries we know nothing. There is no record of it having suffered any severe damage from the earthquakes that twice devastated Antioch in Justinian's reign; and it was spared the destruction that the Syrian mainland underwent owing to the wars against Persia, which resulted in the sack of Antioch. It is probable that the island benefited from the revival of trade across the Mediterranean that followed Justinian's reconquest of the West and the elimination of the Vandals: though it never quite recovered the prosperity that it had enjoyed in late Roman times. However, when the secret of the silk-worm was brought to Justinian by two monks who travelled from the Far East with worms hidden in their hollowed staffs, Cyprus was one of the areas into which the new industry was introduced. Cypriot silks soon became famous and their export added to the wealth of the island.

It is equally unknown whether the island was affected by the terrible war against Persia in the earlier years of the seventh century, when much of the Empire was overrun by the enemy. We know that for a short time the Emperor Heraclius minted coins in Cyprus, perhaps when the Syrian mints were closed by the war. We know that under the same Emperor a new aqueduct for supplying Salamis was completed. We know too that it was in Cyprus that he first tried out the theological doctrine of Monotheletism — the doctrine that Christ had two natures but one will — which he hoped would heal the rift between his Orthodox and his Monophysite subjects. A decree which he sent to the Archbishop Arcadius spelt out the doctrine, which seems at first to have had some success in the island. Heraclius was of Armenian origin; and the doctrine was in general acceptable to the Armenians, of whom there were large colonies in the island. But it only increased the bitterness between the Orthodox and the Monophysites; and if the island Church ever officially adopted the doctrine, it was soon abandoned.

Before Heraclius had died the whole situation in the Eastern Mediterranean world had been drastically altered. The irruption of Arabs from the desert, inspired by the teachings of their Prophet Mohammed, came at a moment when the Christian Empire, exhausted by the long Persian war, was in no condition to oppose them. By 639 all Palestine and Syria were in Arab hands, and by 642 the Arabs controlled Egypt. The Cypriots may have hoped at first that the sea would protect them, as it had done from the Persians. But after their conquest of the Syrian and Egyptian ports the Arabs set about building a fleet. In 649 — the sources also give 647 or 648, but 649 seems the most probable date — the governor of Syria, Muawiya, obtained permission from the Caliph Othman to use the fleet for an expedition against Cyprus. The Caliph agreed, provided that only volunteers were used. The fleet, which consisted of 1500 vessels of all sizes and included a large contingent from Egypt, assembled at Acre and sailed to Constantia-Salamis. Muawiya, who commanded it in person, brought his wife Fakhita with him; and his second-in-command, Ubada ibn as-Samit, also was accompanied by his wife, Umm-Haram, a lady related to the Prophet himself and famed for her goodness. Heralds from the fleet ordered the governor of Con-

The church of *Panayia Angeloktistos,* Kiti. First built in the 5th century, largely destroyed by Arab raids of the 7th century, rebuilt c. A.D. 1000, reconstructed in the 12th century, restored in the sixteenth century

stantia to surrender. When he refused, trusting in the city walls, the Arabs landed and laid siege to the city. After a brief resistance the walls were breached and the invaders poured in, massacring vast numbers of the inhabitants and sacking the city so thoroughly that it never recovered. The Arabs went on to pillage the rest of the island but retired on the news that an Imperial fleet was approaching. According to an old tradition, in the course of the pillaging the 'righteous lady', Umm-Haram, fell from her horse and died, and was buried in Hala Sultan Tekke.

This expedition had been intended as a raid. The Muslim authorities were too far-sighted to devastate so thoroughly an area which they hoped to incorporate in their empire. But Muawiya seems to have demanded an annual tribute from the island and an undertaking that it would not allow itself to be used as a Byzantine base. In 653 or 654, on the grounds that the latter promise had been broken, he invaded the island again, and again massacred many of its inhabitants. Those who

The image shows a mosaic with Greek inscriptions: †ΗΑΓΙΑ † ΜΑΡΙΑ†, ΜΙΧΑΗΛ, ΓΑΒΡΙΗΛ

could took refuge in the town of Lapithos, which after a short siege surrendered to him, on condition that all lives should be spared, though all their possessions were confiscated. Muawiya then decided to leave a garrison of 12,000 men in the island, in a town that he built specially for them, and to encourage Muslim settlers.

For the following thirty years life for the Cypriot Christians was uncertain and miserable. Things improved slightly after the failure of the Arabs to capture Constantinople in 677 and the disasters that they suffered on their retreat. In 678 peace was made between the Emperor and the Caliph, which obliged the Caliph to pay an indemnity to the Emperor; and the treaty was renewed in 685. In neither treaty was there any mention of Cyprus; though there is evidence that the Muslim garrison was withdrawn in about 683. But when the treaty was renewed once more, in 688, between Justinian II and the Caliph Abd al-Malik, a special clause regulated the future of the island. It was to be neutralised; that is to say, neither the Empire nor the Caliphate was to keep troops in the island nor to use it as a military base, and the revenues derived from taxation were to be divided equally between the Emperor's and the Caliph's treasuries. So much is made clear by the Muslim historian Masudi and, as regards the taxes, confirmed by the Byzantine historians Theophanes and Constantine Porphyrogenitus. A third clause, attested

The Virgin attended by the Archangels Michael and Gabriel; 6th c.; apse mosaic church of Panayia Angeloktistos, Kiti

143

by the Patriarch Nicholas Mysticus in the early 10th century, required each of the two communities in the island to give help to the other were it attacked from outside. But, as the same letter makes it clear that neither community was armed, the help must have been economic or at least a refusal to give any support to the invader.

This remarkable treaty remained in force for very nearly three centuries, except for a brief period in the late 9th century when, under circumstances that are unknown, the Emperor Basil I sent troops to occupy the island. It did not ensure unbroken peace. The Byzantine and Muslim navies were allowed access to the island's harbours and often made use of them when assembling ships for a naval campaign. Cyprus was too well placed strategically for either side to abandon this convenience. Presumably each naval command would seek a harbour in a district where its co-religionists predominated, but there was no territorial division. There were Muslim villages side by side with Christian villages, though probably the former were more numerous in the eastern areas. For the collection of taxes and the administration of justice there must have been Byzantine and Muslim Residents permanently established in the island, presumably with fixed seats of residence; and each must have employed officials to see that the taxes were collected and some sort of civil police. The late 9th-century Life of St. Constantine Judaeus tells us that there were regular passenger services to the island to and from Adalia on the Anatolian coast and from Seleucia; and other evidence shows that there were services to Syria. The pilgrim St. Willibald, who visited the island in 723, remarked upon the condominium there between Greeks and Saracens. He was able to travel freely through the island, visiting Paphos as well as Constantia. St. Constantine was alarmed when some Muslims entered a church in which he was worshipping; but his fears were groundless.

Justinian II seems himself not to have had much faith in the treaty. About the time that he made it he embarked upon a scheme to transfer a large proportion of the Greek population to the Anatolian mainland, providing a new home for them on the southern shore of the Marmora, near the city of Cyzicus. A new town was built for the settlers, which he called Nova Justinianopolis; and the Archbishop of Cyprus was induced to emigrate with his flock, on the undertaking that his new diocese, which was to include the whole province of Hellespont, would continue to enjoy the autonomy that Cyprus had enjoyed, an undertaking that was confirmed by the Council *In Trullo* in 691. But already the experiment was proving to be unsuccessful. The transports sent to Cyprus to collect the emigrants, amongst whom were a number of Muslim prisoners of war, ran into a bad storm on the return journey, and many ships were wrecked, with heavy loss of life. A number of Cypriots defected and made their way home. Other Cypriots fled to Syria to avoid deportation. In 698, after Justinian's dethronement, the Emperor Tiberius III sent the whole colony back to Cyprus and at the same time negotiated with the Caliph to have the refugees to Syria returned. The Caliph agreed and sent officials to round them up and to arrange for their transport back to the island.

The paucity of information about Cyprus during the three centuries of the condominium suggests that the island was enjoying a rare period of tranquillity. There were battles off its harbours, as when in 747 a huge Egyptian fleet, assembled to

(opposite page)
Silver bowl with central medallion surrounded by a band of nielloed ornament. In the medallion, in low relief, is the full face bust of a nimbate saint, probably either St. Sergius or St. Bacchus. On the underside are five control stamps of the Emperor Constans II; from Lambousa; D 24.7 cm; A.D. 641–651
British Museum

Silver spoon; from Lambousa; the interior is embossed with the figure of a ram; L 25.4 cm; A.D. 600
British Museum

144

Nine silver plates illustrating the story of David were discovered at Lambousa in 1902. On the evidence of date stamps they were made between A.D. 627 and 630 and their intention was probably to celebrate the victorious Persian campaign of the Emperor Heraclius in 627

Silver plate on footring with relief depicting the Marriage of David and Michal. King Saul presides between them and two pipers play music on either side; from Lambousa; D 26.8 cm (plate) D 11.8 cm (footring); A.D. 627–630 Cyprus Museum, Nicosia

attack the Byzantine mainland, was caught and destroyed by a Byzantine squadron or when in 790 a Muslim fleet, that had assembled in a Cypriot harbour, sailed out and defeated a Byzantine fleet some way off the coast. The Byzantine admiral Himerius put in to Cyprus on his way to sack Lattakieh in 910. On that occasion some of his men landed and slew a few Muslim officials who were no doubt protesting against their presence. The island did suffer three serious Muslim raids, made in each case because the Cypriot Christians had allegedly broken the terms of the treaty. In 743 the Caliph Walid ordered an invasion of the island and carried off a number of Christians, "on suspicion"; but we are not told of what misdemeanour they were suspected. His son, Yazid III, sent them back unharmed a year or two later. In 806 a raid on the island was made on the orders of the Caliph Harun ar-Rashid, "because the people of Cyprus had broken the treaty". Once again we do not know what they had done. The same excuse was given when the Emir Damian of Tarsus raided the island in 912. Probably this was a reprisal for Himerius's sailors' behaviour in 910; or perhaps the Muslims had come to hear of instructions that had been sent from Constantinople to the Byzantine Resident, the *archon* Leo Symbaticius, instructing him to find in Cyprus reliable spies who could go to the Muslim ports, Tarsus, Lattakieh and Tripoli, and report on naval activities there. The Patriarch Nicholas of Constantinople wrote to the Caliph to protest against Damian's raid, linking it to Himerius's men's misbehaviour. He pointed out that the Cypriot Greeks could not do anything to help their Muslim neighbours, as they did not have any arms.

The treaty was certainly breached on the Byzantine side when Basil I occupied the island and made it a *theme*, or province, of the Empire. The circumstances and the date of the occupation are unknown. It lasted for seven years. Then the condominium was restored.

Little is known of the economic life of the island during the condominium. The few travellers' accounts give the impression that it was modestly prosperous. The silk industry was developed; and it seems that the island exported foodstuffs to Syria. The two communities seem to have lived fairly harmoniously together, though it must have been galling to the Christians, who were far more numerous than the Muslims, to see a large proportion of the taxes that they paid going to the Caliph to make up his half-share of the revenue. Both empires used the island as a place to which tiresome dissidents could be sent. They could do no harm there. The iconoclastic Emperors in particular found it a convenient spot to which to exile image-worshipping monks. The Cypriot archbishop never subscribed to the iconoclastic decrees.

By the middle of the 10th century the Caliphate was sinking into decline. Egypt

Hexagonal silver censer. On each side is a medallion containing a nimbed bust as follows: Christ, the Virgin, St. Peter, St. Paul, St. John the Evangelist, St. James. On the base is a set of control stamps of the reign of the Emperor Phocas; from Lambousa; D 10.6 cm; A.D. 602–610
British Museum

147

Silver plate with relief of
David trying on Saul's armour;
from Lambousa; D 26 cm
(plate) D 12 cm (footring); A.D.
627–630
Metropolitan Museum of Art,
New York (Given by J.
Pierpont Morgan)

Large silver plate on
footring, decorated with three
scenes in relief. The top
scene is the meeting of David
and Goliath and shows the
two men addressing one
another in dispute. The
middle scene shows the
actual fight and in the bottom
scene Goliath is on the ground
about to be slain by David. On
the base are five control
stamps of the Emperor
Heraclius; from Lambousa;
D 49.4 cm (plate) D 20.7 cm
(footring); A.D. 627–630
Metropolitan Museum of Art,
New York. (Given by J.
Pierpont Morgan)

Silver plate on footring with
relief of David slaying the
bear; from Lambousa; D 14
cm (plate) D 6.5 cm (footring);
A.D. 627–630
Cyprus Museum, Nicosia

Silver dish with relief of David
as shepherd; from Lambousa;
D 14 cm (plate) D 6.5 cm
(footring) A.D. 627–630
Cyprus Museum, Nicosia

had seceded and soon, under the Fatimid Caliphs, was to annex Palestine and southern Syria. In northern Syria the local emirates were independent in all but name. Under such circumstances there was no more point in the condominium. In 965 the Emperor Nicephorus Phocas reconquered Cilicia and turned his attention to Cyprus. The Egyptians also were interested in the island; but, after defeating their fleet off the mainland coast, he sent troops under the Patrician Nicetas Chalcutzes to occupy Cyprus, which once more became a province of Byzantium.

It can be questioned whether the island benefited from the change. It had its advantages. The Christian islanders could now feel themselves to be full citizens of the great Christian Empire. Many of the Muslims emigrated. Others became converts to Christianity and were absorbed into the Greek population. The islanders no longer had to pay half their taxes to the Caliph. But the Byzantine Empire was the most highly taxed state in the mediaeval world; and the taxes were efficiently collected. The governors sent out from Constantinople were far more powerful than the previous Residents; and their power was resented by the Archbishop, who regarded himself as head of the Christian community. There was constant friction between the civilian government and the Church. The island now contained armed forces to protect it against raiders. But the era of Arab raids was over; and ambitious governors were sometimes tempted to use these forces to defy the central government, thus involving the island in a rebellion.

The first governor to rebel was Theophilus Eroticus, a man who had been governor of Serbia and had failed to crush a revolt there in 1040. Instead of being retired in disgrace he was transferred to Cyprus by the Emperor Michael IV, with whose family he was probably friendly, as it was on the fall of Michael V, Michael IV's nephew, that he decided to rebel. The *protospatharius* Theophylact, the official in control of judical and fiscal affairs, refused to join him; so he tried to stir up the populace against the *protospatharius*, whose office was always unpopular. But Constantinople was warned, probably by the *protospatharius*. A naval squadron was sent to the island by the new Emperor, Constantine IX. The abortive revolt was easily put down and Eroticus was brought as a captive to Constantinople. The authorities did not take him very seriously. They confiscated his possessions and forced him to parade in the Hippodrome dressed as a woman, then set him free.

It was important to have a loyal governor in Cyprus, as he was conveniently placed for seeing to the Empire's interests in Syria and Palestine. He kept a close connection with the Byzantine frontier-officials in northern Syria, who, when unrest across the frontier made travel dangerous, would often send pilgrims to wait in Cyprus till conditions improved. Bishop Lietbert of Cambrai and his fellow-pilgrims were obliged to follow this course in 1055. In their ignorant arrogance they regarded it as an attempt to sabotage their pilgrimage, not realising that it was intended for their safety. In 1027 a treaty with the Fatimids entitled the Emperor to rebuild the Church of the Holy Sepulchre in Jerusalem, destroyed by the mad Caliph Hakim in 1009. The treaty was renewed in 1036; but it was only in 1045 that work was started. It was the Governor of Cyprus who was sent to make the final arrangements for it and for the rebuilding of the walls of the Christian quarter.

The whole situation in the Levant was changed a quarter of a century later when the Turks, mostly under the leadership of the Seljuk dynasty, burst into Anatolia after the disastrous defeat of the Byzantine army at Manzikert in 1071. Within ten years they were in control of all Anatolia, as far as the Aegean and Marmora Seas, apart from a few isolated cities and most of the coast. Meanwhile other Turks had invaded Syria and Palestine, causing utter disruption and confusion there. Cyprus was not directly affected; but communications with Constantinople were continually interupted, especially after the Turkish emir Chaka occupied Smyrna and built a fleet, with which he began to capture the nearby Aegean islands.

The Empire was saved by a remarkable Emperor, Alexius I Comnenus, who took over the government in 1081, when the Empire seemed unlikely to survive. By the time of his death in 1125 he had recovered all the coastal lands of Anatolia, as well as the islands. He re-created the Imperial army to be an efficient fighting-force; but his successes were due more to diplomacy than to warfare. He also depended on the loyalty and abilities of his lieutenants.

He was not always fortunate in them. In 1093 the governor of Cyprus, Rhapsomates, conspired with the governor of Crete, Caryces, to revolt against the Emperor, hoping for help from Chaka of Smyrna. Alexius at once sent his brother-in-law, John Ducas, with a fleet to deal with the rebels. At the news of his approach the Cretans rose against Caryces and slew him. Ducas sailed on to Cyprus. When he landed a small body of troops at Kyrenia he found Rhapsomates encamped with the island militia in the hills above the town. But Rhapsomates was a man with little military experience and a lack of decision. Instead of attacking the Imperial troops as they were disembarking he hesitated; and when at last he marched down against them, several hundred of his forces went over to the other side and the rest showed little desire to fight. Rhapsomates gave up the struggle and fled towards Limassol, where he hoped to find a ship to take him overseas, but was captured at Stavrovouni and sent to Constantinople. His fate is unknown.

The general in command of the small Imperial landing-force was Manuel Butumites, a man who was to have a very distinguished career as a soldier and diplomat. He seems to have acted briefly as governor of the island, till Alexius sent out a new military commander, Philocales Eumathius, and an official of known probity and modesty, Calliparius, to take charge of the judicial and fiscal administration.

According to a legend which there is no reason to doubt, Butumites when he was in the island was cured of sciatica by a monk, Esaias, whom he encouraged to found a monastery at Kykko. Under his patronage Esaias then visited Constantinople, where he cured a daughter of the Emperor of the same complaint. In gratitude Alexius gave him an icon of the Mother of God, attributed to the brush of St. Luke, which remains to this day the holiest icon in the island.

Philocales, who succeeded to Butumites, was, according to the historian-princess, Anna Comnena, our chief authority for Cypriot history during these years, a man of high qualities, prudent, generous, pious and loyal. Though no soldier —

he could not draw a bow nor wield a shield — he was an ingenious strategist. He seems to have had two periods of office in the island, from about 1093 to 1100 and from about 1105 to 1112. In the interval the governor was Constantine Euphorbenus Catacalon. Unfortunately Philocales was on bad terms with the Cypriot Church and its Archbishop, Nicholas Muzalon. After his retirement in about 1110, which was perhaps forced by Philocales, Muzalon wrote a long poem describing the sufferings of the Cypriots at the hands of Byzantine officials and blaming in particular a governor who is certainly to be identified with Philocales. It is a hysterical work. It depicts the inhabitants of the island being cruelly tortured if they did not pay taxes that left them starving, and, significantly, it lays most emphasis on the extortions to which the clergy were subjected and the cruel punishments meted out to those who disobeyed the tyrannous governor. Particular venom is directed against those clerics who supported the lay authorities. It is true that taxation was very severe and that taxes were collected ruthlessly. But the exaggerated picture of an island reduced to penury by wicked officials is clearly the work of a disgruntled and ill-tempered cleric with a grievance. The island was in fact rather prosperous. In 1097 Symeon, Patriarch of Jerusalem, who had retired to Cyprus when life became impossible in the Holy City, was able to send several consignments of foodstuffs from the island to the soldiers of the First Crusade when they were suffering from hunger before the walls of Antioch. In 1105 the threat to withhold the export of foodstuffs to Tripoli was sufficient to make the authorities there comply with the Emperor's wishes. It is unlikely that a starving island should have exported food. If the government had confiscated all the island's produce in order to export it, an enfeebled peasantry would hardly have been in a condition to continue cultivation. It is certain that there had been extortionate governors, as we know from an anonymous work, the *Logos Nouthetikos*, traditionally attributed to Cecaumenus, which mentions Cyprus as a victimised province. Muzalon many years later, in 1147, returned to episcopal life as Patriarch of Constantinople. But his temper had not improved; and everyone was delighted when, four years later, it could be shown that his election had been uncanonical.

Both Butumites in his later career and Philocales when governor of Cyprus were employed by the Emperor to help to deal with the situation that arose on the Syrian mainland out of the advance and ultimate success of the First Crusade. The Crusaders had at first, despite minor misunderstandings, co-operated fairly well with the Byzantines and helped them to recover much of western Anatolia. But when the Crusade moved into Syria there were difficulties. Till the Turkish invasions Byzantium had controlled northern Syria as far south as Lattakieh and including Antioch; and the Emperor had induced the Crusader leaders to restore the area to him. But the ablest of them, Bohemund the Norman, had seized for himself Antioch and the surrounding country. The Emperor was determined to recover the coastal ports; and for that Cyprus was the obvious base, both militarily and diplomatically. His success was limited. He did not object to the Crusaders establishing settlements farther south, in Lebanon and Palestine. The Cypriot governor continued to send provisions and military equipment to the Crusader army. But it is interesting to note that it was in Cyprus that several Muslim princes,

The church of Saints Barnabas and Hilarion at Peristerona dates from the early 10th century. The iconostasis is dated 1549

ousted by the Crusaders, sought temporary refuge. The island itself was not directly affected by troubles on the mainland. In 1099 a Pisan fleet conveying the Archbishop of Pisa, Daimbert, who had been appointed Papal Legate for Palestine, after raiding Corfu and other Greek islands on its way, attempted to land on Cyprus; but Philocales had little difficulty in thwarting the landing.

During the first half of the twelfth century Cyprus enjoyed a period of tranquil prosperity. The establishment of the Crusader states on the mainland opened up new markets for the produce of the island; and it was admirably placed for taking advantage of the new trade routes. The Venetians, who were now the most active traders in the eastern Mediterranean, considered it important enough to demand that the Emperor should grant them the commercial privileges that they had been given, in return for naval help, in other parts of the Empire. It was a time of architectural and artistic activity. The superb frescoes in the church at Asinou were commissioned by Constantine Euphorbenus Catacalon during his period as

Kykko Monastery on Mt. Troodos, founded c. 1100 and frequently rebuilt. Archbishop Makarios, who served his novitiate there, is buried on an adjacent hill

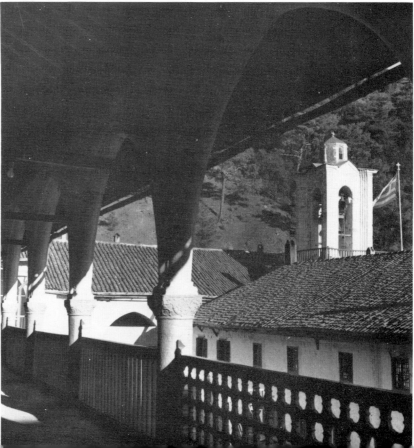

governor, between the two governorships of Philocales; and those of the monastery of St. Chrysostom at Koutzoventi probably date from about half a century later, commissioned by the governor John Comnenus. The governors sent out to administer the island were all men of distinction, such as Philocales, or Catacalon, who had been a successful naval commander and whose son was married to the Emperor Alexius's youngest daughter, or John Comnenus, whom the Emperor Manuel regarded as his favourite cousin. They now bore the title of *doux*, or duke; and they governed the island from the city of Nicosia. New towns were arising. Constantia-Salamis had been replaced by Famagusta, as its harbour seems to have silted up. Kyrenia on the north coast and Limassol on the south coast were the other chief ports of the island. Taxation undoubtedly was high but it does not seem to have been oppressive.

The tranquillity was cruelly broken in 1156. An Armenian principality had been founded in Cilicia, and its Prince Thoros II, was in constant rebellion against the Emperor. A French adventurer, Reynald of Chatillon, who had become Prince of Antioch by marriage with its heiress, had undertaken to invade Thoros's territory to recapture some land that he had annexed. After defeating Thoros but before he had taken over the promised towns he demanded subsidies from the Emperor Manuel, who told him to wait till the task was completed. Reynald therefore made peace with Thoros and planned to raid Cyprus with his help. King Baldwin III of Jerusalem heard of the plan and sent to Cyprus to warn John Comnenus, the governor. But before reinforcements could arrive from Constantinople, Thoros and Reynald landed with a large force on the island. The island militia tried to intercept them but was hopelessly out-numbered, and its commander, Branas, was captured. John Comnenus himself was captured when trying to defend Nicosia. Then the invaders overran the whole island, burning churches, monasteries and houses, taking anything of value that they could find and rounding up the herds and flocks and, since they were too many and awkward to export, forcing the farmers and peasants to ransom them at a heavy price. Then, before the Byzantine forces could arrive, they sailed away with their booty and their captives.

The raid shocked Reynald's fellow-Franks as much as it infuriated the Emperor Two years later the Byzantine army marched on Antioch and forced Reynald to make a humiliating apology. But that could not repair the damage done to Cyprus. Many years were to pass before it recovered its prosperity. Severe earthquakes in 1157 added to the misery; and in 1158 an Egyptian fleet raided the island, capturing the governor's brother and returning home with such booty as they could find. The raid was probably made without the authority of the Egyptian authorities, who hastened to send the governor's brother home with every honour. It is probable that the governor in question was the Emperor's cousin, John Ducas, who certainly held the post in 1161, when the Emperor Manuel married as his second wife Princess Maria of Antioch. He had first negotiated for the hand of Princess Melisende of Tripoli, a lady later famous as the *princesse lointaine* of the troubadours. Her disappointed brother, the Count of Tripoli, lent the fleet that he had prepared to escort her to Constantinople to pirates, telling them to raid Cyprus and any other Imperial territory that they chose: which they carried out with efficiency.

The Monastery of Ayios Chrysostomos (called after St. John Chrysostom, 354–406) or the White Monastery. The original building dates from the 11th century; it is a dependency of the Orthodox See of Jerusalem. The church of the Holy Trinity, one of two attached to the monastery, was founded in 1110 and contains twelfth century wall-paintings.

In 1166 Manuel appointed his cousin Andronicus Comnenus governor of Cilicia, with rights over the government and revenues of Cyprus. The idea of connecting the island with Cilicia was not new. The Emperor John had in 1142 toyed with the idea of turning southern Anatolia and Cyprus into an autonomous appanage under one of his sons. Andronicus was a man of many talents but unstable and, at the time, more interested in amorous adventures than in administration. He soon went off to Antioch, enriched with the revenues of the island, where he seduced the Empress's sister, Philippa of Antioch, then left her for Palestine, where he seduced and eloped with the Queen Dowager, his cousin, Theodora Comnena. The island was left once more impoverished.

These melancholy years saw the emergence of two great Cypriot saints. Nilus, who came to the small monastery of Machaeras in 1172, soon made it one of the most influential establishments on the island. He later became Bishop of Tamasos, and was greatly admired for his piety and his care for the oppressed. But he was overshadowed by Neophytus, who had been a novice at the monastery of St. Chrysostom, and then a hermit in the hills above Paphos. He was not allowed to remain in solitude for long; in the 1170's he founded for his disciples the monastery of New Zion, better known as the Enkleistra. He made himself an outspoken critic of the misgovernance of the island. There was little that he could achieve; but he was so greatly loved by the people that the authorities could not silence him.

In 1176 the Imperial army under Manuel was utterly routed by the Turks at the battle of Myriokephalon, a disaster from which it never recovered. The Empire lost its control over southern Anatolia; and Cyprus was isolated once more. Manuel died in 1180. His widow, Maria of Antioch, took over the regency for their young son, Alexius II. But her incompetence and the favour that she showed to the Latins soon made her hated. The adventurer Andronicus then emerged from exile and marched on Constantinople to take over the Empire. He was an able administrator who tried to stamp out inefficiency and corruption in the civil service. But he was also tyrannical, suspicious and so savagely cruel that he lost all his popularity. After two years he was dethroned and torn to pieces by the furious population of the capital. In his place they elevated a distant cousin, Isaac Angelus, an elderly, amiable and incompetent man, who in his turn was dethroned in 1193 by his brother Alexius, who was equally incompetent and less amiable.

There was a junior member of the Imperial family, Isaac Ducas, who took his mother's surname of Comnenus, and who had been appointed governor of Cilicia

The 12th century church of Antiphonitis, which was part of a monastery until 1965. A narthex was added in the 14th century and an open loggia with pointed arches in the 15th century

157

at the end of Manuel's reign. He could do nothing there and was soon captured by the Armenians, who sold him to the Order of the Templars. At the request of his aunt, ex-Queen Theodora, Andronicus's mistress, Andronicus consented to ransom him and to permit him to return to his precarious governorship, lending him a sum of money on the security of two distinguished Constantinopolitan citizens. Isaac used the money to collect a few soldiers, with whom he crossed the sea to Cyprus, armed with forged letters appointing him as its governor. Once he was established there he threw off allegiance to Andronicus and took the supreme title of *basileus*, or Emperor. Andronicus in his rage tortured and impaled the two innocent sponsors but perished himself before he could take action against the rebel. His successor, Isaac Angelus, tried to buy back his allegiance, and when that failed sent a naval expedition to recapture the island. The Emperor of Cyprus was warned of its approach. Having no ships of his own and hearing that a Sicilian admiral, Margarito, was cruising off the Syrian coast, he hired his services. When the expedition landed Margarito swept into the harbour. Isaac then had little difficulty in forcing the landing-force to surrender. Its leaders were

Machaeras Monastery, founded c. 1148; burnt down in 1530 and 1892, rebuilt in 1900 put to death, except for a few who agreed to take service under him. The common soldiers and the ships' crews were sent back unharmed to Anatolia, while Margarito made off with the ships and the ships' officers.

Independence under its own monarch might have been the best temporary solution for Cyprus. But Isaac had a difficult task. His usurpation was resented by many Cypriots; and he had aroused the bitter enmity of Constantinople. The island was still impoverished after three decades of disasters; and soon its foreign trade was to be disrupted by Saladin's conquest of the Kingdom of Jerusalem, after the battle of Hattin in 1187. This not only deprived Cyprus for the time being of one of its main markets, but it involved a political threat. A Crusade was certain to come east to try to recover the lost lands; and as a base for operations Cyprus would be invaluable to the Crusaders. Isaac was aware of the danger. As soon as possible he entered into relations with Saladin, hoping for his help in the event of a Crusader attack. But it is hard to see how Saladin could have come to his assistance. Nothing came of the negotiations.

Had Isaac been a more popular ruler he might have survived. But his financial exactions, from which the wealthy suffered as much as the poor, lost him the good will of classes that might have supported him. He was personally detested for his ungovernable rages and wanton cruelties. His high-handedness offended the Church and caused St. Neophytus to write bitter diatribes against him. It may be that his many enemies exaggerated his crimes. But when the crisis came his only loyal supporters were some, and not all, of his troops.

In the spring of 1191 news came that King Richard of England had set out from Sicily on his way to fight in Palestine. At the end of April three ships from his fleet appeared off Cyprus. Two were wrecked on the coast, but the third, containing his sister, Queen Joanna of Sicily, and his betrothed, Berengaria of Navarre, anchored off Limassol. Isaac hastened to the town and invited the royal ladies to come

The Monastery of Ayios Neophytos, founded by the hermit of that name c. 1170. His original cell is preserved, decorated with contemporary paintings; of the buildings the earliest are from the fifteenth century.

159

ashore. They refused, fearing to be used as hostages, but asked permission to send ashore for water and provisions. Isaac forbade this and began to fortify the coast. About a week later King Richard arrived with his main fleet. He considered that his sister and his betrothed had been insulted and landed with some troops at a nearby bay and marched on Limassol. The Italian merchants in the town welcomed him gladly and even the Greeks, in their dislike of Isaac, were friendly. Isaac, who had retired to the slopes of Troodos, then offered to negotiate, if given a safe-conduct. He visited Richard's camp and in an interview agreed to pay the King a sum of money, to allow his men to buy provisions free of custom dues, to send a contingent to join the Crusade and to offer his daughter as a hostage. But his visit to the English camp made him think that Richard was not so formidable after all. When he returned to his own camp he repudiated the agreement.

Unfortunately for him, that very day Richard was joined by a number of distinguished lords from Palestine, come to welcome him, and each with his escort of knights. On 12th May Richard married Berengaria in the chapel of St. George at Limassol, and on 13th May the remainder of the English fleet arrived. Seeing his mistake, Isaac moved to Famagusta, but realised that he could not hold it against a combined naval and military attack. He retired to Nicosia, sending his wife, an

Armenian princess, and his daughter, his only child, to the castle at Kyrenia, hoping that they might if need be escape to Armenia. In Nicosia he collected all his troops and marched down to meet the English army at the village of Tremithus. After a sharp skirmish, his troops, who were said to have been armed with poisoned arrows, were routed. Isaac fled to Kantara; and Richard entered Nicosia without opposition, many of the inhabitants even welcoming him. There Richard fell ill; and Isaac hoped to hold his four northern castles, St. Hilarion, Buffavento, Kantara and Kyrenia, till the King tired of his venture and went away. But Guy of Lusignan took command of the English army and marched on Kyrenia, capturing it together with Isaac's wife and daughter. He then blockaded St. Hilarion and Buffavento. Richard, as he informed an envoy from King Philip of France, had no intention of leaving the island till Isaac had been punished; and he pointed out how valuable possession of the island would be for the pursuance of the Crusade.

By the end of May Isaac realised that he was beaten. He surrendered unconditionally, asking only that he should not be put in irons. So he was brought before Richard loaded with silver chains. When Richard left the island a few days later, Isaac was brought with the fleet and later handed over to the Hospitallers. He died, still a captive, in about 1195. His wife and daughter were attached to Queen Joanna's household.

The Akheiropiitos Monastery ('built without hands') near Lapithos. The church is of the early Byzantine period with an apse containing the remains of paintings. A cruciform domed building with a domed narthex and a porch were added later

161

The Church of Panayia Phorviotissa at Asinou. The main building dates from 1105 and the domed narthex was added c. 1200. The wall-paintings are among the finest in Cyprus and have recently been carefully cleaned

Isaac's surrender had left the whole island in Richard's hands. His first act was to extract all the ready money that he could from it. Then he confirmed the laws and institutions that had existed in the Emperor Manuel's time. Latin garrisons were placed in all the castles, and two Englishmen, Richard of Camville and Robert of Turnham, were appointed justiciars, to govern the island till Richard should decide on its fate. The Greeks soon found that they had not gained from Isaac's fall. They were to take no more part in the government of their land. As a symbol of their subservience they were ordered to shave off their beards. A new era had begun.

162

IX
THE FRANKISH
PERIOD 1191–1571

Richard the Lionheart and the Templars 1191–1192
The Lusignan Dynasty 1192–1489
The Venetians 1489–1571

In coming under the rule of French-speaking foreigners from the West Cyprus suffered the same fate as did most of the rest of Greece and indeed many other territories in the Southern and Eastern Mediterranean. The great expansion of Latin power into the Greek-speaking territories of the Empire came thirteen years after Richard's intervention in Cyprus, with the capture of Constantinople by the Fourth Crusade in 1204. That was perhaps not originally intended, except by the Venetians; it might have been avoided, since nothing in history is inevitable; but the overthrow of the Greek ruler of Cyprus was even more accidental. None of the leaders of the Third Crusade coveted the island. Richard was dragged into its acquisition against his will and began at once to take urgent steps to pass it on to someone else. Nevertheless there was a certain inevitability about it. The Kingdom of Jerusalem and the other states founded by the Crusaders had for the moment the strongest fleets in the Eastern Mediterranean, thanks to the support of the Italian maritime republics: it was natural that Cyprus should yield to their control as it had done in the past to all other powers who had dominated the waters around its shores. Before long, when the strength by land of the Moslem powers had become too great to allow the descendants of the Crusaders to cling

The Royal Arms of Cyprus showing the arms of Lusignan, Cyprus, Jerusalem and Armenia

to their Syrian coastal strip, Cyprus took over the role of the last military bastion of
the Cross against the Crescent and the great entrepot of East-West trade. It was
rewarded, for a time, by great prosperity. The foreign rulers became notorious for
their luxurious living; but their subjects profited little.

The Greeks call this period of their history the Frankokratia, the rule of the
Franks; it is scarcely regarded as preferable to the succeeding Tourkokratia. The
Peloponnese, the ancestral home of the Cypriots, presented almost the same
picture under a family from Champagne as Cyprus did under a family from Poitou.
Both had a feudal system of land tenure and inheritance. In peacetime the barons
were as turbulent as a favourite cliché of mediaeval history asserts. In war they
combined personal courage with military incompetence. The consequent
fatalities, and the effects of an unfamiliar climate, meant that there were frequent
breaks in the dynastic succession, with Queens as regents for minor heirs.
Women indeed play a prominent part, though mainly as transferrers of hereditary
rights. In the end the bright silks and plate-armour of the reigning houses yield
place to the mercantile and calculating Venetians.

Before that the Frankish kingdoms had done their very best to assure their own
destruction. None of them could stay at peace either internally or with their neigh-

Berengaria leaving Cyprus

164

bours. There were civil wars and murderous conspiracies throughout their history and on the classical plains of Boeotia as in the streets of Famagusta rival Latin forces brought a special enthusiasm to mutual massacre. Although the French-speaking noble houses were much given to feuding a certain edge was given to the struggle when Spaniards, especially Catalans, were involved, as in fifteenth-century Cyprus. Undoubtedly the most destructive influence in the long run was the intense rivalry between the Italian mercantile cities and especially Venice and Genoa. Most historians blame the Genoese for weakening the powers of the Government of Cyprus, and for subordinating its interests to those of their trade with the Moslem states. Venice, whose arms and intrigues had been mainly responsible for ruining the Empire of Constantinople, was to Cyprus little more than the final receiver in bankruptcy.

Richard soon found evidence of what he suspected from the start: that Cyprus would be more of a trouble to him than an advantage. The Greek inhabitants had certainly been glad to be rid of Isaac but they soon rose in revolt against the foreign conqueror. Richard's governor, the Englishman Robert of Turnham, put down the rising and hanged a Greek monk who had been proclaimed Emperor. No doubt this strengthened his desire to disembarrass himself of the unwanted possession. He was pleased to find that he could pass it on to the military order of the Temple at the reasonable price of 100,000 dinars of which only 40,000 in cash down. The Templars were also faced by a revolt; they took more drastic action and massacred so many Greeks in Nicosia that blood ran in the streets. For a long time afterwards a stone was pointed out marking the point the flow reached. They also ravaged all the villages of the plains, driving the inhabitants to take refuge in the mountains. This was not what the Templars wanted and they appealed to Richard to cancel the sale. He agreed because it would help him in his complicated but well-intended intrigues to settle the affairs of the kingdom of Jerusalem if he could

Church of Panayia tou Arakou, Lagoudera, completely painted in 1192 with a unique series of classicising wall-paintings

165

The Archangel Gabriel, part
of the Annunciation; 1192,
classicising style; north-east
pendentive, Church of Panayia
tou Arakou

bestow Cyprus, on the same financial terms, on Guy de Lusignan. Local bankers scraped together 40,000 dinars, the Templars were reimbursed and the deed was done. A dynasty lasting three hundred years was founded.

Guy de Lusignan (1192–1194) had been King of Jerusalem in right of his wife Sybil, mother of King Baldwin who died at the age of seven. She had married apparently for love since he was poor, "easy-going and far from clever" as one historian describes him, and disliked by most of the prominent barons of the kingdom. He came from a reasonably distinguished Poitevin family but was the least distinguished of three brothers. He also managed to get himself captured by the Saracens in the battle of the Horns of Hattin where, according to Chesterton, "the hope of the world went down" and where, in more sober truth, the greater part of the Kingdom of Jerusalem was lost. He was released in 1188 but his rule over the remaining coastal strip was contested. In 1192 he was ousted in favour of Henry, Count of Champagne; in recompense he took over Cyprus, to hold as a fief from Richard for his lifetime.

Although the other Crusaders thought him stupid ("simplex et minus astutus") he followed a sensible policy in Cyprus. He offered the fullest assurance to the Greek inhabitants that there would be no more massacres and they could all go back to work in security. To gain the support he needed for his colonial rule he appealed to the remaining barons of Palestine who had been made landless by Saladin, or to their widows and children. Instead of clinging to the few coastal cities still in Christian hands they should come to Cyprus where they could hold by feudal tenure wide estates rich in corn and vines. According to one chronicler he was acting on the advice of Saladin. If so, it was good and disinterested advice, and the basis of the constitution of the Kingdom of Cyprus.

Guy reigned for less than two years. He never took the title of King of Cyprus but regarded himself as still King of Jerusalem. He was succeeded by his brother Aimery (1194–1205). During his reign a complete new ecclesiastical establishment for Cyprus was brought into effect whereby the Latin Church took over the administration of the dioceses from the Greek Orthodox clergy and bishops. He also regularised the international position of his state by doing homage to the Western Emperor, Henry VI, and receiving in return recognition as King of Cyprus. Not long afterwards he was able to call himself King of Jerusalem as well, by the

Christ Pantocrator, surrounded by a host of angels and the Preparation of the Throne in medallions; 1192, classicising style; dome, church of Panayia tou Arakou, near Lagoudera

167

same means as his brother; for he married Isabel, widow of Henry of Champagne. His second crown brought him few advantages; the resources and manpower of Cyprus were used to defend Acre and the remaining territories on the Syrian coast while the island was exposed to raids by the Sultan al-Malik al-Adil. In reprisal he raided the Egyptian Delta, but he was glad to make a treaty with the Sultan in 1204 which gave him some advantages in Palestine. On the whole he is the King of Cyprus against whom there is least to say; cautious, prudent, and reasonable the only thing known to his discredit is that he is supposed to have brought on an early death by eating far too much fish at one sitting.

His son Hugh I also had a short reign, from 1205 to 1218; he was only ten when he succeeded so that it lasted effectively for eight years. He took part in the Fifth Crusade, which achieved nothing, and died suddenly in Tripoli at the age of twenty-three. He had been married for eight years to Alice d'Ibelin, of a crusading house famous in Palestine; his only son, Henry, was born only about nine months before his death. When he succeeded as Henry I (1218–1253) a long regency was certain. That was a state of affairs thoroughly familiar in the crusader kingdoms of the Levant because the men, especially if active in war and politics, died much younger than the women. It was a dispensation generally welcome to the principal barons because it left them free from restraint to pursue their own policies. In the case of Henry I the regency lasted nearly fifteen years and the reign a surprising

The Birth of Christ; 1192, classicising style; church of Panayia tou Arakou

168

thirty-five years; but his nature was exceptionally easy-going — he was called Henry the Fat and was as lethargic in spirit as in body — so that the leading men were rarely incommoded by a royal initiative. It was not a successful reign from the point of view of Cyprus. On the other hand it must be admitted that there were later kings with conventionally preferable qualities who caused greater damage.

Queen Alice became Regent of the Kingdom and guardian of her infant son; she was assisted by her two uncles Philip and John d'Ibelin in succession. One of her first acts, whose effects were to be long-lasting and damaging, was to grant extensive commercial privileges to the Genoese. It included the right of establishment in Famagusta, the principal port. The main event of the first part of the reign was the armed attempt of the Emperor Frederick II to seize the regency in virtue of the homage done to his predecessor by King Aimery. Frederick of Hohenstaufen, known as *Stupor Mundi*, the astonishment of the world, because of his knowledge of languages, poetry and law, married in 1225 Yolande, the heiress of the Kingdom of Jerusalem. By her he had a son, Conrad IV of Jerusalem. It was in right of that son that he sailed for the East in 1228 to take over what remained of the Kingdom of Jerusalem. His journey is sometimes counted as the Sixth Crusade. It resulted in his obtaining from the Sultan of Egypt, by negotiation, possession of Jerusalem, Bethlehem, Nazareth, Sidon, Lydda and some other places and the promise of a ten-year truce. In Cyprus he was in the

The Ascension of Christ (detail); 1192, classicising style; church of Panayia tou Arakou, near Lagoudera

169

long run unsuccessful. To begin with he received recognition as suzerain of the island from John d'Ibelin, now acting as Regent in place of Queen Alice, and from the principal barons so that when he returned to the West in 1229 he could leave the direction of affairs in the hands of his adherents, five of whom acted as his "bailies" or representatives. The Cypriots, under the leadership of John d'Ibelin, soon went over to opposition. The wars lasted four years, with a brief intermission. The castles of Hilarion, Kantara and Kyrenia, seized by the Imperialists, were twice besieged and twice captured. A famous battle was fought at Aghirda, at the foot of the pass leading across the Pentadaktylos range, in which John d'Ibelin and his son Sir Balian d'Ibelin won an unexpected victory over the Imperialists. Throughout these struggles, which are written up in the brightest colours of chivalry by the chroniclers, especially by the poet Philippe de Novare, King Henry the Fat played no active role. He had been prematurely crowned to guard against Frederick's pretensions but his supporters took great care that he should not be exposed to danger.

He did take part, when he was twenty-one, in the Seventh Crusade led by King Louis IX of France. He had been host to St. Louis since September 1248; the next eight months were spent in Nicosia, in leisurely and repetitive discussions of plans of campaign. In May the two kings embarked at Limassol and sailed for Damietta,

David, Isaiah, Jeremiah, the Preparation of the Throne; wall painting, classicising School of Constantinople; in the church of Panayia tou Arakou, Lagoudera; 1192

170

for it had been decided that the only way to safeguard the Kingdom of Jerusalem was to destroy the power of the Sultan of Egypt. (This was probably a sound decision; it had been the view of all the sensible Kings of Jerusalem.) The Latin Archbishop of Nicosia came too, and died in Egypt. King Henry stayed only briefly, though he left behind a strong force of 120 knights, with their accompanying infantry, under his relation Baldwin d'Ibelin. The Cypriots distinguished themselves next year at the battle of Bahr-al-Saghir but in April 1250 were forced to surrender with the whole of the army. Meanwhile King Henry had been widowed for the second time, taken as his third wife, in September 1250, Plaisance, Princess of Antioch, and died in 1253 having at last begotten a son, Hugh II, who succeeded at the age of a few months.

Another regency for an infant king may give a good opportunity to break off the

Wall painting of King Hugh I (1205–1218) from the Templars chapel at Cressac, France

171

dynastic chronicle and consider the nature and organisation of the Kingdom of Cyprus. The most important fact about its nature was that the ruling class was a small stratum of West Europeans, French-speaking and predominantly of French origin, and that the subject population was overwhelmingly Greek with a few Armenians and Syrians. The state was organised on the purest feudal principles. Indeed it had a written constitution, the Assizes (i.e. ordinances) of Jerusalem, a document often quoted by English and French historians of feudalism who can find nothing so elaborate and consistent in the looser practice of their own countries. The island was divided into King's land and fiefs held by barons (and ecclesiastical institutions) on condition of rendering him military service. The King was the sovereign liege of all the barons who had originally received their lands from him; like Guy de Lusignan himself the first barons had come from Palestine, most of them having lost their lands there to the Saracens. The original settlers were said to have numbered 300 knights and 200 mounted sergeants. The principal constitutional body was the *Haute Cour* or High Court, the equivalent of the curia Regis of Western Europe, which consisted of the whole body of barons. It had executive, legislative and judicial powers. No fief-holder could be punished

Aerial view of the Abbey of Bellapais

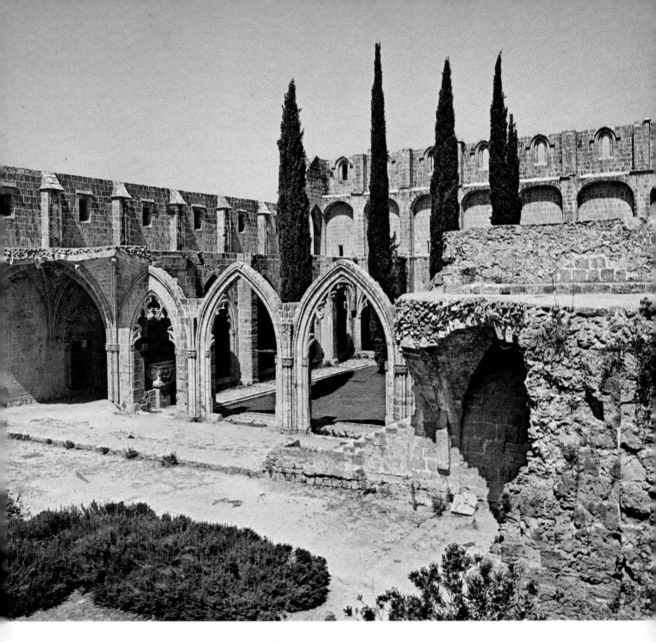

by the King without its judgment. For non-noble Franks there was a Lower Court or *Cour des Bourgeois*.

The Greek subject classes were divided into three. The lowest and most numerous consisted of *parici* or serfs who were bound to the soil, paid an annual poll-tax and rendered two days a week forced labour to their lords, who also took one-third of their agricultural produce, and were entirely under the jurisdiction of their lords in all criminal matters. In the second class were the *perperiarii* (from hyperperon, the standard Byzantine coin) who were so called because they had partly compounded with their lords for their servile dues by paying an annual tax of fifteen hyperpera. The third class was of the free men or *lefteri* who were released from feudal dues either by purchase or by favour and held their lands by free tenure.

The Abbey of Bellapais, three miles south-east of Kyrenia. Founded c. 1200 by King Aimery as a house of Augustinian canons, it later belonged to the Premonstratensians. The church is from the 13th century. The long building to the north of the cloisters is the well-preserved refectory

Wall-paintings in the narthex of the church of Panayia Phorviotissa, Asinou, dated by an inscription over the lintel to 1333. The theme of the decoration is the Last Judgment. In the apse personifications of Earth (left) and Sea (right); below St. Peter leads the Just to Paradise; in the pendentives the Apostles in four groups of three; at ground level the Archangel Michael (right), three saints (left). The style of the paintings reflects that of the late Comnenian period

Many travellers visiting Cyprus during the Frankish period, after commenting enviously on the wealth of the ruling class, say that the peasantry get no benefit from it but are wretched slaves, oppressed with heavy taxes. Others describe them as cheerful, indolent people who console themselves with the excellent local wine. It is likely that in fact the peasants were materially no worse off than when under either Byzantine or Turkish rule. But material well-being is not everything. They resented their subjection to the foreigners, for the Lusignans made no effort to bridge the legal and social gulf between themselves and their Greek subjects. The Normans in Sicily and South Italy had been brilliantly successful in creating a real national feeling and a fusion of races — and there they had had a third element to assimilate, the Arabs. Other Normans in England achieved even more lasting results in reconciling conquerors and conquered. It seems that in other parts of France there was a less generous, and less effective, political outlook.

Even more serious to the Greeks than their own reduction in status was the treatment of their church. The Lusignan kings, who regarded the Orthodox church as schismatic, put themselves under the authority of the Roman see. Nicosia became the seat of a Latin Archbishop in 1196, with suffragans in the dioceses of Paphos, Limassol and Famagusta. The four sees were endowed by Aimery with lands and tithes. The Greek incumbents were driven out in 1220 and made to live in villages. Some Latin monasteries were founded in the island, of which the spectacularly beautiful Bellapais is the best known, and some Greek monasteries were taken over by Latin religious orders. But the most important Orthodox monasteries continued and monastic life flourished.

The first eight years of the reign of Hugh II (1253–1267) were dominated by his mother, Plaisance of Antioch, who acted as Regent. She appears to have been a woman of strong character and is described by one chronicler as "one of the most valiant women in the world". In 1258 she made a dramatic appearance at Acre, where the crusading spirit of mutual massacre had reached a peak in an all-out war between the Venetians, the Pisans and the Templars on one side and the Genoese, the Spaniards and the Hospitallers on the other. She was able to persuade the Venetian side, then for a time in the ascendant, to recognise her son as King of Jerusalem. The title was rapidly losing its value as the Sultan of Egypt took

The Triumphant Entry of Christ into Jerusalem; first. half of the 13th century; St. John Lampadistis, Kalopanayiotis

175

The Cathedral of Ayia Sophia (the Selimiye Mosque) in Nicosia. Construction began under Archbishop Thierry, from the Ile de France in 1209; consecrated in 1326. In 1570 it was converted into a mosque; wood engraving; The Graphic 1878

advantage of the Franks' quarrels to pick off their castles one by one. Three years later Plaisance died and the Regency was taken over by Hugh of Antioch, son of Prince Henry of Antioch and Isabel de Lusignan. When Hugh II died childless at the age of 14 the original Lusignan line became extinct.

Hugh of Antioch changed from being Regent to being King as Hugh III (1267–1284). He adopted his mother's name and thus founded the second Lusignan dynasty.

Hugh III was one of the best of the Kings of Cyprus; the competition is pretty weak. The affairs of Syria pre-occupied him more than Cyprus. This was the time when the approach of the Mongol power out of Central Asia, friendly to the Frankish Christians and hostile to the Egyptian Sultan, seemed to offer a new chance of survival. It did; and the rivalry and bitterness of the Christians, especially the Venetians and the Templars, threw it away gladly in exchange for a final chance to harass their enemies, the Genoese and the Hospitallers. Hugh attempted to play a mediating role. At one point he was obliged to throw in his hand and return to Cyprus when the intrigues of the Temple brought the recognition of Charles of Anjou instead of himself; but at the end of his life he was back in Syria, endeavouring to form a united front. All the time the power of the Mamelukes, the white slave rulers of Egypt, was growing, under two successive forceful Sultans, Baibars and Kalaun.

Hugh died in Tyre in 1284 and was succeeded by his elder son John I. He reigned for just over a year (1284–5) and died in Nicosia, not without suspicion of poison. His younger brother, Henry II (1285–1324), was then crowned as his successor, although he was only fourteen. He reigned for almost forty years, but it was an unhappy and ineffectual reign, partly because he suffered for most of it from epilepsy which prevented the usual kingly activity and deprived him of the respect of his subjects. In 1286, with the affairs of the Kingdom of Jerusalem in their customary confusion, he was acknowledged as King and crowned in Tyre. It was only to preside over the downfall of the Kingdom at the hands of the Mameluke Sultan al-Malik al-Ashraf. In spite of his youth and his illness he fought

Interior of the Cathedral of Ayia Sophia, now the Selimiye Mosque

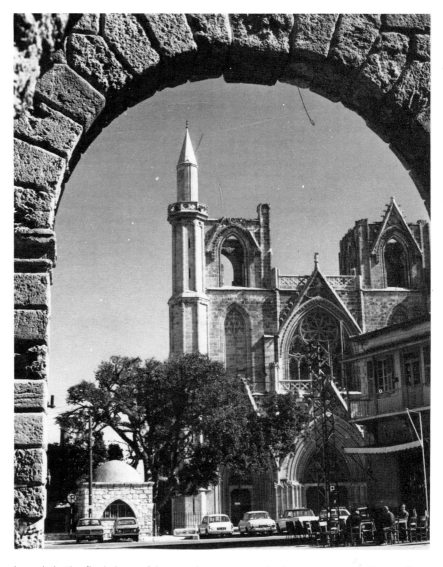

bravely in the final siege of Acre and was among the last to escape to Cyprus from the harbour after the land walls were stormed. Only the island of Ruad remained in Christian hands for another thirteen years until 1303. Three years later Henry was the victim of a coup d'état by his ambitious younger brother Amaury, who deprived him of all authority, had himself proclaimed "Governor" and finally drove Henry into exile in the Armenian Kingdom of Cilicia. His exile was ended when Amaury was murdered, apparently on personal not political grounds, by one of his closest adherents. The restored Henry II reigned for another fourteen years. His epilepsy had abated but he remained a feeble and unimpressive ruler. Why Dante described him in the *Paradiso* as a beast, who made Nicosia and Famagusta lament, is unknown; locally he had a good reputation as a pious ruler and a man of courage.

The Cathedral of St. Nicholas Famagusta, seen through the ruins of the Palace of the Proveditore

178

The disappearance of the last coastal strongholds of the Kingdom of Jerusalem was of great advantage to Cyprus. Its consequences are the principal reasons for the great prosperity which marked the fourteenth century. To begin with, it was no longer necessary for Henry II and his successors to pour out their money and military resources in vain attempts to preserve the Frankish foothold in Syria. On the positive side Cyprus gained from its position as a Christian stronghold surrounded by Moslem states. It was ultimately untenable, and was almost of necessity bound to fall when its neighbours came under a strong, unitary, military state; but two and a half centuries are a good long time. Immediately it became the main entrepôt for oriental trade, equalling in importance Constantinople and Alexandria. The merchants of Famagusta became notorious for wealth and ostentation. The proceeds of trade spread throughout the island; as a result the standard of living of the nobles improved spectacularly. The German traveller Lindolf of Suchen saw them out hunting the moufflon with leopards. "In Cyprus

The Cathedral of St. Nicholas (the Lala Mustafa Mosque) in Famagusta. Built in the early fourteenth century and consecrated in 1326 it was severely damaged during the siege of 1571 and converted into a mosque the princes, nobles, barons and knights are the richest in the world. They spend all their money on the chase. I know a certain Count (Hugh d'Ibelin, Count of Jaffa) who has more than five hundred hounds and every two hounds have their own servant to guard and bathe and anoint them." Even the subject classes found themselves living more at their ease.

Henry II died in 1324 and was succeeded by Hugh IV (1324–1359), son of his brother Guy. His reign illustrates the advantages of the new situation of Cyprus. He lived in peace with all his neighbours, amusing himself with literature and hunting. His only harassment was from pirates who were attracted by the increase in the wealth of Cyprus and in the numbers of the merchant ships using Cypriot ports. Evidence of the same kind is given by the heightened interest of Venice and Genoa; other merchant cities also obtained privileges in the island including Florence and Montpellier. There was a murderous riot between Venetians and Genoese at Famagusta in 1345, but this was the sort of thing that happened all over the Levant and scarcely ruffled the prosperity of this peace-loving king.

His son and successor Peter I (1359–1369) was his precise opposite. It is in keeping with Gibbon's view of history as little more than the register of the crimes, follies and misfortunes of mankind that he is by far the best-known mediaeval King of Cyprus. Villon in France and Chaucer in England wrote about him; the peasants in the villages of Troodos still sing songs about him. Admittedly their themes are different, one celebrating his love of war, the other his love of women.

King Peter was determined to wage war with the infidel in the spirit of a crusader born out of time. His first expedition was to Cilicia, where he captured the city of Adalia and massacred "all that ever were within none except" according

Thirteenth-century stone relief, probably from a tympanum over a door, showing Christ in Majesty surrounded by a mandorla supported by angels and flanked by scriptural scenes; below the Virgin *orans*, the Archangel Gabriel and Apostles
Victoria and Albert Museum

to Froissart. In preparation for his second he went on a long mission to Western Europe to gather support. He was received everywhere with great enthusiasm but little real help. There is a tradition in the City of London that he was feasted there in the winter of 1363 by the Master of the Vintners Company in the company of the Kings of England and Scotland. He was nearly three years on his travels.

On his return, in 1365, he led a very large expedition against Alexandria. This was in principle, as already remarked, a sensible move. If he could have established himself on the Egyptian coast he might have altered significantly the balance of power in the Levant. This was possibly his intention; but perhaps because he could not control his troops he made no serious attempt to exploit his rapid success in capturing Alexandria and withdrew the force to Cyprus after a few days in which the city was thoroughly sacked. The fleet returned with an enormous booty. The report of the sack spread throughout Europe. In the Canterbury Tales Chaucer recounts that his knight had been at Alexandria, as previously at Adalia. If so he showed a taste in massacre at variance with the well-known compliments with which he is introduced in the Prologue. A recent work has argued that Chaucer wrote ironically; he did not intend to present the knight as an ideal of chivalry but as a brutal mercenary fighting for pay and plunder. If so his flattering words about King Peter in the Monk's Tale may not represent his

"The Feast of the Five Kings." The Master of the Vintners' Company of London entertaining Peter I of Cyprus in 1363 with the kings of England, Scotland, France and Denmark (the presence of the last two kings is not authentically attested); from a picture by Chevalier Taylor in the Royal Exchange. (This painting is at the offices of KEO, in Limassol)

181

genuine opinion.

These warlike exploits brought King Peter the "renown" of which Villon speaks but they were very expensive. He raised money partly from his own subjects, by selling their freedom to the perperiarii at a reduced rate, and partly from abroad, which increased the hold of the Venetians and Genoese on the trade of Cyprus. He had another side to his character. He was apparently devoted to his wife, Eleanor of Aragon, and took her nightgown with him on his travels when he was parted from her; but he also kept at least two mistresses. These activities were resented by the nobles, who in addition feared his increasingly tyrannical treatment of them in flagrant disregard of the laws. One morning in January 1369 three of the leading barons forced their way into his bedroom and stabbed him.

A woman donor, detail from the composition of the enthroned Virgin Mary with the child Christ; 14th century; south apse of the narthex, church of Panayia Phorviotissa of Asinou, near Nikitari. (Her cloak-like veil is of the type introduced into the island by refugees from Syria, after the fall of Acre in 1291, and was widely used until the 15th century)

His son Peter II (1369–82) was mild-mannered and lethargic, and only fifteen when he succeeded. For all the contrast with the preceding reign, this one gave Cyprus what was probably its most decisive push on the downward path. The trouble began in 1372, when the king was crowned with the crown of Jerusalem in Famagusta. A quarrel began between the Genoese and the Venetians immediately after the ceremony about who should take the right-hand rein of the

King's horse when he came from the cathedral. This privilege had in the past been claimed by the Genoese but on this occasion the Venetian consul took it by force. That night at the coronation the brawling broke out again. The Cypriots, who hated the Genoese because they were grasping and arrogant on land and pirates at sea, took the side of the Venetians. Genoese shops were looted and burned and many Genoese were wounded and some killed. In Genoa the affair was written up into a massacre.

The Italian maritime republics believed that they could only maintain their trade with the Levant and their colonial possessions there by taking violent reprisals against any state that ill-treated their nationals. Genoa pursued this policy with particular relish. An expedition was sent to Cyprus which ravaged the entire island and plundered both Famagusta and Nicosia. The king and his mother fell into their hands by a trick involving the most blatant breach of faith. Venice was unable to help because she saw herself imminently threatened by what became the War of Chioggia against Genoa and her mainland allies. The Cypriots were reduced to guerrilla attacks on the occupying force. Finally, in 1374, they were forced to accept the Genoese terms. These provided for the payment of a tribute of 40,000

The presentation of Christ in the Temple; second half of the fourteenth century; Ayios Nicolaos tis Stegis gold florins a year, a fine of 2,012,240 gold florins to be paid in instalments over 12 years, and a down payment of 90,000 gold florins to reimburse the expenses of the fleet that invaded them. When the 90,000 had been paid the Genoese would hand back Nicosia and the rest of the island except Famagusta. The loss of Famagusta marked the end of Cypriot prosperity. As it happened, its possession did very little good to Genoa. The interminable internal wars of the Franks in the Levant almost invariably resulted in no advantage to either side.

In spite of the ostensible cause for the murder of Peter I his widow, Eleanor of

Sgraffiato ware — a type of glazed pottery dating largely from the fourteenth and fifteenth centuries; (left) bowl, H 12.1 cm; (right) goblet H 12.5 cm British Museum

Aragon, pursued his murderers with passionate vindictiveness. She got the Genoese to execute the better-known ones but she was convinced that her brother-in-law John, known as Prince of Antioch, had been a co-conspirator. For six years she let his suspicions die down until he felt it safe to accept an invitation to dinner in the palace. After dinner a covered dish was brought in. The Queen took off the cover and on the dish was the bloodstained shirt of her husband. "Do you know whose this was?" she asked. It was the agreed signal for some Italians, concealed in the room behind the Prince's back, to rush out and kill him. The King, who had been persuaded of his uncle's guilt, nevertheless soon thought it time to send his mother back to Catalonia. It was the last time he asserted himself. In 1382 he died at the age of 29. His lethargy had increased to such a degree that he was the second King of the house of Lusignan to have the sobriquet of "the Fat".

Peter II died without lawful issue and was succeeded by his uncle James I (1382–1398) who at the time was a prisoner in Genoa, having been seized by a more than usually perfidious trick. It was three years before the Genoese let him out on very severe terms including the outright cession of Famagusta. The King had also to agree that all ships coming to Cyprus should discharge only in Famagusta. This prohibition was often ignored but it contributed to the ruin of the island's trade. The King's son and heir had been born in prison in Genoa in 1374 and baptised Janus, after the mythical founder of the city rather than the appropriately double-faced god; he was retained as a hostage and only allowed to return seven years after his father, in 1392. To pay off the Genoese demands the king was forced to impose greatly increased taxes. He solaced himself with hunting. The Lord of Anglure, a French traveller who visited Cyprus in 1395, described him as a pretty fine-looking man who spoke French well enough; he praised the King's skill at hunting. In 1393 he added to his titles that of King of Armenia, the kingdom having disappeared and the last King having died in exile. Sir George Hill claims, on rather thin evidence, that he was the only King of Cyprus to take an interest in the arts.

King Janus, his son and successor, who reigned from 1398 to 1432, was the third of the Lusignan Kings to be described as fat; however, the chroniclers record that he was also tall, and good looking. His first concern, as was natural and necessary, was to drive the Genoese from Famagusta but in two campaigns, interrupted by treaties in 1403 and 1414, he was unsuccessful. In its weakened state it was natural that Cyprus should appear a suitable prey to its external enemies. The Sultan of Egypt sent an expedition against it in 1425 which ravaged a great part of the south of the island. A larger one was mounted in 1426. In a battle at Khirokitia the Mamelukes defeated the full force of the kingdom. Janus himself was taken prisoner. Nicosia was captured and devastated. After two years' captivity in Cairo Janus was ransomed at a great price and returned broken in health and spirit. He

The Castle of Buffavento in the Pentadaktylos range. It was originally built in the 12th century and enlarged under the Lusignans; dismantled by the Venetians had been forced to accept the suzerainty of the Sultan and to pay a yearly tribute. The finances of Cyprus were exhausted and Janus, who never recovered from his humiliation, died poor in 1432. The century of prosperity was over.

King John II (1432–1458), Janus' only son, is described by Sir George Hill as "effeminate but not unattractive" and by Pope Pius II, a contemporary, as "cowardly and vile in spirit though handsome to look at" and "living a life of sloth, gluttony and lust." He was certainly ordered about by his women, two wives and a mistress, all Greek or with Greek connections. His first wife was Medea, of the Paleologi of Montferrat, and his second Helena Palaeologina, daughter of the Despot of the Morea and grand-daughter of the Emperor Manuel II. Her tyranny over her husband, mitigated only by occasional bouts of ill-health, is celebrated in popular song and legend. The mistress, Marietta of Patras, is supposed to have been of a milder nature; in a fight with the Queen, in the enthusiatic presence of the King, she had her nose bitten off. However, she was the mother of James the Bastard, loved and spoiled by his father when alive and his eventual successor. Queen Helena, though disapproved of as a virago, was popular with the Greeks inasmuch as she was devoted to the Orthodox Church. It is in this reign that there can be noticed an improvement in the status of the Greek population and a show of

The Castle of St. Hilarion, in the mountains south of Kyrenia. The present building dates from c. 1220, with fourteenth-century additions, and stands on the site of a Byzantine castle. It stood sieges on several occasions and was partially demolished by the Venetians in the sixteenth century because of shortage of man-power to defend it

greater solidarity with the alien regime at least on the part of the more prosperous of them.

John's daughter Charlotte was another of those forceful women who make the history of Cyprus so entertaining. She intimidated her father and dominated her second husband Louis, son of the Duke of Savoy. As the only legitimate heir she was recognised as Queen regnant in 1458, with the right of succession to Louis. Her illegitimate half-brother James was the complete opposite of his father, except in good looks, being active and ambitious. He had been involved in several murders before his father's death and he was not slow to try his hand at usurping Charlotte's throne. He fled to Egypt, where the Sultan was also captivated by him, and, having received from him a promise to be a faithful subject, conferred the kingdom on him by right of suzerainty and supplied him with ships, soldiers and money to make good his claim. With a fleet of 80 ships under the Egyptian commander-in-chief he landed at Ayia Napa in September 1460 and advanced boldly on Nicosia. Charlotte and Louis took refuge in Kyrenia, whose strong castle stood a siege for four years. Next year James began operations against Famagusta. In 1464 he was finally successful on both fronts. Queen Charlotte, showing the strength of character she had inherited from her mother, went on repeated journeys to the West pleading for support; she was unsuccessful, and Kyrenia castle, whose garrison had been reduced to famine by the siege, was surrendered by the treachery of its commander. Famagusta was surrendered by its Genoese garrison when attempts to revictual it failed. James II was now established firmly on the throne and controlled the whole island.

To have regained Famagusta meant the end of a parasitic growth which had for long sapped the strength of Cyprus. But it came too late. The revenues had been mortgaged and capital exhausted. The tribute to Egypt was a heavy burden which

(Opposite page)
The Castle of Kyrenia. Originally Byzantine it was enlarged and developed in the late thirteenth century and extensively remodelled by the Venetians, who turned it into a modern artillery fortress. Though often besieged, with varying success and for long periods at a time, it was never taken by storm. Wood engraving
Illustrated London News 1878

The Castle of Kantara, at the eastern end of the Pentadaktylos range. Originally built in the ninth century it was greatly strengthened and enlarged under the Lusignans; the Venetians partially demolished it, as they did St. Hilarion and Buffavento. The name is Arabic, meaning 'bridge'. Wood engraving
Illustrated London News 1878

Coats of arms over the eastern entrance to Kolossi castle. In the centre above, the arms of Lusignan, quartering Jerusalem, Cyprus and Armenia; below, the arms of Louis de Magnac, who rebuilt the castle in the mid-15th century; to right and left above, the arms of Jean de Lastic and Jacques de Milli, Grand Masters of the Order of St. John

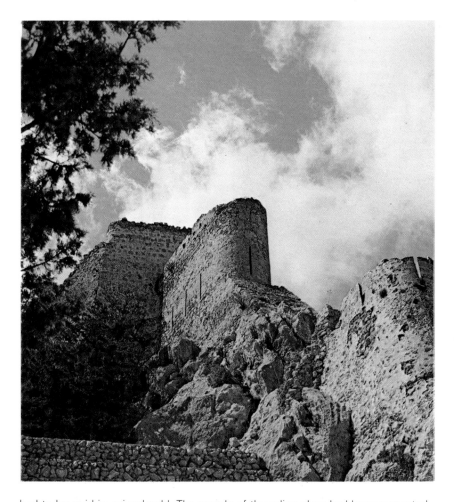

had to be paid in coined gold. The morals of the ruling class had been perverted, treachery was everywhere and the political basis of the kingdom was undermined. Some writers claim that James was popular with the Greeks because he was half Greek on his mother's side. (So was Charlotte, who spoke little French but too much Greek for Pius II's liking.) If so they concealed their feelings very well because no evidence is preserved. James himself certainly treated the serfs on his estates very harshly. When it came to the choice of a wife he broke with his father's Greek connections and married a Venetian, Catherine Cornaro. The Venetian state, with prudent foresight, adopted Catherine as a daughter; the legal effect would be that if the crown came to her, and if she then died without heirs, Venice would inherit. In fact when James died in 1473 (having reigned since 1460, or 1464 counting from the surrender of Kyrenia) he left the kingdom to his posthumous child, for Catherine was pregnant, and to her as Regent.

Catherine's child was a son, James III, but he reigned only for a year (1473–74). She herself remained Queen for 15 years until 1489. It was not a happy reign. There were still many supporters of Charlotte in the island, and the ex-Queen continued

The Castle of Kantara.

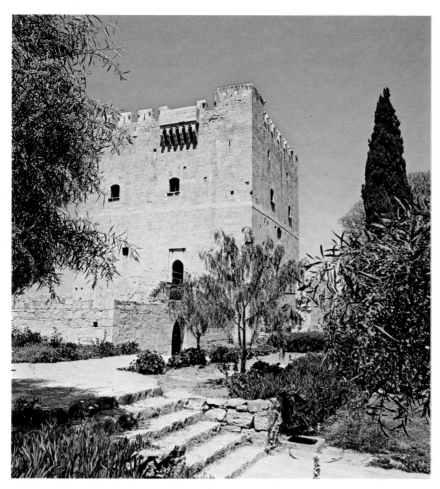

her intrigues until she died in 1485. (She bequeathed her rights to the Duke of Savoy and the arms of Jerusalem, Cyprus and Armenia still appear in the great shield of the former royal house of Italy.) In addition there was a strong party which supported the aspirations of Ferdinand II of the Aragonese dynasty of Naples, for a large number of Spaniards, especially Catalans, had settled in Cyprus during the past two reigns. In 1473 the last-named party fomented a conspiracy that began with the murder of the Queen's uncle and principal adviser, Andrew Cornaro, and nearly brought the whole island under control; it was put down by the arrival in mid-winter of the Venetian fleet with reinforcements. The party that favoured Queen Charlotte, headed by a Venetian malcontent Mark Venier, plotted to assassinate Catherine in 1479. The conspiracy had gone far, and the King of Naples was ready to send a fleet to assist, when it was betrayed in the usual way and suppressed by the Venetians with their usual ruthless severity. The internal divisions in the island with the increasing external threat from the Ottoman Empire now convinced the Venetians that they would do better to assume direct responsibility. The agent to persuade the Queen to abdicate was George Cornaro, her brother. Catherine was reluctant. She evidently had not the same attachment to Cyprus as Charlotte, last heiress of a long

The castle of Kolossi, rebuilt in the mid-fifteenth century. This was the headquarters, or Commandery, of the Order of St. John of Jerusalem, the Knights Hospitallers

1. Base silver denier of Guy de Lusignan, Lord of Cyprus, 1192–94

2. Base gold besant of Hugh I, 1205–18

3. Base gold besant of Henry I, 1218–53

4. Base gold besant of Henry II, 1285–1324

5. Silver gros of Hugh IV, 1324–59

6. Silver gros of Peter I, 1359–69

7. Silver gros of Peter II, 1369–82

8. Silver gros of James I, 1382–98

9. Silver gros of John II, 1432–58

10. Silver gros of Charlotte, 1458–60

11. Silver gros of James II, 1460–73

12. Silver gros of Catherine, 1474–89

British Museum

Ten miniature compositions depicting the legend of the Discovery of the Holy Cross; wall-painting, church of the Holy Cross of Ayiasmati; now dated to c. 1494 line of kings, but she would have liked to remain a Queen all her life. After some persuasion, and the promise of an estate at Asolo with the same civil list that she had had in Nicosia, she agreed to yield the kingdom to the Republic. Her farewell to Cyprus took place at Famagusta, from where she sailed direct to Venice. Her formal abdication took place in St. Mark's. The Saint's lion flag was already floating over all the castles in the island.

The Signory of Venice had the greatest reputation in Europe for wisdom and the state was both rich and also powerful at sea; but in its colonial territories its administration was inefficient and corrupt. One reason for this was that in their fear of allowing individuals to become too powerful, the controlling oligarchy insisted on restricting the terms of office-holders. In Cyprus the government was in the hands

The Presentation of the Virgin Mary in the Temple; Post-Byzantine local revival style; 1494; church of the Holy Cross of Ayiasmati, near Platanistassa

194

of a Lieutenant and two Counsellors (collectively known as the three Rectors) and a Captain to command the army. All these changed every two years. The Venetian state also had a reputation for parsimony. In Cyprus this was shown by the scant numbers and inadequate training of the defence forces, and the delay in strengthening the fortifications of Nicosia and Famagusta. Taxation was heavy but insufficient, in many years, to meet the costs of administration. On the other hand the profits from the salt monopoly brought in a large surplus of revenue which went direct to Venice.

The old feudal class and the Greeks were equally discontented. The former found themselves excluded from power. Although many of them were more interested in hunting they resented being placed in an inferior position to Italian officials, especially since the first act of the new regime was to abolish the *Haute Cour*, the symbol and safeguard of noble status. The oppression of the Greeks is described by Martin von Baumgarten, a Tyrolese pilgrim who visited the island in 1508. "All the inhabitants of Cyprus are slaves to the Venetians, being obliged to pay to the state a third part of all their increase or income . . . (they have to work for the state two days a week) . . . And what is more there is yearly some tax or other imposed on them

The Virgin Mary *Orans* Blachernitissa type in the conch of the apse, Stavros tou Ayiasmati; 1494

195

The Nativity, wall-painting in
the church of Stavros tou
Ayiasmati, Platanistasa; 1494;
in post-Byzantine local revival
style by Philip Goul

Silver gros of Catherine

with which the poor common people are so flayed and pillaged that they hardly have wherewithal to keep soul and body together". There must have been some elements of the population who were better off than this because when the Venetians, desperate to raise money, began selling off the old crown land they found sufficient buyers. Nevertheless the general discontent was demonstrated in 1562 when two Greeks, a schoolmaster and a troop commander of the light cavalry, raised a hopeless rebellion. The colonial masters could not count on the hearty support of the Greeks even against the Turks. Many serfs had already voted with

Catherine Cornaro — by Titian
Uffizi Gallery, Florence

197

their feet by fleeing to Turkey. There is some evidence to show that under Venice the population had been reduced to little over 100,000 from the half million it had reached in the prosperous Lusignan days of the fourteenth century.

For the greater part of their rule the Venetians tried hard to avert the Turkish danger, which increased in 1517 when the Ottomans conquered Egypt, by diplomacy and bribery. It seems likely that the only effect of this policy was to convince the Porte that they would never fight. In 1566 Selim succeeded Suleiman the Magnificent as Sultan; it was generally believed that he would try to make his name by a new conquest, which would also redeem his father's failure to capture Malta in 1565. For this purpose Cyprus was an obvious choice since it was now surrounded on three sides by Ottoman territory. Accordingly in March 1570 he sent an envoy to present a formal demand to the Council of Ten for immediate cession of

Queen Catherine Cornaro
(School of Bellini)
University of Sydney,
Australia

198

Cyprus. The insulting terms of his message were designed to preclude acceptance. The Signory took up the challenge. They also tried to put together a relief expedition with the help of the Papacy and King Philip II of Spain. It was a disgraceful failure for which the Spanish admiral John Andrew Doria, of Genoese extraction, was mainly responsible, acting on secret instructions from Philip. The fleet got no farther than Castellorizo and turned back in September. Meanwhile in July a Turkish expeditionary force had landed on the south coast. Its commander was Lala Mustafa Pasha, Beylerbey of Damascus. The number of soldiers he brought with him is unknown. At the siege of Famagusta next year he commanded something like 200,000 all told but it is known that he had received strong reinforcements. Perhaps the first échelon of the invaders was only half as large.

St. George and St. Theodore, wall-painting in the church of Ayios Nikolaos tis Stegis, Kakopetria; fifteenth century

199

The Venetians had been proceeding in a leisurely way with improvements to the defences of Nicosia and Famagusta since 1567. They gave priority to the latter, which they expected would be the first objective of the enemy. In fact Mustafa moved first on Nicosia. It was ineptly defended by the Lieutenant, Nicholas Dandolo. He had little competence in military matters but continually overruled his subordinates who had much more. The siege lasted from 25th July to 9th September. After the walls had been surmounted the remnants of the defenders offered to surrender. Dandolo thought, for some reason, that he would receive special treatment. Instead he was massacred with the rest and his head sent to the commander of Famagusta, to which the Turkish army now transferred.

The Captain of Famagusta, Marcantonio Bragadin, of a distinguished Venetian family, was a commander of a much more resolute character. He was supported by Astorre Baglione, a professional soldier from Perugia. The defence of Famagusta is one of the greatest epics of siege warfare recorded in history. Against Mustafa's two hundred thousand men, with 145 guns, the Venetians had some three to four thousand regular Italian infantry, two to three hundred cavalry and about four thousand Greek militia, with 90 guns. The siege lasted from 16th September 1570 to 1st August 1571. On that day the defenders had been reduced to some four hundred men and a few barrels of powder. The walls had been breached so thoroughly that it was said a horse and cart could drive across the moat and into the city; provisions had long been so short that defenders were dying of hunger; in spite of which six full-scale assaults by Turkish infantry had been repulsed. Bragadin offered capitulation. It was accepted by Mustafa in flattering terms. When he and his surviving officers came out, after receiving the acknowledgement of surrender sealed with the Sultan's seal, they were at first received with elaborate courtesy. At a certain moment Mustafa gave the pre-arranged signal for the massacre to begin. Bragadin alone was reserved for a more prolonged fate. Mustafa himself cut off his ears and nose; he was kept waiting for

"Venice pays homage to
Catherine Cornaro"
Hans Makart

The Virgin Mary *Orans* attended by the Archangels; post-Byzantine style; church of the Archangel, Galata. (The Church is known as that of the Archangel but is dedicated to the Virgin Mary by inscription.)

The Church of Panayia Podithou Galata, erected in 1502; contains paintings in the Italo-Byzantine style. (The Gothic openings in the roof are recent.)

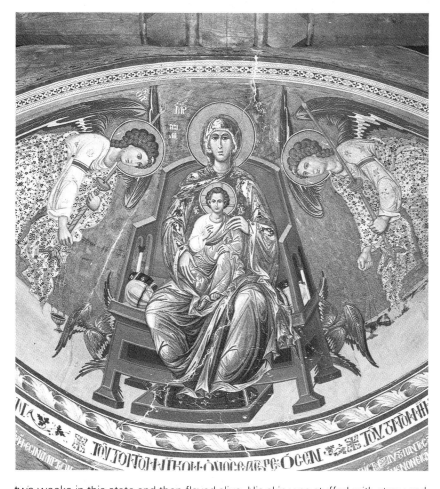

two weeks in this state and then flayed alive. His skin was stuffed with straw and taken to Constantinople in triumph. A patriotic Venetian later stole it and it now rests in an urn in the church of SS Giovanni e Paolo in Venice.

Cyprus was annexed as a province of the Ottoman Empire and Lala Mustafa Pasha became the first Governor.

The buildings of the Frankish period make the biggest impression on the visitor to Cyprus. The walls of Nicosia and Famagusta, the Gothic cathedrals in the two cities, the mountain-top castles of the Pentadactylos range and the great sea-girt castle of Kyrenia: it is these that are illustrated in tourist brochures and remain afterwards as the most abiding memories. They are, indeed, very fine in their own fashion. The two cathedrals are outstanding examples of the best French Gothic style. The military architecture illustrates the development of the art of fortification as practised in the area that first gave it birth, from the early period which still re-flected memories of Roman practice down to the age of artillery. The design and workmanship are also of the highest aesthetic value. But their fashion is not Cypriot but French or Venetian. For indigenous art during this period you must look

Virgin Mary and Child attended by the Archangels; Italo-Byzantine style; 1502; Panayia Podithou, Galata

202

to literature or mural painting.

There is a fair amount of folk-poetry which can be ascribed to the Lusignan period, some even dealing with themes of the court, such as the "Arodaphnousa" cycle which derives from stories about Queen Eleanor and Joanna l'Aleman, wife and mistress of Peter I. Of formal literature in Greek the best examples are from the fifteenth century, the historical writings of Leontios Machairas and George Bustron. Both write in a Cypriot dialect of Greek but in a form closer to French chroniclers, with great vigour and liveliness of description. It is interesting to note that they are generally sympathetic to the Frankish rulers and feel a certain solidarity with them.

Cyprus has preserved more early mural paintings, especially in remote churches of the Troodos mountains, than any other part of Greece. The experts' appreciation of the style of Comnenian and Palaeologan painting is largely based on Cypriot specimens, many of which are securely dated. The paintings at Kalopanayiotis in the Monastery of St. John Lampadistis are from the first half of the thirteenth century. Frankish influence is to be detected in a number of details but the essential spirit of the art is Byzantine. The assimilation was in any case very easy because the Romanesque style which dominated western art at the time of the early Crusades drew its inspiration to a large extent from Byzantium. The late Comnenian

The Adoration of the Magi; early 16th century; *Katholikon,* Monastery of St. Neophytos, near Paphos

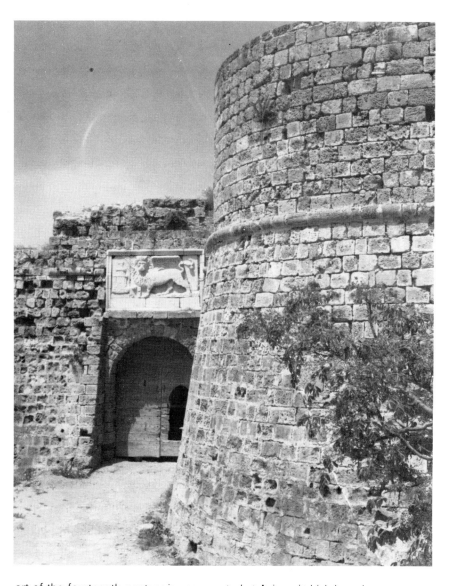

art of the fourteenth century is represented at Asinou (which has also some out-standing paintings from the very beginning of the twelfth century) and at St. Nicholas of the Roof. From the fifteenth century there is a culminating series in the late Palaeologan style in the Monastery of St. Neophytus near Paphos. The finest of its scenes shows the departure of the Magi, the three crowned kings riding away on their horses between the hills. There is an illusory third dimension to the composition which gives an air of distance, magic and romance. It may not be fanciful to think of it as figuring the fading out of the Lusignan kings who had come a long way from the plains of Poitou to rule a legendary realm on the wilder shores of the Levant.

The Citadel of Famagusta, known as Othello's Tower in allusion to Shakespeare's tragedy. In its present form it dates from the Venetian reconstruction

Lusignan Genealogy

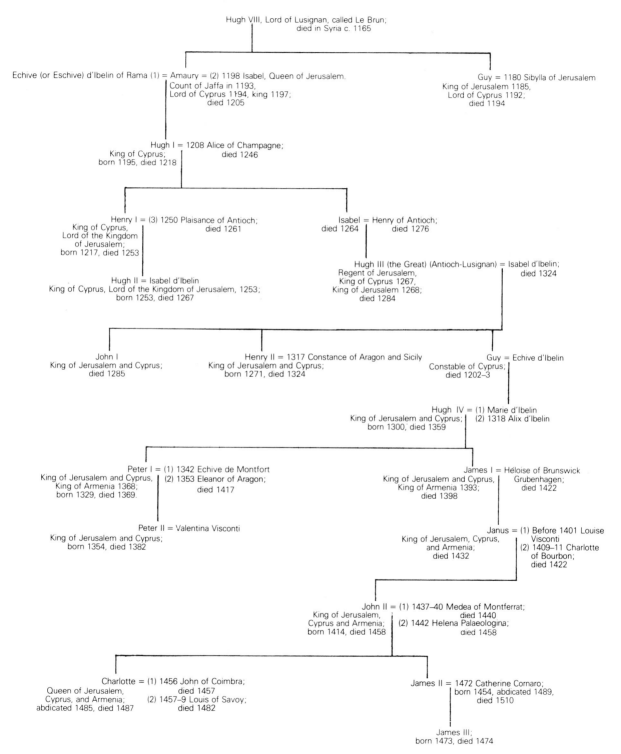

Hugh VIII, Lord of Lusignan, called Le Brun;
died in Syria c. 1165

Echive (or Eschive) d'Ibelin of Rama (1) = Amaury = (2) 1198 Isabel, Queen of Jerusalem.
Count of Jaffa in 1193,
Lord of Cyprus 1194, king 1197;
died 1205

Guy = 1180 Sibylla of Jerusalem
King of Jerusalem 1185,
Lord of Cyprus 1192;
died 1194

Hugh I = 1208 Alice of Champagne;
King of Cyprus;   died 1246
born 1195, died 1218

Henry I = (3) 1250 Plaisance of Antioch;
King of Cyprus,   died 1261
Lord of the Kingdom
of Jerusalem;
born 1217, died 1253

Isabel = Henry of Antioch;
died 1264   died 1276

Hugh III (the Great) (Antioch-Lusignan) = Isabel d'Ibelin;
Regent of Jerusalem,   died 1324
King of Cyprus 1267,
King of Jerusalem 1268;
died 1284

Hugh II = Isabel d'Ibelin
King of Cyprus, Lord of the Kingdom of Jerusalem, 1253;
born 1253, died 1267

John I
King of Jerusalem and Cyprus;
died 1285

Henry II = 1317 Constance of Aragon and Sicily
King of Jerusalem and Cyprus;
born 1271, died 1324

Guy = Echive d'Ibelin
Constable of Cyprus;
died 1202–3

Hugh IV = (1) Marie d'Ibelin
King of Jerusalem and Cyprus;   (2) 1318 Alix d'Ibelin
born 1300, died 1359

Peter I = (1) 1342 Echive de Montfort
King of Jerusalem and Cyprus,   (2) 1353 Eleanor of Aragon;
King of Armenia 1368;   died 1417
born 1329, died 1369.

James I = Héloise of Brunswick
King of Jerusalem and Cyprus,   Grubenhagen;
King of Armenia 1393;   died 1422
died 1398

Peter II = Valentina Visconti
King of Jerusalem and Cyprus;
born 1354, died 1382

Janus = (1) Before 1401 Louise
King of Jerusalem, Cyprus,   Visconti
and Armenia;   (2) 1409–11 Charlotte
died 1432   of Bourbon;
                            died 1422

John II = (1) 1437–40 Medea of Montferrat;
King of Jerusalem,   died 1440
Cyprus and Armenia;   (2) 1442 Helena Palaeologina;
born 1414, died 1458   died 1458

Charlotte = (1) 1456 John of Coimbra;
Queen of Jerusalem,   died 1457
Cyprus, and Armenia;   (2) 1457–9 Louis of Savoy;
abdicated 1485, died 1487   died 1482

James II = 1472 Catherine Cornaro;
born 1454, abdicated 1489,
died 1510

James III;
born 1473, died 1474

(opposite page)
Monument to Marcantonio
Bragadin in the church of SS
Giovanni e Paolo, Venice. The
urn contains his skin,
recovered from
Constantinople in 1580

(Right)
The Monastery of Ayia Napa
on the Cape Greco peninsula
in south-eastern Cyprus; built
by the Venetians in the
sixteenth century

Token money issued during
the siege of Famagusta; the
obverse pledges "the
inviolable faith of Venice" to
its redemption
British Museum

X
THE TURKISH
PERIOD 1571–1878

The three hundred years of Turkish rule left fewer "footprints" in Cyprus than comparable periods under other rulers. The Ottomans were not interested, at least in this impoverished province, in adorning their new possession with fine buildings; on the contrary they regarded with indifference the slow decay of the architectural heritage left by the Venetians and the Lusignans. Even the strong fortifications of Nicosia, Kyrenia and Famagusta, which the Venetians had re-modelled along the latest lines of military science, and whose value the invaders had themselves experienced, were allowed to crumble. Their garrisons also dwindled and degenerated. In a sense, however, they can be said to have created the image which the nineteenth century formed of Cyprus: part of the romantic Levant of the Victorian steel engravings which juxtapose the Gothic arch and the minaret in a framework of palm fronds, with a piece of classical ruin to heighten the effect. Time stood still. The island found itself in a backwater of affairs. Surrounded by the possessions of a slowly declining empire it suffered in obscurity from an administration which was not so much actively oppressive as slothful and inefficient. The burdens on the peasantry became heavier and both intellectual activity and commercial prosperity slumbered.

Two consequences of the conquest were to be of great importance for the future. The first brought a change in the composition of the population. Grants of land and houses were made to Turks from the victorious army, and other Turks from Anatolia were persuaded, in some cases compelled, to immigrate. Nearly all

Seventeenth-century Arms
of the Ottoman Empire

the statistics of population in the sixteenth century are unreliable but there seems to be a general agreement among historians that the new settlers numbered about 20,000. This includes the permanent garrison whose official strength was 1000 infantry (janissaries) and 2666 cavalry (spahis). What proportion this figure bore to the Greek population is unknown but the first census, taken in 1572, is said to have shown a population liable to pay the 'kharaj', or poll tax, of about 85,000. These were by definition Christians, since Moslems were exempt. Included among them were Armenians, Maronites and Roman Catholics of various origins, known for convenience as Latins; all subsequent figures show these made up only about one per cent. In consequence there was for the first time in Cyprus a settled Moslem community, and one whose members were almost entirely of pure Turkish origin. Nothing similar had been seen there for two millennia.

The second great change was slower to appear: the gradual rise to political power of the Orthodox ecclesiastical establishment. The assumption of political rights and duties by religious leaders was a characteristic of the Ottoman empire. It was an essential part of their political theory. The Turks were a conquering, military caste like the Normans in England or the Visigoths in Spain. They originated in Central Asia and never quite lost traces of their nomadic origins. Their way of life was adapted to continuous warfare and their conversion to Islam pro-

Copper-plate engraving illustrating the Turkish invasion; published by Balthasar Ienichen in 1571 and based on a map by Hans Rogel Augsburg 1570 National Maritime Museum, London

Copper-plate engraving of the siege of Nicosia, showing Turkish dispositions; from *Isole che son da Venezia . . .* published by Simon Pinargenti in Venice in 1573. It is a close copy of one published by Giovanni Francesco Camocio in Venice in c. 1570 Museo Storico Navale, Venice

vided them with a theological justification for this predisposition. In Islamic theory a state of permanent war with the non-Moslem world was both inevitable and meritorious. Only true believers could take part in it, and the poll-tax was the price non-Moslem Ottoman subjects paid for exemption from military duties. For the purpose of tax-paying and to ensure orderly behaviour and security against rebellion each religious denomination was organised into a community known as a *milet*. The largest of them in the empire was the one that consisted of all Orthodox Christians. This united not only Greeks, though they formed the majority, but also Slavs and Romanians. The titular leader was the Ecumenical Patriarch of Constantinople, the highest ecclesiastical authority in the Orthodox church. It was with him that the Sultan and his ministers dealt at the capital; the provincial authorities in Cyprus recognised the Archbishop as the responsible leader of the

Greek population.

The light in which the Ottoman Government regarded their non-Moslem subjects can be seen from the name of *rayah* which was commonly applied to them: it means "cattle". Theoretically they were mere possessions of their rulers, who had, on the same theory, the right to their services and their property. But the prudent herdsman takes good care of his herd. The Turks, who had been notable cattle-grazers in their nomadic life on the steppes, were aware of the desirability, in principle, of keeping their *rayah* contented and prosperous enough to pay their taxes. Mehmed II, the Conqueror under whom the system was first elaborated, was partly Greek himself and, though a pious Moslem, wished Christians well. As Sir Steven Runciman comments in his *The Great Church in Captivity*, he wanted them to enjoy peace and prosperity and to be content with his Government and an asset to it.

Orthodox Patriarchs, Archbishops and Bishops had been accustomed to the *milet* system since the time when the first Christian cities had been occupied by Moslem conquerors in the seventh century. (It had been copied by the early

Rare wood-cut of the siege and capture of Nicosia showing the break-in of Turkish troops in the southern sector of the defences (north is at the bottom of the page); issued as a separate sheet with no indication of author, date or place of issue but probably in Venice shortly after the capture. The title is *Nicosia Regal(e) Citta Di Cipro Combatuta Da(i) Turchi*

211

Caliphs from the Persians). They knew it was their duty to care not only for the spiritual but for the material needs of their flocks, and that that usually involved standing up to Ottoman governors against corruption, oppression and excessive taxation. In Cyprus the role of the Archbishop, supported by his suffragan bishops and the abbots of the principal monasteries, went rather further. With the progress of time he became responsible for the collection of tax and, to a large extent, for the administration of the island. He had direct access to the Sultan. He could send messages under his seal — with the impression in the imperial red that Zeno had granted to his remote predecessor — which the Governor could do nothing to stop even though he might himself be impugned in them.

This was only a particularly striking example of a practice common throughout the empire of leaving civil administration in the hands of subjects, especially Greeks. The Sultans of the period of the greatest Turkish successes realised that their Moslem subjects had little aptitude for or inclination towards the management of civil as opposed to military business. They were willing to leave it, as they left commerce, to the Greeks. The highest office in what we would call the Civil Service, that of Grand Dragoman of the Porte, was always held by a Greek.

Copper-plate engraving of Famagusta under siege by the Turks (north is to the right) showing the fortifications in detail and the dispositions of the besiegers and ships bombarding; published by Giovanni Francesco Camocio in Venice c. 1571
Museo Storico Navale, Venice

Similarly in Cyprus a Greek was Dragoman of the Saray, the Governorate. The title means literally interpreter; because senior Turkish officials were disinclined to learn Greek they had to use an intermediary, who was never slow to take advantage of his opportunities. There were some notable Dragomans, during the eighteenth century in particular, who grew rich from the exercise of this delegated authority. The Greek church, which had occupied such a lowly position under the Latins, found itself under the infidels not merely restored to supremacy in religious affairs but endowed with secular authority as well.

For the Greek Cypriots Turkish rule began well, after the sufferings brought by the conquest. Taxes were reduced well below the level which had ruled under the Venetians. They were soon to rise again; but far more important in the long term was the abolition of all feudal tenures. At a stroke the peasant acquired an inalienable and hereditable right to land. Those who for centuries had been mere bondmen on the soil were now on payment of a trifling sum constituted its possessors, with the right of succession to their descendants.

The first Governor after the conquest was Muzaffer Pasha. His title was Beylerbey, or Bey of Beys, and in order to live up to the importance of this rank a

Oil painting entitled "The Fall of Cyprus 1571" by Bonaventura Peeters (b Antwerp 1614 d. Hoboken 1652) Collection H.C. Perry

213

The Bülyük Khan was built by Muzaffer Pasha immediately after the occupation of the island in 1571 "for the benefit of foreigners". The rooms are arranged on two floors round a courtyard in the middle of which is an octagonal mosque built over a water tank; From a drawing by Archduke Luigi Salvatore 1873

proper Pashalik had to be constructed. This was done by adding to the island four districts of the mainland. One of them was the Sanjak of Ichil, thus recreating the old Roman province of Cyprus and Cilicia. Muzaffer was a Pasha of three tails and had under him two Pashas of two tails at Famagusta and Paphos. The "tails", badges of rank in the higher levels of the Ottoman administration, were actual horses tails attached to a pole as a standard, a reminiscence of Turkish nomad days. This establishment was before long found to be excessive. During the century after the conquest the island suffered severely from locusts and from plague. Many of the rayahs had fled the country to Crete and the Peloponnese. The amount at which the island was assessed for tax remaining the same, those who remained had to pay more. A census taken in the 1640s was reported to have calculated that the Christian population had been reduced to 25,000. As a first step the two Pashas of Famagusta and Paphos were removed, the establishment of headquarters in Nicosia was reduced and efforts were made to persuade Cypriots who had emigrated to return. It is generally accepted by all historians who wrote of the seventeenth and eighteenth centuries that these efforts were unavailing.

Travellers comment on the contrast between the potential fertility of the island and the smallness of the population, whereby large areas were left desolate.

As an economy measure the Ottoman administration decided, in or shortly after 1670, to abolish the Pashalik. The island of Cyprus, minus the four Anatolian sanjaks, was put under the Kapudan Pasha, the Commander in Chief of the Navy. This meant that it was treated in the same way as the islands of the Aegean or, in

Column of grey granite from Salamis erected by the Venetians in Konak Square (now Ataturk Square) Nicosia; overthrown in 1570, it was later re-erected. It originally was surmounted by the lion of St. Mark
From a drawing by Archduke Luigi Salvatore 1873

the terminology of the time, Rhodes and the Archipelago. As one of these Admiralty properties Cyprus was administered on behalf of the Kapudan Pasha by a deputy, in Turkish a Müssellim. He received a fixed salary of 15,000 piastres annually (rather under £2,000) but since he had had to bid for his post he took steps to extort as much extra as possible during his usually short period of office. Under the new system however, according to the Archimandrite Kyprianos in his history published in Venice in 1788, the Müssellim was not so powerful or so rich as the senior officials in Nicosia, the Aghas who controlled the financial administration as tax collectors or tax farmers. Their wealth, their prestige and their influence at Constantinople had made them the real rulers of the island. Another result was jealousy and rivalry among themselves and in about 1680 one of the resulting clashes led to armed conflict. Out of it arose, as self-proclaimed "leader" of Cyprus, Mehmed Agha Boyajioglou who headed the first rebellion of Cyprus. It was a purely Turkish affair in which none of the Greeks were involved. Kypríanos says his rebellion lasted seven years in all. He made a point of sending the poll-tax proceeds regularly to Constantinople, which no doubt delayed the taking of action against him. It could not have been rapid in any case since one of the facts revealed by the rebellion is that the Sultan had no sufficient force in Cyprus that he could use to assert his authority. It was necessary to bring in troops from Karamania, on the south coast of Asia Minor, under a local commander. After a siege of Nicosia, and a hectic pursuit of Boyajioglou to and fro across the island, he was caught and executed.

The revolt of Boyajioglou, and the reason for it, caused the Ottoman administration to decide that the time had come for another change. With all deliberate speed, that is to say in 1703, about thirteen years after the restoration of order, the island was transferred from the jurisdiction of the Kapudan Pasha and given to the Grand Vizier as a personal fief, for which the Turkish is *hass*. The Grand Vizier was the equivalent of the Sultan's Prime Minister, the head of the administration. It was so powerful a post that, except when held by persons of the greatest strength of character and political shrewdness, it never remained long in the same hands. Cyprus was certainly one of the least of the great man's preoccupations. As the

The Haidar Pasha Mosque, built in the late fourteenth century as the church of St. Catherine, in the Flamboyant Gothic style
From a drawing by Archduke Luigi Salvatore, 1873

Cyprus, Lemnos, Chios, Mytilene, Euboea, Cythera, Rhodes; copper-plate engraving; G. Mercator; first published by Hondius, Amsterdam 1606
Finopoulos collection

Admiral had done he appointed a deputy or Müsellim who also was the Muhassil, or collector of taxes. The Muhassil was appointed annually by the Grand Vizier, who invariably chose the highest bidder. Alexander Drummond, who was the British Consul in Aleppo not long afterwards, recorded in the course of his visit in 1745 that the current holder of the post had made a profit of 250,000 piastres (£31,250) in his one year whereas the total government revenue of the island was

310,000 piastres (£38,750).

In the year of Drummond's visit the administrative arrangements were altered again: Cyprus was taken from the Grand Vizier and made an independent province once more under a Pasha of three tails. The reason for the change is not known; the Grand Vizier was given an annual sum in compensation. The second Pasha of

The Monastery of St. Barnabas, west of Salamis. The church, dating from the Byzantine period, was rebuilt in 1756 and restored after earthquake damage in 1941

this dispensation, Abu Bekr, is celebrated in history as the only Turkish governor of whom nothing but good is recorded. Even the violently critical Drummond speaks of "the old gentleman's public spirit. While he was Pasha of this island in the year 1747 he formed the noble design of bringing water from the spring of Arpera to supply the people of Larnaca. A work worthy of a great and good man, which might have cost him above fifty thousand piastres or six thousand two hundred pounds." This money came from his own pocket in the form of a charitable foundation. The aqueduct was about six miles long and at three points can still be seen on the right-hand side of the road from Nicosia, shortly before the entrance to the town.

The good Pasha had one successor of whom little is known except that he finished the aqueduct in 1750; but shortly thereafter the island was returned to the Grand Vizier who reintroduced the system of Muhassils. Taxes both ordinary and extraordinary were exacted with growing rapacity. By general consent Chil Osman Agha who arrived in 1764 was the worst of all the governors. According to Kyprianos he was deeply in debt because he had put in a very high bid for his office. He was determined not only to recoup what he had paid but also to gain "fantastic wealth" on top of it. Within a few days of his arrival he announced to the Archbishop through the Dragoman that the tax paid by the Greeks would be more

220

than doubled. The Archbishop, Paisios, declared that it was impossible for the rayahs to pay such a sum; he demanded, and was allowed, to send a delegation to the Vizier. After much delay the delegation returned with a *firman* or imperial order addressed to Chil Osman ordering him, with threats, not to exact more than the sum fixed by the imperial rescript and to repay all that had been levied in excess of it. The order was brought to Cyprus by one of the Vizier's own staff. It should have been read out in court but the governor asked that it should be communicated to him in the Saray, the Government House. The Archbishops and the Bishops, and numerous senior officials both Greeks and Turks, were summoned to attend the ceremony. Only the first part of the order had been read when part of the floor of the room collapsed precipitating the ecclesiastics and others (including Kyprianos the historian) into a basement. The Pasha remained in safety on a surviving portion of the floor. Foul play was at once suspected and stories of rafters and columns being sawn through, with ropes to pull on at the right moment, rapidly circulated. At least the interruption came very conveniently. The messenger from the Grand Vizier was not endangered by the collapse as he was sitting too close to the Pasha who consequently had to resort to the supplementary measure of poisoning his coffee. It was frustrated by the timely provision of an antidote.

This spectacular example of political manoeuvring gave immediate rise to the second revolt in Cyprus. The Molla, the Islamic religious head, summoned the governor to appear before him, as he had the right to do, but when he three times refused the Nicosia mob, Greeks and Turks together, invaded and burned down the Saray and killed Chil Osman with some eighteen others. There was a similar but less violent outbreak at Larnaca. Then came the reckoning. The surviving authorities composed a report which was conveyed to the Vizier by his messenger, who in the light of his own experiences could be relied on to put a fair

The fort at Paphos harbour. Standing on the remains of the ancient breakwater it replaced a castle built in 1391, demolished by the Venetians. An inscription over the door records its reconstruction by the Turks in 1580–92 complexion on events. The Vizier and the Sultan were appeased, a new moderate governor was appointed; but there was a price to be paid for the rebuilding of the Saray, compensation for looted property and the blood money of the victims. Turks and Christians agreed to allow the new governor, Hafiz Effendi, to assess the amount required, and the Bishops and the Aghas worked out that it could be covered by a payment of 14 piastres a head by Christians and 7 by Turks. This was accepted by the former but the Turks, accusing Hafiz of deliberate over-assessment, broke into open insurrection headed by Khalil Agha, the Dizdar or fort commander of Kyrenia.

Khalil's insurrection, which lasted over a year, was a serious affair because he was supported by so many of the Turkish inhabitants. The Archbishop, escaping from the island with difficulty, went to Constantinople to appeal for an imperial force to be sent to restore order. Once again the weakness of the military forces at the disposal of the Governor was revealed since a special expeditionary force from

Janissaries on their way to archery practice. The regular infantry of the Ottoman Empire, they were raised by forced recruitment among Christian children
Paris, Bibliothèque Nationale

Karamania had to be sent. It took a long time to arrive but eventually Khalil was driven to shut himself in the castle of Kyrenia. For two months it resisted all attempts at a storm. Eventually Khalil was tricked into giving himself up when provisions began to run short. He was executed with the bowstring in violation of his safe-conduct; the heads of two hundred of his supporters were sent to the Sultan as proof of the suppression of the rising.

The Russo-Turkish war of 1769 to 1774 affected Cyprus to the extent that the Russian fleet soon gained complete dominance in the Eastern Mediterranean after it had destroyed the Ottoman fleet at Cesme, on the coast opposite Chios. The result was not only to hamper the island's maritime trade but also to impose on it

Cypriot iconostasis (H 4.20 m, W 4.60 m.) of carved, painted and gilded pine-wood; exact provenance unknown; dated 1757–1762
Berlin Staatliche Museen

extra expense for the maintenance of the military reinforcements sent there. These afflictions were, however, almost forgotten in the extraordinary episodes which marked the period as governor of Haji Baki Agha. He may not have been the worst governor but no other was more picturesquely reviled by his contemporaries and by posterity.

Baki was a Cypriot by origin, from the village of Klavdhia, about six miles east of Larnaca. He is described by Kyprianos as a one-eyed, illiterate woodcutter. Obviously a generous allowance must be made for the conventions of Levantine political abuse. His subsequent history shows that he possessed much personal charm, which enabled him to ingratiate himself with persons of influence, and intelligence sufficient to allow him to rise to high office and to administer it with at least as much competence as his predecessors and successors. He cannot have been as ugly as he is described since his first appointment, as governor of Adalia in Karamania, was allegedly due to having gained the favour of a member of the harem of a notable of the island. His next post was as chief magistrate of Larnaca. In 1771 the Governor of Cyprus, Ismail Agha, made him Defterdar, head of the financial administration and the senior Agha of Nicosia. A new governor arrived in 1775. Allegedly he intended to dismiss Baki because he knew him of old — or because he would have liked to give his post to a nominee of his own; but he died before he could give effect to his intention. Baki's enemies naturally accused him of having poisoned the governor, and when the deputy governor died about a month later this was also supposed to be his work. In spite of these hostile mutterings he had such support from the Turkish senior officials and clergy, and from the Bishops, that he became governor, first on an acting and then on a permanent basis. In the latter capacity he ruled for six years, an unusually long term. The evidence even of his enemies credits him with being a good administrator and if he made a very large fortune by corruption and illegal extortion he did no more than many other governors had done. For some reason, however, he has remained a well-known figure in folk-memory; "Baki Agha the tyrant" is the very type of the bad Governor.

Travellers from Europe who visited Cyprus in the seventeenth and eighteenth centuries are eloquent about the heavy taxation imposed. "The impositions upon the island are such as you never heard of" says Drummond, who goes on to give full details of the poll-tax and the other regular taxes. In addition there were always special impositions known as *avanie*, brought in whenever the governors thought they could squeeze something extra out of the peasants. After all, as Drummond has just explained, they were only in office for a year and had had to pay a great

View across the salt lake of Larnaca of the Hala Sultan Tekke on the site of the burial place of the maternal aunt of the prophet Mohammed, Umm Haram. As a place of pilgrimage it ranked next after Mecca and Medina. The mosque with its minaret was built in 1816 by the Governor Seyyid Mohammed Emin

225

bribe to obtain it: if they were to recoup these expenses and make a fortune as
well they could not afford to be nice in their methods. As Drummond
concludes . . . ''The method of levying these impositions is very strange: no time
is fixed for payment, but when the officer empowered shall make his demand if
the unhappy man cannot produce the money, he must undergo imprisonment, the
bastinado or some other torture; if he is possessed of any effects, houses, lands,
cattle or other moveables they are instantly sold at an undervalue to satisfy these
cormorants, who set his wife and children adrift without remorse or compunction;
nay, they even make sport of their misery.'' What made things even more
poignant for the Greek peasantry was the prominent part played in the tax-
gathering machinery by their own religious leaders, the Archbishop and Bishops.

226

In accordance with the Ottoman theory whereby the religious leaders of the various communities in the Empire were responsible for the secular behaviour of their flocks, it was reasonable that they should have powers to enforce obedience. After all, it was the Archbishop who would be held responsible if the community rebelled or failed to pay its taxes. A hundred years after the conquest, in about 1660 according to Kyprianos, the Archbishop and his suffragans were formally recognised as "official guardians and representatives of the rayahs." To make them effective in this role they were given the right of direct access to the Sultan with petitions and complaints. In 1754 they were made responsible for the actual collection of taxes. They constituted in effect a second source of authority set over against the governor. They had also the advantage that his tenure was ephemeral whereas they lasted longer. They were able to establish a more continuous relationship with the officials in Constantinople whose favour they, like the governors, obtained by bribes. There was another advantage in that the Dragoman of the Saray, the man through whom all official business between the administration and the Greek Cypriots was conducted, was a Greek appointed by the Archbishop. At the beginning of the nineteenth century the Dragoman Hajigeorghiakis Kornesios was described as the most powerful and the wealthiest person in Cyprus. This special position of the higher clergy is always commented on by travellers during this period of Ottoman rule. The British diplomat Turner in 1815 goes so far as to say that "Cyprus is in fact governed by the Archbishop and his subordinate clergy." The French consul at Larnaca a few years before had strongly condemned the Archbishop and the Dragoman and their subordinates, the tax-collectors, for oppression so serious that they drove the Christians from the island. Sir George Hill takes a more judicious view of the conflicting evidence: although the Archbishops often made themselves unpopular with their flocks by their demands for money the best of them took seriously their duty to protect against oppression the faithful committed to their change.

The aqueduct of Larnaca built by Abu Bekr Pasha in 1747; from a drawing of 1878 showing the Channel Fleet in the anchorage
Wood engraving
Illustrated London News, 1878

The consequences of the Greek War of Liberation, starting in 1821, showed the

227

other aspect of the Archbishop's position. In the plans of the Philike Hetaireia (Friendly Society), the first movers of the insurrection, Cyprus was naturally included, along with all other Greek territories, among those to be liberated. It was recognised that its position was difficult because of its distance from the Peloponnese, the first focus of the movement, and because it was surrounded on North, East and South by predominantly Moslem countries. On the other hand the Turkish garrison was small and inefficient and the Greek insurgents had reasonable grounds to hope that they could successfully challenge the Ottoman navy. Agents from the Society came to Cyprus in 1818 and Kyprianos, Archbishop since 1810, was enrolled as a member; he pointed out, however, that for the reasons already given he could contribute no more than a promise of money, and supplies if ships could be sent to fetch them. The latter promise was fulfilled when in July 1821 the Greek naval commander Canaris was secretly revictualled at an anchorage on the north coast. The governor, Mehmed Silahshör (known as Küchük, or Little Mehmed) was aware of what was going on, for it is rare in Cyprus for anything to be kept secret. Greatly alarmed, he asked the Sultan for troops and for permission to execute all the leading Christians in the island. Some 4,000 troops were sent from Syria but the Sultan, for the moment, preferred merely to disarm the Christians. This was done in April and May 1821. Küchük Mehmed began executing Christians in any case and sent a further message detailing 486 prominent persons of whom he would like to make an example. Kyprianos told a British traveller, who has left a moving account of him in his last days — "highly eminent for his learning and piety as well as for his unshaken fortitude" — that he knew the governor was only waiting for an opportunity to kill him.

Very shortly afterwards the Sultan — who had just executed the Ecumenical Patriarch — sent his assent to Mehmed's proposal. On 9th July the three Bishops were beheaded and the Archbishop was hanged in the square in front of the Saray. Next day the Abbot of Kykko and other clergy were executed. The property of the church was plundered: that was indeed one of the main motives of the Aghas of Nicosia in urging severity on the not unwilling governor. As a further step an order was enforced that all Christians were to pull down the upper storey of their houses since only Turks were allowed to have houses with an upper floor. This order remained in force until the British occupation in 1878. The French consul reported on 6th August that in the whole of Limassol there remained only two Greeks, a few porters, and the governor's executioners.

Massacres continued and became worse when the Sultan felt bound to call on the Pasha of Egypt for help in Cyprus as in the other insurgent Greek territories. The Egyptian troops were as badly disciplined as the Syrians who had preceded them. The number of Greeks fleeing from the island increased; out of this emigration many for the first time went to Egypt. Küchük Mehmed had made so much money from confiscating the property of those he massacred —greed had probably been a stronger motive with him than fear or hatred — that he was able by bribery to prolong his tenure for an extra year.

In 1833 three insurrections broke out, inspired by the sudden imposition by the governor Said Mehmed of a new, arbitrary and heavy tax. The last known of them

(Opposite page)
Bellapais; Lacroix-Lemaitre; after Cassas 1799; steel engraving; Paris 1853

Mosque in Famagusta; Lacroix-Lemaitre, after Cassas 1799; steel engraving; Paris 1853

229

is the one called the revolt of the Giaur Imam. It was led by a wealthy Turkish land-owner from Tremithusa who claimed support among the Christians, from which circumstance he was given the nickname of 'infidel'. He appears to have been driven to it by a personal insult but he capitalised on the resentment aroused by the new tax to occupy the whole district of Paphos. He held out for about three months, murdering people whose wealth he coveted, until finally crushed by government troops who outdid him in atrocities against innocent people.

The Greek War of Liberation marks the beginning of the process which transformed the Ottoman Empire into "the sick man of Europe." The nineteenth century was full of death bed repentances and promises of reforms. Intentions were good, results were negligible. Sultan Mahmud II began the process but the first codification came with his successor and eldest son, Abdul Mejid I, who in his first year 1839 issued a charter of reforms. These provided for regular and published scales of taxation and the abolition of tax-farming, an improvement in the system of justice and the strict prohibition of bribery and corruption in the administration. None of the reforms were applied in Cyprus any more than in other Ottoman provinces. When in 1856 the Sultan issued another version of the original *Hatti Sherif* or noble writing, the Kadi of Nicosia (the Chief Judge) assured the Turks that it would have no more effect than the earlier version. As Sir Charles Eliot wrote in 1908, in his influential work *Turkey in Europe*: "The reforms of Mahmud and Abdul Mejid . . . and the establishment of parliamentary government

230

by the present Sultan (Abdul Hamid II) were measures which would have revolutionised any ordinary country but they have simply collapsed in Turkey without result and without fuss."

When in 1840 a new governor Talat Effendi was sent with the express purpose of introducing reforms, especially in taxation, the Turks began to arm themselves. Their aim was to intimidate the administration against tampering with the old system from which they had profited. Troops were again brought from Karamania but the intimidation was successful; the introduction of the reforms was indefinitely postponed. So was the promise of the institution of a commercial court in Larnaca. As a result of the confusion the collection of taxes had been suspended and the subsequent demand for arrears caused more emigration of taxpayers. Over the next few years, however, there came a change in the method of collection. The Archbishop no longer guaranteed the tax, assessed it and collected it through his own officials; instead it was collected direct by the

Larnaca; steel engraving drawn by S. Bough after Cassas. The Imperial Family Bible, 2nd part. London 1858 Finopoulos collection government. From this period the ascendancy of the hierarchy began to diminish although the Archbishop still remained the Rayah-vekili, the representative of the Christian rayahs, a title which the Greeks, stressing race rather than religion, translated as Ethnarch.

From 1849 to 1861 Cyprus was included in the Pashalik of Rhodes, which was the provincial capital of the islands of the Aegean. During this period the governors changed rapidly. Some were octogenarians and some permanently drunk but even the more competent never had enough time to do any good. After seven years as an independent province it was transferred to the newly-formed Vilayet or Governor-Generalship of the Dardanelles. This made for even greater inefficiency because the Governor-General had his headquarters at Chanak. Since all important powers were centralised in his hands both administrative and judicial business was subjected to great delay. After two years the island was put back under the jurisdiction of Rhodes. It was to the Governor-General of the Archipelago, with his seat at Rhodes, that Sultan Abdul Hamid addressed the order to transfer Cyprus to British administration in 1878.

There are not many significant remains of the Turkish occupation to be seen in the island. The fort at Paphos is a poor specimen of military architecture and in any case largely based on a Venetian original. Nicosia was the centre of government and the majority of its inhabitants were Turks; the principal architectural remains are here. The Great Khan built by Muzaffer Pasha in the sixteenth century is a respectable, functionally designed building. The seventeenth century saw the construction of the Tekke of the Mevlevi Dervishes, now a museum, as a centre for this mystical Sufi brotherhood. Perhaps the most attractive specimen of Turkish architecture in Cyprus it is built in a decent, unpretentious style well suited to the engagingly austere ideology of a sect that has suffered in Western eyes

Hajigeorghakis Kornessios (Great Dragoman of Cyprus 1779–1809). He is holding a diploma with the Sultan's cipher
Cyprus Museum, Nicosia

233

from its appellation of the "Dancing Dervishes." The small Arab Ahmet Pasha mosque has its admirers among those who are attracted by Ottoman eighteenth century architecture. The best specimen of this is undoubtedly the Halah Sultan Tekke in which is the tomb of Umm Haram, the maternal aunt of the Prophet Mohammed. The tomb, built in 1760, incorporates a megalithic dolmen but the mosque and tekke were added in 1816. Romantically placed in a grove of palm trees with a salt lake in front the tekke is the embodiment of the old Levant.

Of all the periods of which there is historical record this is without doubt the unhappiest and least prosperous. Cyprus was of no particular importance to the Ottoman Government. It was neither a frontier province nor of strategic value: for a regime whose interests were primarily military that meant that it was regarded solely from the point of view of how much money could be made out of it. There were, it is true, enlightened Sultans, especially in the earlier period of the occupation, who were able to take a long-term view. They might treat their provincial subjects as sheep but, like the Emperor Tiberius, they preferred them shorn not flayed. Their orders were well conceived but always disobeyed. Because the only system of administration they could imagine was based on unrestricted autocracy their civilian officials held on a servile tenure posts which they had purchased by bribery. The interests of these officials were directly opposite to those of the Sultans. They could only take short-term views. They must recoup by oppression and corruption, as quickly as possible, the expenditure which had won them their chance of a fortune. The judgement of Captain Savile in 1878 is temperate and reasonable: "It seems that in Cyprus it is not so much the laws themselves but rather the administration of the laws which needs reform. The Ottoman Government is noted for publishing innumerable *firmans*, laws and ordinances, which leave but little room for improvement as regards either completeness or natural equity; and it has been either the disregard or maladministration of these laws which has done so much injury to the country."

The principal change brought about by the Ottomans, as has been already mentioned, was the introduction of an extraneous ethnic element. The new Turkish settlers, however, rapidly divided into two unequal parts, different both in their own eyes and in those of the Greeks. On the one hand were the Aghas, the representatives in Nicosia of the oppressors of the island, and on the other the Turkish peasantry who suffered as much as the Greeks from the exactions of the tax-gatherers, among whom some Greek magnates could be numbered. As many travellers attest, relations in the countryside were as friendly under the Ottomans as they remained until the second half of the twentieth century.

XI
THE BRITISH PERIOD

1878–1960

It should not have been a matter for surprise that Cyprus came into British hands in the last quarter of the nineteenth century. The reasons were strategic and political though that does not imply that it was itself of strategic value. Cyprus appears to occupy a central position in the Eastern Mediterranean but in fact is not on the way to anywhere in particular. Its ports are of no great commercial importance. For naval purposes the only one that was thought to have possibilities as a base, Famagusta, was then not capable of being one and was never properly developed into one during the eighty-two years of British rule. The lesson of history is that so far from bringing advantage to a country that seeks to dominate the area Cyprus has always fallen, as though inevitably, into the hands of whichever country was in fact already dominant there. It is not a positive aid but a passive adjunct to power. Britain's acquisition of Cyprus was not for the sake of adding to the Empire and certainly not for the sake of Cyprus itself; it was a commitment accepted to serve other and more distant purposes.

Since the day in 1683 when the flood-tide of Turkish conquest had fallen back from the gates of Vienna the Christian powers in emulous contest had planned the division of the Sultan's European territories. In due course the weakness of the Ottoman Empire began to menace the peace of Europe as much as its strength had done in the past. The first main contestant for the reversionary estate was the Hapsburg dynasty under the successive titles of the Holy Roman Empire, the Austrian Empire and Austria-Hungary. Its aim was to expand its rule into the Balkan peninsula, much of which had belonged earlier to the Hungarian kingdom

The emblem of the two lions of Richard Coeur de Lion was used during the British period on the official flag and some coins

236

to which the Hapsburgs were the heirs. Very soon, however, imperial Russia stepped forward as the chief rival of the House of Othman both because of its sympathies with its Orthodox co-religionists and also because the Hapsburgs, unlike the Romanovs, had always had to occupy themselves with western Europe as well. France, allied to the Turks in the sixteenth century and with long and valuable commercial ties with them, had been stimulated by Napoleon's romantic ideas of oriental conquest; the Bourbon and Orleans monarchies which succeeded him pursued similar policies under the more respectable pretext of protecting the Latin Christians of the Levant. Napoleon III was at times thought to have considered the acquisition of Cyprus. The whole system of conflicting claims was a high concern of European politics under the general designation of "the Eastern Question." The British were comparative late comers.

The Royal Navy had been actively engaged in the Mediterranean since the seventeenth century but its dominant influence there, especially in the Levant, dated from the beginning of the nineteenth. British policy there differed from that of the other powers by being inspired by extra-European motives. They were imperial motives. Throughout the nineteenth century the word Empire meant India.

The British landing at Larnaca;
wood engraving
Illustrated London News, 1878

237

CONVEYING BAGGAGE

CAMP OF CHEFLIK PASHA

C.R.   MINOTAUR GATE NICOSIA

BARRACKS BAFFO
NICOSIA

Africa was merely an inconvenient piece of land that got in the way of a voyage from Britain to India; the posts occupied on the two coasts for the purpose of suppressing the slave-trade were "millstones round our neck" as Disraeli called them; the only parts of Africa of any interest were those that commanded the way round, the Cape and the isthmus of Suez. The Cape was safe enough. In the Eastern Mediterranean British policy would react to any hostile threat but there was one which inspired special fear. The power which was making most of the running against the Turks, Russia, was also the one whose empire in Central Asia was expanding most rapidly. The occupation and colonisation of one independent Asian state after another was bringing the Russians closer every day to the frontiers of India. A series of successes in wars against the Turks seemed to presage a time when the Czar would not be satisfied merely with the annexation of additional Ottoman provinces but would take over, either as a protectorate or in full possession, all the territories of that empire whose imminent demise Nicholas I had confidently predicted in 1853.

In London strategic opinion was unanimous in holding that any further advance by Russia would fatally endanger imperial communications. The key issue was Constantinople and the Straits, that is the Bosphorus and the Dardanelles. In consequence, throughout the nineteenth century it was an axiom of British policy that Turkey should be supported against Russia, preferably by diplomacy only but if necessary by arms. The Crimean war was an example of the latter. It also demonstrated the difficulties of giving military support to the Sultan, for although in the circumstances it was remarkably successful as an amphibious operation, the fact that the British-French expeditionary forces had no base nearer than Marseilles caused grave difficulties of supply. The restrictions imposed on Russia by the Black Sea clauses of the Treaty of Paris in 1856 were satisfactory so long as they lasted, but Alexander II took advantage of the defeat of France in 1870 to repudiate them. In the succeeding decade Russian military strength was augmented (introduction of universal conscription in 1874), the struggles for freedom of the still-enslaved Christian nations of the Balkans became sharper and the highest levels of the Imperial government began to espouse with fervour the Pan-Slav cause which called for independence for Serbs, Macedonians, and Bulgars under Russian inspiration and control.

The most serious of the Russo-Turkish wars was the one that broke out in 1877. Its origin was the Russian desire to rescue Serbia and Montenegro, which had been defeated in war by Turkey, and to liberate the enslaved Christian nations of the Balkans; and also, naturally, to exploit that liberation to produce as much political and military advantage as possible. In Britain it found a Conservative government in power under Disraeli with, for the first time in his life, an unassailable majority in Parliament. In spite of a growing wave of public opinion against the Turks, stirred up by reports of the atrocities committed in Bulgaria, he was determined to pursue "the old Crimean policy". Besides, on this occasion it looked as though the Russians really would reach Constantinople. The city was within their power. Nothing but the indecisiveness of Alexander II held them back. The British countermove was to send the Mediterranean Fleet through the Dardanelles into the Marmara to anchor in sight of the Seraglio. Troops from the Indian Army were brought to Malta. Plans were made to use them to seize either Cyprus or Alexandretta (Iskanderun) as a base for operations in support of the Sultan. A popular song by G. W. Hunt expressed the mood and added a word to the vocabulary of politics:

We don't want to fight but, by jingo, if we do
We've got the ships, we've got the men, we've got the money too.
We've fought the Bear before and while Britons shall be true
The Russians shall not have Constantinople.

The Russians flinched from Constantinople but imposed on the Sultan the annexationist Treaty of San Stephano. So exorbitant were its terms that the other

European powers insisted on its being submitted to a special Congress in Berlin. As with all successful international conferences the main points of contention were the subject of secret, separate negotiations beforehand. Britain and Russia worked out an accord. It allowed the victors a reasonable share of the spoils of war, especially at the eastern end of the Sultan's Anatolian dominions, while reducing their aspirations in the Balkan peninsula and the region of the Straits. Simultaneously the British and Turkish governments were conducting a parallel set of preliminary negotiations. For if the old Crimean policy was to be followed and Britain was to protect Turkey against Russian aggression then Turkey must be shown to be worth preserving. Public opinion in Britain was doubtful, on moral grounds, even though an alliance with the Sultan was accepted as being in British interests. Accordingly in the new agreement the British government's undertaking to assist the Sultan to defend his possessions in Asia (but not in Europe) against

Cartoon showing the Sultan as Humpty-Dumpty being put back on his wall (the Asian frontier in Anatolia) by Disraeli, assisted by Cyprus *Punch*, 1878

Hoisting the British flag in
Nicosia; wood engraving
Illustrated London News, 1878

any further Russian aggression was balanced by stringent conditions accepted by the Ottoman government. Not only did they promise reforms of administration for the benefit of their Christian subjects — an easy and by then conventional formality which had already produced several admirably expressed but wholly disregarded constitutions — but they agreed to the appointment all over Anatolia of British "Military Consuls" who would report regularly on the non-performance of the Sultan's promises. This would give London a desirable leverage. Finally the island of Cyprus was to be handed over to be administered in the name of Queen Victoria while remaining formally part of the Sultan's dominions.

One reason for the acquisition of Cyprus was that the preliminary agreement made by Salisbury, the British Foreign Secretary, and Shuvalov, the Russian Ambassador in London, had conceded Russian territorial claims not only to the fortresses of Kars and Ardahan in the Caucasus but also to the Black Sea port of

"Triumphant entry of Captain Swain into Levkonico"; wood engraving
Illustrated London News, 1878

Batum. So agitated was popular opinion that these concessions, when revealed, would be hard to defend unless there was some positive gain. In this role the Cyprus Convention contributed to the success of the Congress of Berlin. "This is progress," said Bismarck when he heard of it. Disraeli commented to the Queen, "Evidently his idea of progress is seizing something." The other reason was the practical requirements of this pro-Turkish policy. The announced intention was to use Cyprus as a *place d'armes*: not a strong point or even a naval base but a convenient location where troops could be assembled if they were to be sent to join the Turkish forces in the Caucasus or, a strategic possibility which loomed large at the time, in the Euphrates valley. Experience had shown that Malta was too remote. Many other possibilities were considered but rejected. A fairly strong favourite at one time was Stampalia (Astypalaea), which has indeed an excellent port but not much room for troops.

The link with the Russo-Turkish frontier continued throughout the British period. In the original agreement it was provided that if Russia gave back the two fortresses and Batum Cyprus too would be returned to the Sultan's direct administration. (Kars and Ardahan but not Batum reverted to Turkey in 1921 as part of the terms of a Soviet treaty with Ataturk's government.) At the time of independence in 1960 the link was again in evidence since the NATO commitment towards Turkey was the principal reason why Britain required bases in the island.

243

Such were the circumstances in which Cyprus in 1878 found itself playing, quite unexpectedly, a leading role in the politics of Europe. It was destined to be only brief. The reasons for this were once more extraneous ones. In 1880 the Conservative government was defeated at the elections and Mr Gladstone became Prime Minister. His ideas on foreign policy were succinctly but sufficiently expressed in the undoing of what he called "Beaconsfieldism". He had described the Cyprus Convention as an "insane covenant" and an "act of duplicity not surpassed, and rarely equalled, in the history of nations"; he was hardly likely to take serious steps to exploit it. His critics pointed out that he took none either to annul it. His sentiments were strongly anti-Turk, as he had demonstrated during his famous electoral campaigns in Midlothian; on the other hand by recalling the military consuls from Anatolia he gave up the best chance of ensuring an improvement of Turkish methods of rule. There was therefore little prospect of Cyprus being used for the purpose for which it had been acquired and only four years had passed when its function as the principal British base in the Eastern Mediterranean was finally superseded. In 1882 began the occupation of Egypt, which provided not only the far superior facilities of Alexandria but also direct control over the Suez canal. Cyprus was by-passed.

The actual process of occupation was picturesque and peaceful. On 4th July, 1878, the Channel Fleet under command of Vice-Admiral Lord John Hay arrived at Larnaca from Crete. On the 6th he was officially informed of the signature on 4th June of the Cyprus Convention but was given no instructions about what action he was to take. After waiting for another two days he went ashore and met the Kaimmakam or local commander, described as a man of mild and indolent temper; it was evident that there would be no opposition. On 10th July the engagingly named H.M.S. Salamis arrived from Constantinople with the Ottoman Commissioner, Sami Pasha, who brought with him the Imperial *firman*, addressed to the Governor of Cyprus through the Vali of the Archipelago, directing him to hand over the administration of the island. A copy for the Admiral was brought by a British official, Walter Baring, who became Secretary to the Government after the transference of power. Sami Pasha and Walter Baring were sent to Nicosia to inform the governor and on the 12th Admiral Hay set off for the capital in a wagonette. He overtook on the way a detachment of fifty sailors and fifty marines and drove in unescorted. After calling on the Governor, Ahmed Bessim Pasha, at the Saray he was present the same afternoon at a brief flag-raising ceremony in front of the Turkish army barracks. In a short address to the crowd he promised justice for all on an equal basis. The only other speaker was a Greek Cypriot, George Kepiades, who expressed the joy of the Cypriots at the prospect of liberty and progress.

After the excitement of the diplomatic bargaining table and the battles in the Balkan passes and at the approaches to the Bosphorus which preceded them the

Greek Orthodox priests blessing the British flag at the Kykko *Metokhi*, Nicosia, in the presence of the High Commissioner; wood engraving
Illustrated London News, 1878

245

actual implementation of the Cyprus Convention passed off in a markedly humdrum manner. There was nothing to match the scenes of horror which had accompanied the transfer of power from Venice to the Turks; it was to prove a strange coincidence however that Venice and Britain ruled Cyprus for the same length of time, eighty-two years. Turkish military strength had run down as explained in the preceding chapter; the first British force to arrive was a detachment from the Indian Army contingent in Malta four hundred strong. The existing Gendarmerie, the Zaptieh, were taken over by the incoming administration and after being purged and retrained were found fully adequate to maintain order in a well-behaved and largely crime-free island. For indeed Cyprus never became a *place d'armes*. Except in war time and, later, during the EOKA campaign, there was no garrison to speak of, merely a company of infantry borrowed from a unit serving in Egypt. The military nature of the occupation began to disappear very soon. The first High Commissioner was a soldier, Lt. Gen. Sir Garnet Wolseley, who went on to become both a Viscount, a Field Marshal and Commander in Chief of the Army. He served for less than a year and was succeeded by another military man, Colonel (later Major General) Sir Robert Biddulph; but thereafter Cyprus, having been transferred from the Foreign Office to the Colonial Office, was ruled by civilians appointed from the career service of the latter. Their title reflected the anomalous position of the island so long as the Sultan's ultimate sovereignty was upheld. As a post it did not rank particularly high compared with other colonies. It was not quite the backwater it had been under the Ottomans but it was no longer a centre of world interest.

The proceedings of the Congress of Berlin are not of a nature to commend themselves to the more enlightened ideas of today, or even of 1918 when

New pier and government offices at Limassol; wood engraving Illustrated London News, 1881

President Wilson proclaimed as one of his Four Principles "Peoples and Provinces shall not be bartered about from sovereignty to sovereignty as if they were but chattels or pawns in the game." (He overlooked this admirable principle when disposing of, for instance, South Tyrol.) Neither the people of Cyprus nor the people of Britain were invited to express their views. On the other hand there was fairly general agreement in 1878, shared and vigorously expressed by Gladstone, that the fewer people under Turkish sovereignty the better. Certainly this was the view of the Cypriots. Turkish rule had been corrupt, grasping and desperately inefficient even when not actively oppressive. The mood in which they looked forward to British rule was expressed by Archbishop Sophronios in his address of welcome to Wolseley: "We hope, therefore, that from now on a new life begins for the people of Cyprus; a new great period, which will become memorable in the annals of the island. We hope that all shall be instructed without distinction of race or creed, that law is the king of all; that all shall have equal rights and equal responsibility before the law; that all shall be used to treading the good road, that is to say, the road of truth, of duty and of liberty." The other component of that mood was made clear to Wolseley by the Bishop of Kition, welcoming him to Larnaca. "We accept the change of government inasmuch as we trust Great Britain will help Cyprus, as it did the Ionian Islands, to be united with Mother Greece, with which it is naturally connected."

Before taking up the theme raised by the Bishop of Kition, which will dominate the rest of this history, it will be as well to say something about the differences

The first British High Commissioner, Sir Garnet Wolseley, receiving Turkish notables in the Konak on the occasion of Bairam; wood engraving
Illustrated London News 1879

247

The British Kaimakam hearing
an assault case at Ephtakomi;
wood engraving
Illustrated London News, 1878

produced by the transition from bad government to good, even if often parsimonious, government. It is notoriously difficult to describe the achievements of administration without going into details. And generalities are liable to sound suspect. Nevertheless the progress made in those eighty-two years is plain to see. Roads were built on a scale unparalleled in other Mediterranean islands where previously there had been one rough track connecting Larnaca with Nicosia. Nineteenth-century travellers had called Cyprus the unhealthiest of all Ottoman provinces: the provision of hospitals and medical services eradicated the endemic diseases, especially malaria, and favoured an increase of population from 186,000 in 1881 to an estimated 660,000 in 1978. One of the most remarkable successes of the British administration was the reafforestation of the mountainous regions and the creation of a Forestry Service that was a model for and a teacher of the other services in the Empire. It fulfils the same role in the Near East of today; and so does the Veterinary Service which has transformed animal husbandry. Legislation against usury and the steps taken from an early date to provide agricultural credit meant that the grip of the moneylenders was lifted from the peasantry. Co-operatives were encouraged: the rise in quality of agricultural products, especially wine, and their successful marketing, are evidence of their value. Cyprus trade unions, most assiduously fostered by the colonial administration, have a stability and responsibility which it is unlikely they would have acquired if their development had been left to indigenous talent. Nor had individual enterprise been behindhand. Greeks are admittedly outstanding as businessmen but the Greek Cypriots under colonial rule benefited from a stable currency and preferential markets and, of course, were spared from the war, the enemy occupation and the civil war which the mother country suffered.

Education calls for special mention. In 1880 the High Commissioner, in a dispatch to the Colonial Secretary, proposed that for the future all education should be through the medium of English. This was consistent with policy in, for example, India. There, in the formative period of British rule, the authorities had positively favoured Oriental languages, especially Persian; but Macaulay's famous minute and an advancing self-confidence had discarded Hafiz in favour of Wordsworth and Shakespeare. Lord Kimberley, Secretary of State in Gladstone's newly elected government, would not hear of such treatment for Greek, which was still one of the two bases of British higher education. In a decision as important as any, and taken within two years of the occupation, he insisted that Greek should be the language of education throughout the island, with Turkish similarly used in the schools set up for the minority. From then on the schools for the majority followed the official Greek curriculum, which was in itself largely modelled on the German system. As a result the history and the literature which children studied from their earliest youth were those of the mother country and the objects towards which their patriotism was directed were the Greek Royal Family and the Greek flag.

Cyprus was given a constitution on the usual colonial model in 1882. It provided for a Legislative Council of twelve elected and six official members (the latter

English graves in the churchyard of St. Lazarus Larnaca; wood engraving Illustrated London News 1878

The harbour of Famagusta;
wood engraving
Illustrated London News, 1878

being colonial civil servants) presided over by the High Commissioner, who had a casting vote. The elected members were divided in proportion to the numbers of Christians and Moslems shown in the census of 1881, viz nine to three. This meant that if the officials voted with the three Turkish members they had an equality with the Greek members and the High Commissioner's casting vote would carry the day. The Council's powers were limited, especially on financial matters; although the annual budget was laid before the Council and voted on it could be enforced whatever the result by the use of the High Commissioner's reserve powers. This constitution remained in force until 1931. It was not affected by the change in status of the island which took place in 1914 when, as a consequence of the state of war between Turkey and Britain, the latter declared that it had been annexed to the British crown. (The change was regularised in 1925, when Cyprus was declared to be a Colony; the title of High Commissioner was changed to Governor.) There was justification for the complaint, made particularly by the Greek Cypriots, that they had less control over their own affairs than was the practice in many other colonies where the standard of popular education was much lower. It was not their only or most serious complaint. For in contrast to the Asian or African territories the aspiration of the majority of the Cypriot people was not for greater self-government leading to independence; it was for transfer to another Crown than the British, for reunion with the rest of the Greek people. The demand for Enosis, the Greek word for Unification, was the only important issue in politics.

The strength of nationalism as a political emotion was one of the distinguishing features of nineteenth-century history as exemplified in particular by the struggles for unification in Germany and Italy. The Greeks were no less persistent in pursuit of it. The comparatively small nation-state created in 1831, with its capital in

Athens, was inspired from its start with the ambition to bring together all the Greek lands which remained unliberated, and fought several wars with this object; the inhabitants of those lands shared the same ambition. In Cyprus there had been no chance under the Ottomans for public demonstrations of nationalist sentiment. The same was true, for example, of Chios or Mitylene and Cyprus was much more distant from Athens being the furthest removed to the east and south of all the Greek islands. The arrival of the British at once released the Cypriots' inhibitions. There was no danger of the savage repression which had been unleashed in 1821; the new rulers were open to argument, allowed free speech and freedom of the press and had even fostered the Hellenic heritage by their educational policy. Besides, there was always the precedent of the cession of the Ionian Islands to which the Bishop of Kition had appealed in the first days of the transfer of power.

From 1878 onwards the hope for unification never dimmed. It would be tedious to detail all the various, almost annual, manifestations which are recounted at length in Sir George Hill's fourth volume. The wording of resolutions and memorials scarcely varies over eighty odd years. From time to time the memorialists received some encouragement. For example Gladstone twice, in 1880 and in 1897, made public statements in favour of Enosis; but on both occasions he was in opposition; when in power he took no action. The independence of Crete in 1898 roused great expectations because it was accomplished by

Ruins of the palace of the Proveditore at Famagusta; wood engraving
The Graphic, 1878

concerted action by all the European powers. In 1907 an even greater stimulus was given by the visit of Winston Churchill, then Parliamentary Secretary at the Colonial Office and its spokesman in the House of Commons. In reply to a memorial he declared that it was "only natural that the Cypriot people who are of Greek descent should regard their incorporation in what may be called their mother-country as an ideal to be earnestly, devoutly and fervently cherished. Such a feeling is an example of the patriotic devotion which so nobly characterises the Greek nation." In 1915 they discovered, after the event, that their great ideal had come momentarily within their grasp, only to be taken away again. When Bulgaria, joining the alliance of Germany, Austria and Turkey, declared war on Serbia the Greek government under Venizelos was ready to go to war with Bulgaria as its treaty obligations to Serbia required; but it was unconstitutionally dismissed by King Constantine, who thought Germany was going to win the war. The British Government, concerned about the fate of Serbia, offered to cede Cyprus to Greece in return for the fulfilment of its obligations. Zaimis, Constantine's stop-gap Prime Minister, refused. Although Venizelos later in the war overthrew Constantine and brought Greece on to the side of the Allies the offer was not repeated.

Coming down from Troodos to winter quarters; wood engraving
The Graphic 1880

On every occasion the Greek petitions for Enosis were put forward representatives of the Turkish minority petitioned in the contrary sense. Occasionally, as in 1907 during Churchill's visit, the Turks mounted riotous demonstrations. Normally, however, they did not feel it necessary to equal the fervour of the Greek Cypriots because they were confident that the British had no intention of relinquishing control. They were content with their status. There was no evidence of resentment when in 1914 they found themselves suddenly British rather than Ottoman subjects in consequence of the annexation. They were spared the upheavals that other parts of the Ottoman Empire suffered. Indeed life in Cyprus continued very much in the old pattern, as it had been in Thessaly or

Archbishop Sophronios (1865-1900) lying in state wearing the imperial purple robe; the priest on his right holds the imperial sceptre. Archbishops of the Church of Cyprus are buried in a seated posture

Macedonia or Eastern Asia Minor before the Balkan Wars and the First World War had broken it. There were Greek villages and Turkish villages and mixed villages as well; Greek Cypriots and Turkish Cypriots lived amicably as good neighbours. But the minority thought that they might not get on so well if they were forced to become Greek citizens. Some of the better-educated reflected that in Crete, where Moslems had once, in the eighteenth century, been a majority, they were now not even a minority since the remaining ones had all been obliged to emigrate. It was not, however, a burning question until the second half of the 1950s; for the present the Turkish Cypriots were content with their prosperity and confident it would continue.

The Greek Cypriots were naturally also conscious of their increasing prosperity. They did not however allow it to distract from the pursuit of their national aims. The politically conscious element kept them constantly before the mind of the public. British officials often expressed surprise at this disregard of the economic factors to which modern political theory tends to attribute predominant influence; but in this they showed a lack of understanding of the Greek national character. One British Governor was reported as declaring, with puzzled emphasis, that he had never met anyone who could show that the Cypriots would be better off if united with Greece. Whether this was true or not, personal advantage was not the moving force for Enosis.

In October 1931 there took place the most serious demonstration up to then in favour of Enosis. The guiding organisation was a recently-formed "National Radicalist Union" which declared as its principal aims "the fanatical pursuit of the Union of Cyprus with the Greek political whole." A leading role was played by the Bishop of Kition, who addressed a meeting in Limassol calling for civil disobedience. In Nicosia the principal part was played by the chief priest of the Phaneromeni church, Dionysios Kykkotis, who unfurled a Greek flag and declared "I proclaim the revolution." A march on Government House resulted in a riot in the course of which it was burned down. The authorities reacted by bringing in a company of troops from Egypt; order was restored in a comparatively short time. Ten Greek Cypriots, including the Bishops of Kition and Kyrenia, were deported. The constitution was suspended, political parties were forbidden and the press censored. The flying of the Greek flag was prohibited by law.

For the rest of the 1930s the expression of support for the cause of Enosis was restricted almost entirely to London, Athens and New York. In Athens it was discouraged by the Venizelos Government. The London Cypriot Committee was especially active. A change of mood in the island and among the political organisations abroad came with the Italian invasion of Greece in October 1940 as a result of which Britain and Greece became allies. Recruitment to the Cyprus Regiment rapidly increased; in all some 30,000 Cypriots are recorded as having served in the forces. The Greek flag was flown in triumph to celebrate frequent Greek victories in Albania. After the German invasion in April 1941 had rescued the Italians and occupied the whole of the country including Crete it appeared that Cyprus was in imminent danger. The appearance was misleading because Hitler, unsettled by the very heavy casualties in Crete, had personally forbidden any

254

further parachute operations; but this could not be known at the time. In spite of the threat the Cypriot population showed no sign of wavering in its support for the Allied cause. In recognition the prohibition of political parties was rescinded; in October 1941 a meeting at Skarinou led to the foundation of AKEL, the Progressive Party of the Working People. Before long it was joined by a Cyprus National Party (KEK) and a Pan-Agrarian Union of Cyprus (PEK). In 1943 municipal elections were allowed in the principal cities. Throughout the war, however, the national aspirations for Enosis were not strongly pressed.

The British Labour Party, returned to power in 1945 at the end of the war, was naturally anxious to introduce representative government in a colony which had been under direct rule for fourteen years. A non-career Governor was appointed in the form of Lord Winster, who had been a Labour Member of Parliament and a Minister. The Secretary of State for the Colonies announced proposals for a democratically elected legislature, a ten-year plan for economic development and social progress, and an amnesty. The Government's intentions were described as aiming at the establishment of a more liberal and progressive regime. It was an intention fully in line with the Attlee declaration of August 1945, that Britain regarded itself as under an obligation to develop self-government in all its colonial possessions. To other colonies the policy was welcome, and it has been duly implemented; but to the Cypriots it was unacceptable. The recently elected Archbishop, Mgr

View from the gardens of the new Government House, now the Presidential Palace. The arches in the foreground were taken from the Bedestan in 1906

Leontios of Paphos, declared on 13th July, 1947, that any deviation from the enotist solution of the Cyprus problem would mean the prolongation of an unbearable servitude. He ended his proclamation with the slogan "Enosis and only Enosis", which he appears to have been the first to formulate. Two days earlier the newspaper Eleftheria, not one of the more extreme, had declared in a leading article that the people of this Greek island would reject even the most perfect constitution if it did not provide for Enosis. This attitude was generally maintained against later constitutional proposals though there were occasional critics who would have favoured self-government as a stage to Enosis.

In August 1948 the constitutional proposals were abandoned in the face of the general opposition. Lord Winster resigned as Governor and was succeeded by a career Colonial official. No effort was made to impose a constitution, as some had feared and others secretly hoped; the initiative was left to the Cypriots. It was seized by the Church. Archbishop Leontios died only a month after his enthronement and was succeeded by Makarios II, who had been Bishop of Kyrenia. The election was regarded as a triumph for the right; his predecessor had been strongly supported by the left but Makarios was vigorously anti-Communist and a veteran nationalist who had fought as a volunteer with the Greek army in the Balkan War of 1912. At the end of 1949 he announced that the Church would organise a plebiscite throughout the island on the question of Enosis. The proposal appears to have been brought forward at the suggestion of the Bishop of Kition, later Archbishop Makarios III. Voting in the plebiscite took place from 15th to 22nd January, 1950; it was held in the churches and women cast votes for the first time. The qualifying age was eighteen. The vote consisted of signing a page of a register under the rubric "I demand Enosis" or on a separate page to indicate opposition. The result was highly favourable to the organisers: out of 224,747 on the electoral role 215,108 or 96% voted for Enosis.

The 1st of April, 1955, marked the beginning of the campaign which led directly to the transformation of Cyprus to its position today. The aim was to persuade the colonial authorities, and the Government in London, that it would be impossible to maintain their position in the face of the demands for unification. The attack began on that day with explosions directed at Government buildings and continued with attacks on officials and on Cypriots who were considered collaborators. The organiser, Lt. Col. (later Lt. Gen.) George Grivas was a Cypriot by birth who had served in the Greek army from 1916 to 1945. He adopted the code-name Digenis; his followers were known as EOKA, the National Organisation of Cypriot Fighters. In 1950 the Bishop of Kition had been elected Archbishop at the early age of 37 and took the name of Makarios III. He took seriously his duties as Ethnarch to direct the political aspirations of his flock. In 1956 he was deported to the Seychelles. This was shortly after he had opened negotiations with Sir John Harding, a distinguished soldier who had been appointed Governor. The interruption of these negotiations was unfortunate since the two men appeared close to agreement.

The struggle of EOKA continued throughout 1956, during which time Cyprus was used as a base for the Anglo-French operation against Egypt. (This was the only time during the British period that it was used for the military purposes for which it was ostensibly acquired.) At the end of the year further constitutional proposals were put forward, based on a study by Lord Radcliffe. They provided for a very full degree of self-government and have on occasions since 1960 been regarded by Greek Cypriots with retrospective favour and regret; at the time they were unacceptable because Enosis was excluded. In 1957 the new British Prime Minister, Harold Macmillan, released Makarios from the Seychelles but banned him from Cyprus. He was given a hero's welcome on arrival in Athens. Not long afterwards Macmillan took the decision that it was not necessary in British interests to retain the whole island as a base; it would be sufficient to have bases on the island.

In their pursuit of union with Greece Grivas and his followers formed an opinion which later proved mistaken about the likely views of the Turkish Cypriots and the Government of Turkey; the same was generally the case with their sympathisers and supporters in Athens. The Turkish Cypriots were contented with the *status quo* and strongly averse to being forced into Greek nationality. They feared that they would become second-class citizens; they would certainly find themselves a tiny minority in the whole population of Greece after having been a respectable one in Cyprus. It was not necessary, as many Greek Cypriots then and later suspected had happened, for British officials to point out the disadvantages of Enosis, at least to the educated class of political leaders. As for the Government of Turkey both Greek Cypriots and Greeks held firmly that it had no right whatever to intervene. They were no doubt correct on this point, as a matter of international law; but they also held that Ankara was not in the least likely to intervene. This was an error. Whether or not the Turks were moved by ethnic solidarity they had serious strategic objections to an extension of Greek territory to a position off their south coast within easy reach of their ports of Mersin and Alexandretta. Once seized of this point — which may have been fallacious if the arguments given above about Cyprus's minor strategic importance are valid — they were able, thanks to their

Sir John Harding, Governor of Cyprus, visiting The Wiltshire regiment at Aghirda camp

258

geographical position, to block the solution that appeared the most natural outcome of the anti-colonialist struggle and prevent Cyprus from following the precedent of Crete.

The original demand of the Turkish Cypriots was that if the British withdrew Cyprus should be transferred to Turkish sovereignty. Subsequently the solution favoured was the partitioning of the island between Greece and Turkey, which was commended under the name of "double enosis." (The dividing line usually proposed by the Turks was the 35th parallel of latitude, which would produce an almost equal bisection.) Both these solutions were regarded with horror by the Greeks. Nevertheless these were the slogans chanted by the Turkish rioters both in Turkey and in Cyprus during 1958. Meanwhile the Government in Athens was coming to the conclusion that an end must be put to the conflict at whatever cost. In 1957 Sir John Harding was succeeded by Sir Hugh Foot, a regular Colonial officer, as Governor.

The vital negotiations which led to the creation of the independent Republic of Cyprus were between Athens and Ankara. They were concluded in Zurich in February 1959. Later in the same month they were embodied in the agreed result of the London conference, but the essential principles had already been accepted before either the British or the Cypriots joined in. Cyprus was to renounce both Enosis and partition and there were to be stringent safeguards for the minority. There could be no doubt that the head of State must be Greek, nor, for that matter, that he would be Makarios, but the Vice-President was to be Turkish. More productive of contention, but considered vital for purposes of stability, the minority would have a veto on tax laws and there should be separate Greek and Turkish municipalities. The Greek, British and Turkish Governments entered into a Treaty of Guarantee to maintain this settlement. After months of argument two areas became British bases under full sovereignty; their territory was restricted by exquisite bargaining to ninety-nine square miles.

Archbishop Makarios and Dr Fazil Küchük were elected President and Vice-President of the Cyprus Republic. Grivas left the island, unsatisfied, for further retirement in Athens. On the night of 15th and 16th August, 1960, the Union flag was lowered and the flag of Cyprus was raised. Cyprus had become independent once more after 470 years and for the first time since 1191 was under a Greek ruler.

The traces of British rule, twenty years after its end, are naturally manifold. English is an official language. The law courts and the administration are British in inspiration. The largest colony of Cypriots abroad is in Britain, not Greece, mainly concentrated in London. Of material remains, such as an archaeologist of the future will unearth, the principal features will be sought in the infrastructure: bridges, dams, hospitals and the best road system in the Levant. The Presidential Palace, once Government House, has been lovingly reconstructed on the original design after its destruction in 1974. A handsome building, suited to its purpose and reminiscent in its architecture of the best local styles, it serves as the best monument to what a contemporary historian has called "Britain's moment in the Middle East."

XII
INDEPENDENCE
AND INVASION

"Cyprus, Reluctant Republic" is the title of a book by Stephen Xydis, one of the more serious works on the achievement of Cypriot independence. The adjective is well-chosen. The majority of the population was glad to see an end to the conflict between the established forces of order and the patriotic resistance but surprised to find what the final result had turned out to be. It was not for an independent Republic that EOKA had struggled; its martyrs had died in the hope that their sacrifice would hasten the day when Cyprus became a province of the Kingdom of Greece. Many consoled themselves with the thought that self-government, though rejected earlier on as a danger to Enosis, might still be used to achieve the national aims, no doubt after a shorter or longer period of transition. The obstacles, however, were formidable. A complicated constitution entrenched the rights of the Turkish Cypriot minority. Contingents of troops from mainland Greece and Turkey were stationed on the island. An international treaty to which the parties were Cyprus, Greece, Turkey and the United Kingdom provided that Cyprus should maintain its constitution and its independence, to the exclusion of either Enosis or partition. In the event of a breach of these provisions Greece, Turkey and the United Kingdom undertook to consult together. A declaratory clause added that each of the three guaranteeing powers reserved the right to take separate

The emblem of the Cyprus Republic, a dove, holding an olive branch, with the date of Independence

The signing of the Treaty
granting independence to
Cyprus by Sir Hugh Foot, last
British governor; on his right
President Makarios, on his
left Vice-President Küchük

The first ceremonial hoisting
of the flag of Cyprus over the
Parliament Building in Nicosia

action to restore the *status quo* if concerted action proved impossible. (This was believed to have been inserted on the insistence of the Turkish negotiators.) So far as the written word could prevail, therefore, all possible steps had been taken that could render permanent the results of the international agreement which had given birth to the Republic. Some hoped and some feared that they might not prove adequate.

The Constitution which formed the basis of this settlement provided that the executive power should be vested in a Greek President and a Turkish Vice-President, elected by their respective communities. The Council of Ministers was to consist of seven Greeks and three Turks; one of the latter must be given the portfolio of either foreign affairs, defence or finance. The legislative power was vested in a House of Representatives of 35 Greeks and 15 Turks, also communally elected. The Turkish members were given in effect a veto over all legislation dealing with electoral law, finance or municipalities. Two Communal Chambers were to deal with religious affairs, education and culture and communal activities. The five main towns were to have separate Greek and Turkish municipalities with their own elected Councils. In the civil service the same proportion of 70:30 for Greek and Turkish officials was prescribed as in the House of Representatives; in the army the proportion was to be 60:40. Both these ratios were favourable to the Turkish Cypriots since the demographically correct proportion was 81:19. A Supreme Constitutional Court was established under a neutral president to decide on the validity of legislative or executive actions which might be challenged as unconstitutional. The Constitution could be amended if two-thirds of both the Greek and Turkish members of the House of Representatives voted in favour.

In November 1959, over six months before independence, Archbishop Makarios was elected as the first President of the future Republic by the voters on the Greek communal roll. He had a majority of two thirds over his opponent, John Clerides, receiving 144,501 votes out of 216,254. For the office of Vice-President Doctor Fazil Küchük was returned unopposed. On 31st July, 1960, elections were held for the House of Representatives. Thirty of the Greek Cypriot seats were won by the party sponsored by the Archbishop known as the Patriotic Front; the other five went to AKEL, the Progressive Party of the Working People, whose candidates were, by agreement, unopposed. All the fifteen Turkish seats went to Dr Küchük's Turkish National Party. On 16th August Cyprus became independent. On 21st September it was admitted as a member of the United Nations on the sponsorship of Greece, Turkey and the United Kingdom. On 16th February the House of Representatives voted by 41 votes to 9 to apply for membership of the Commonwealth and this was agreed by the other members on 13th March. In 1961 Cyprus, in vindication of its claim to a share in the foundation of European civilisation, became a member of the Council of Europe.

Archbishop Makarios was the dominating figure in Cypriot politics in the 60s and 70s. He was born in 1913 into a peasant family living in a village on the south-western slopes of Mount Troodos. He was destined for the Church and became a monk in Kykko Monastery; from 1938 to 1948 he studied theology in Athens and Boston. In 1948 he was elected Bishop of Kition and Archbishop in 1950. After leading the struggle against the colonial administration he was President of the Republic from 1960 until his death in 1977. His easy ascendancy and unchallengeable authority did not derive only from his office, although as Archbishop and Ethnarch (and later Head of State) he combined both spiritual superiority and political leadership; it came from his strength of character and intellect. He had an exceptionally powerful mind which was quick to follow logical connexions and to forecast the future. In his public speeches he had a lucid eloquence whose effect was reinforced by his dignified and benevolent appearance. The principal criticism made of him as President is that he did not do enough to restrain extremists, whose behaviour contributed to the feeling of insecurity of the Turkish Cypriot community.

The Archbishop quickly launched himself into international affairs. At the United Nations Cyprus joined the Afro-Asian group and played an active role in group discussions. At that time President Nasser was Makarios' closest associate. He also joined the non-aligned nations and was a prominent figure at the Belgrade and Cairo summits in 1961 and 1964. He did not, however, overlook his Commonwealth connections which to some extent duplicated, and strengthened, his

Archbishop Makarios with, behind from right to left General Grivas and Mr Glafkos Clerides

Group photograph of Commonwealth Heads of Government, Buckingham Palace 1977. President Makarios is on the Queen's right

attachment to the Third World. These newly-found associates were prepared to give whole-hearted diplomatic support, but only to a completely independent Cyprus; they were not likely to agree to their newly-liberated comrades being swallowed up by Greece, a NATO country. Some of the more conventionally-minded Greek Cypriots thought that Makarios' foreign policy might as a result work against the pursuit of national aims; indeed some people, who had suspicions about the depth of his attachment to Enosis, thought that this contradiction was in his eyes one of its attractions. These suspicions were never wholly laid at rest during his first fourteen years as President.

In internal affairs Makarios' influence was equally paramount. (In this sphere his activities were hampered by precisely opposite suspicions held of him by the Turkish Cypriot leaders: that he was under the control of the Greek government and intended to bring about reunion as soon as possible.) Economically the island's prosperity not only remained but increased; politically the first three years were marked by a growing estrangement between the Greek Cypriot and the Turkish Cypriot communities. It proved impossible to operate the elaborate provisions of the constitution. Having been imposed from outside on the Greek Cypriots they were regarded by them with dislike and ill-will, while the Turkish Cypriots obstinately clung to every detail. The latter used their veto to prevent the passing of financial measures; in February 1963 the Supreme Constitutional Court declared that the government had no right to collect income tax or customs dues. The provisions about the apportionment of posts in the civil service were not put into effect. In fact the Constitution appeared to have broken down entirely. At the end of November 1963 Archbishop Makarios put to his Vice-President Doctor Küchük thirteen proposals for its amendment. In the meantime both communities were secretly organising clandestine military forces.

Makarios' thirteen proposals, which would have had the effect of reducing the safeguards provided for the minority community, were indignantly rejected by Ankara on 16th December before any reply had been made by Doctor Küchük, who at the time was believed by the Greek Cypriots to be not wholly hostile to them. A week later, in the early morning of the 23rd, fighting broke out in Nicosia between the two communities. It later spread to other places. On Christmas Day both sides agreed that they would observe a cease-fire which would be supervised by British troops from the Sovereign Base Areas. This agreement was formalised on the 26th. It is from then that the "Green Line" in Nicosia dates, a neutral zone between the Greek Cypriot and Turkish Cypriot areas of the city to be guarded by the British and subsequently by UN troops. These last began to arrive in March 1964, by which time their presence was required throughout the island. The force was known as United Nations Forces in Cyprus (UNFICYP) and included contingents from Canada, Denmark, Finland, Ireland, Sweden, and the United Kingdom under an Indian commander. Originally they were to serve for three months, but they were still in the island after eighteen years had passed.

Many Greek Cypriots left places which had come under Turkish control and there was an even greater influx into them of Turkish Cypriots who felt it unsafe or inadvisable to remain in the more extensive areas still controlled by the Government. The result was that for the next ten years the authority of the Government of the Republic extended over by far the greater part of the island but there were definite Turkish Cypriot areas where that authority·was not respected. The largest extended from the northern half of Nicosia almost as far as the northern coast, but there were similar enclaves in all the main towns except Kyrenia, and also others in inland districts. On the north coast the Turkish Cypriots held the area around Kokkina and Mansoura; this was their closest point to Turkey and there was an evident danger of the landing places there being used to bring in arms and troop reinforcements. The Government decided to eliminate this enclave, using the newly-formed National Guard. General Grivas was allowed to return from his honourable exile in Greece to take over command of it. The attack, in August 1964, was only partially successful. Mansoura was cleared but the smaller enclave of Kokkina held out, assisted by the intervention of the Turkish Air Force. It continued to exist, under close blockade of all the landward approaches, for the next ten years.

This was the last serious fighting for some time although both sides strengthened their military capacity with the aid of troop reinforcements from Greece and Turkey. In addition the two "mother-countries" supplied officers and NCO's to train and command the Greek Cypriot and Turkish Cypriot local forces. The

The front of the Presidential
Palace; above, after
destruction in the coup of July
1974; below as now restored.

Right: The Archiepiscopal
Palace; above, showing
damage inflicted in July 1974;
below, as restored

Swedish soldiers of UNFICYP relaxing in a village coffee shop

contingents of UNFICYP patrolled the borders of the enclaves. A proposal for a settlement was produced in March 1965 by the mediator appointed by the Secretary-General, Señor Galo Plaza, a former President of Ecuador. Its principal features were that Cyprus should in effect revert to the form of state provided by the 1960 constitution with additional written safeguards for the minority and further declaration against either Enosis or partition. The demand that Enosis should be formally renounced might have caused embarrassment both in Nicosia and in Athens but fortunately for them the Turkish government took only a few hours to denounce it and declare that Galo Plaza was unacceptable as a mediator. This rejection came before the Turkish Cypriot leadership had been able to make any comment.

In November 1967 a serious clash near Kophinou between Greek Cypriot forces under the direct command of Grivas and the local Turkish Cypriot forces was followed by an ultimatum from Ankara to Athens. The Greek government consisted of a military junta which had seized power in a *coup d'état* in the preceeding April. It accepted the Turkish demands with only minor exceptions to save face. In consequence Grivas was again banished from the island and all the Greek

Mainland troops who had been introduced clandestinely to the number of about 7,000 were likewise withdrawn. One result of this show-down was a greater tranquillity; another was that on the Greek Cypriot side the Archbishop was accused of having compromised Enosis. His critics were joined by all three of his suffragan Bishops. Nor did Grivas remain inactive in his second Athenian exile even though his advancing years might have excused him from taking the field again. In 1971 he returned in secret to Cyprus and established what he called EOKA-B, the Second National Organisation of Cypriot Fighters. His operations had no positive result and in January 1974 he died, still in clandestinity, at the age of seventy-five.

It was in that year that, for the first time, a Greek Government took the lead in a course of action to further the union of Greece and Cyprus. Hitherto it had been the Cypriots who had expressed their enthusiasm for the achievement of their national aspirations while the Greeks, though making their own feelings clear, had refrained from anything that might look like undue infuence. The initiative may have derived from internal exigencies of the junta. Their popularity had long before disappeared; they possibly hoped to restore it by a triumph such as no earlier

Intercommunal meeting in 1977 between President Makarios and Mr Rauf Denktash under the auspices of U.N. Secretary General Dr Waldheim government in Athens had been able to achieve. They had the means, since the Cyprus National Guard was still commanded by Greek officers who would accept their orders. Makarios had some advance warning; on 2nd July 1974 he wrote to the President of Greece to demand the withdrawal of the Greek officers. The challenge was accepted. On 15th July troops of the National Guard attacked the Presidential Palace. The violence of the attack, which laid the building in ruins, made it evident that the intention was to kill Makarios. In this the conspirators were unsuccessful. He made a daring escape; while Nicosia radio was announcing his death he got safely to Paphos and from there broadcast to the people of Cyprus. Undiscouraged the conspirators proclaimed as the new President Nicos Sampson, who had played an active part in the original EOKA.

The Turkish Government, purporting to act under the Treaty of Guarantee, ordered intervention by its armed forces. On 20th July the first landings began in the neighbourhood of Kyrenia. The Sampson regime immediately collapsed. Glafkos Clerides, who under the constitution was the person authorised to act in the President's absence, was sworn in. Makarios had by then gone to the United

In a refugee camp after the Turkish invasion and occupation of northern Cyprus, 1974

Nations to rally support. The Turkish bridgehead was expanded to cover the greater part of northern Cyprus. The area seized, which was still in their hands eight years later, amounted to forty per cent of the territory of the Republic and some seventy per cent of its productive capacity. Greek Cypriots fled to the unoccupied zone in numbers estimated at 200,000. There was heavy loss of life both in the course of military occupations and in attacks on civilians. Property was destroyed and looted; the same is true also of cultural monuments and antiquities. Since the invasion immigrants from Turkey have been brought in. The northern half of Cyprus has lost both its Hellenic character and its prosperity. This forcible partition of the island has been maintained until the present day. The unoccupied zone has, in contrast, shown a remarkable economic recovery. The standard of living remains high and is rising.

Archbishop Makarios returned to Cyprus in December 1974. He died in office in August 1977 and was succeeded by Spyros Kyprianou.

The case of Cyprus has been before the Security Council of the United Nations

Intercommunal meeting in 1979 showing centre, Dr Waldheim, U.N. Secretary General, with President Kyprianou on his right and Mr Rauf Denktash on his left

Mr Andreas Papandreou, Prime Minister of Greece, being welcomed at a public meeting in Nicosia by Mr Lellos Demetriades, the mayor. On the right, President Kyprianou and Archbishop Chysostomos

since July 1974. The Council has passed judgement on the case in a series of resolutions. The essential element in these can be briefly expressed. As the highest organ of international law it has declared that justice requires that all states should respect the sovereignty, independence and territorial integrity of the Republic of Cyprus, and called for an immediate end to foreign intervention and the withdrawal without delay of foreign troops. These are demands which are fully within the competence of the Security Council, whose decisions all members of the United Nations are pledged to respect. Meanwhile discussions have continued over the past seven years between Greek Cypriots and Turkish Cypriots to determine what constitutional arrangements would be acceptable to allow the two communities to live together in amity when the military occupation has been lifted.

272

EPILOGUE

Nine millenia have left many footprints in the soil of Cyprus. The first Cypriots whose culture the ordinary man can grasp are the stocky, round-headed inhabitants of Khirokitia with their village of circular houses on the slope above the bed of the river Maroni. It stands by the side of a main road; it has been most intelligently excavated; the walls of the houses are palpable and their functions clearly to be perceived. If ever a neolithic civilisation can be said to speak plain to the ordinary layman it is here in Cyprus. But with this exception the Stone Age is something to be studied in books or in museums. As with the succeeding Early and Middle Bronze Age there are ingenious and beautiful artefacts to be admired; speculation can play on the evolution of international relations, and maritime trade, in the Eastern Mediterranean at the turn of the third and second millenia; but it is from the fourteenth century B.C. that the continuity of the history and culture of Cyprus really begins, with the coming of the Greeks.

The land to which they came was the same in geographical outline as the present Republic, apart from the differences in coastal areas that have been caused all over the Mediterranean by variations in sea level. The climate was no doubt much the same although when the island was still covered with its original vegetation this would have produced milder summers than the austere heat that strikes the dried-up plains of the twentieth century. There was more water, retained by the forest cover; there were even running rivers. It was a rich land for agriculture, and brought riches to the miner too, as soon as the great copper deposits began to be worked. It was well provided also with harbours, the sea-level being higher; in fact Enkomi and Kition, for the shipping of their time, gave better shelter and easier access than do the commercial harbours of today. They were close to the coasts opposite where a higher civilisation was already in full development in Phoenicia and Egypt. It was a desirable land for colonisation, a sweet land to borrow a phrase from Leontios Machairas, whose attractions for Arcadian settlers from the Peloponnese outweighed those of the Ionian coast or the precarious trading outposts of Cilicia and the Levant.

The political history of Cyprus begins with the Greeks. The word itself attests that origin since it means the science, or art, of conducting the affairs of the *polis*, the city. There were, indeed, two or three Phoenician cities also before long but the dominating stamp was given by the Greeks. And this is where continuity begins. Down the centuries the line runs true, with minor and occasional deviations. Though interested parties have from time to time attempted to draw a distinction between the Cypriots and the inhabitants of the rest of Greece, the testimony of history is too plain to allow the attempt any plausibility. There are of course certain interesting variations to be noted; this was only to be expected since Greek states, wherever they were situated, never followed the Egyptian pattern of solidifying into a rigid mould. Thus monarchies survived in Cyprus longer than in other Greek states — if you except Sparta and Macedonia. At the turn of the eighth and seventh centuries they seem to have been swept by a passion for Homeric poems — the same could be said of Chios. At about the same time they acknowledged for a brief space the supremacy of the Assyrian Empire. It does not appear to have incommoded them any more than the Ionians were by their subjection to Lydia. They came under the Persian Empire a century and a half later; so did the Greeks of Asia Minor, Thrace and Macedonia. They joined the Ionian revolt. Defeated, they fought under Xerxes' banner in the campaign that ended at Salamis and Plataea; so did the Thebans. When Alexander destroyed that empire and set himself on the Great King's throne the Cypriots found that their traditional monarchies were back in fashion again. It was not long before they were to come under another monarchy, the Macedonian dynasty of the Ptolemies, just as though they had been any other province of Greece that had fallen under the domination of one of the deified kings who claimed part of the fractured succession to the universal monarchy of Alexander.

The Ptolemies yielded to the arms of Caesar's heir. The most vigorous of a line famous for the martial prowess of its women, Cleopatra VII, after she had vainly staked on a throw for the mastery of the world all the wealth of Egypt and the Roman legions that her captive Antony could command, poisoned herself rather than allow herself to figure in a Roman triumph. Her realm of Cyprus had already come under the grasping rule of the Roman Republic. Cicero, most eloquent of the Latins, had ruled it, unwillingly indeed but more than competently. As an imperial province of the unarmed class, to which Augustus assigned it to gratify the Senate and preserve a constitutional appearance, it conformed peaceably to the same pattern as the other Greek-speaking provinces. When St. Paul went to Paphos he felt himself as much in Greece as when he went to Corinth. It would not have occurred to him to think he was anywhere else. Nor did the Cypriots notice anything different when the Empire was divided and they found themselves under Constantinople rather than Rome. They did not regard themselves as Byzantines — they could hardly do so since that technical and scholarly term had not yet been invented. They did not then call themselves Hellenes either, since the theologians had given that name the meaning of pagans. They knew that they were Romans; they also knew they were Christians.

In coming under the rule of the Franks the Cypriots once more kept company with the other Greeks. There was a Frankish King of Cyprus, just as there was a Frankish Duke of Athens and a Frankish Prince of the Morea. The Cypriot subjects of the Lusignans continued to call themselves Romans. If they ever thought of their co-religionists in the Peloponnese, from which their ancestors had come three thousand years earlier, they might have reflected with justice that while they in their sea-girt isolation had remained unmixed in blood the Moreotes were in large measure derived from Slav and Albanian invaders. This *limpieza de sangre* may have carried with it some difference in character, a thing quite customary in isolated communities. The language is to this day a little archaic, as in West Virginia. The Hellenic character survived the experience, again shared by Cyprus with all the other Greek lands, of incorporation in the Ottoman Empire.

The Ottoman occupation of Cyprus was not in essence any different from what happened in, for instance, Thessaly or in Crete which, like Cyprus, had been conquered by the Turks from the Venetians. The British occupation was more unusual but that experience too had been shared by the Septinsular Republic of the Ionian Islands. Even the deployment in a Greek island of an international peace-keeping force had been seen in Crete in the years following 1898. In fact throughout the centuries since the fourteenth before Christ nothing happened in Cyprus which could not be paralleled elsewhere in Greece. There was nothing to modify the essential character of the Great Greek Island.

As in other countries of Greek speech the vicissitudes of history left many splendid monuments in Cyprus. The remains of the public buildings of the Greco-Roman city of Salamis, the theatre of Curium, the mosaic floors of the imperial governor's palace at Paphos, are reminders of that splendidly homogeneous culture which marks the Roman lands from Newcastle-on-Tyne to Jordan. The painted churches which nestle in the valleys of Troodos are inspired by the same spirit as their sister churches from Sicily to Serbia to the Ukraine. The first wholly exotic element enters with the Lusignans. The cathedrals of Nicosia and Famagusta are examples of the purest Ile de France Gothic architecture. Their conversion into mosques has preserved them from the hand of the restorer. The great castles hold so much of the spirit of Romance that if it had not existed the word would have had to be invented to describe Hilarion, Kantara, Kyrenia, Buffavento whose names fall upon the ear like the echo of a vanished world.

The British legacy is on the surface the most eminently visible today, from the pillar-box on the street-corner to the thrifty architecture of public buildings. Government House, now the Presidential Palace, is an exception because more magisterial; but it too is in a romantic Cypriot-Gothic style. It has so taken the fancy of the Cypriots that after one Greek faction had burned it down the restored Republican government lovingly rebuilt it and set over the entrance porch once more the strongly-carved Royal Arms and Cipher of their previous sovereigns of the House of Windsor. The real British legacy is to be sought in the very widespread knowledge of the English language, in the uniforms of the police and to a great extent in their behaviour, in the traditions of an impartial civil service and an incorrupt and principled administration of justice, and in the confidence and ability of the commercial and financial community. Cypriots now look on good government as the normal thing, which it is certainly not elsewhere in the Near East; they have a standard against which to measure shortcomings. Countries such as Lebanon admire Cyprus as an example and value it as a refuge in times of trouble.

It would be too gloomy a task to speculate about what will be the mark left on the island by the period which begins with the Turkish invasion of 1974. The brutal partition, enforced by an army of occupation which has repeatedly shown itself capable of deliberate destruction of monuments, has swept away much that had remained unchanged for centuries. A way of life has ceased to exist. The villages where the bell-tower of the church and the minaret of the mosque rose side by side have changed utterly. A piece of the old Levant has been brought violently into the divided Near East of the twentieth century. Part of the Hellenic heritage, an island which like Crete should long ago have rejoined the Hellenic political community, is held in jeopardy by unlawful violence. For Europe the lesson is clear. Justice denied to one country flashes a warning signal to all the others. The funeral bell for Cyprus, to borrow John Donne's phrase, tolls as well for the other nations of mankind.

CHRONOLOGICAL TABLE OF EVENTS

(Early dates are very approximate only and between 4500 and 2500 B.C. they are obtained from calibrated radiocarbon (Carbon-14) determinations; earlier radiocarbon dates cannot yet be calibrated to calendrical dates but the earliest are likely to be far in excess (c.1000 years) of the quoted range.)

B.C.

7000(?)–5300	**NEOLITHIC**
	(?) Colonisation of Cyprus by farmers from Syria or Cilicia: deer herding(?)
5000–4000	Earliest pottery-using groups and signs of regionalisation.

4000–2500	**CHALCOLITHIC**
	Emergence of metal-users and settlement of west Cyprus

2700–1900	**EARLY CYPRIOTE (EARLY BRONZE AGE)**
	(Arrival of people from Anatolia; ox-plough cultivation starts; sporadic exchanges with Levantine mainland)

1900–1600	**MIDDLE CYPRIOTE (MIDDLE BRONZE AGE)**
	Beginning of contacts with the Aegean
1900–1750	First mention of *Alasia* (probably Cyprus) and its export of copper in Near Eastern historical records
1650–	Start of large-scale pottery export to Levant and Egypt; fortifications and development of urbanisation in Cyprus

1600–1050	**LATE CYPRIOTE (LATE BRONZE AGE)**
c.1550	Development of Enkomi as major port
c.1400	Large-scale imports of Mycenaean pottery begin
c.1375	References to Alashiya in Tel el-Amarna documents
c.1220	Enkomi and Kition destroyed by Sea Peoples; rebuilt shortly afterwards. First settlement at Maa-Palaeocastro
c.1190	Second settlement at Maa-Palaeocastro. Beginning of immigration of Achaeans. Foundation of Palaepaphos
c.1150	Second wave of Achaean settlers
c.1080	Third wave of Achaean settlers
c.1050	Enkomi abandoned

1050–950	**CYPRO-GEOMETRIC I**
	Consolidation of Cypriot kingdoms

950–850	**CYPRO-GEOMETRIC II**
	Obscure period

850–750	**CYPRO-GEOMETRIC III**
	Phoenician colony at Kition. Royal tombs at Salamis, first burials
750–600	**CYPRO-ARCHAIC I**
709	Seven Cypriot Kings pay homage to Sargon II of Assyria
709–c.663	Assyrian domination
673/2	Ten Cypriot kings pay homage to Esarhaddon of Assyria
c. 663–569	Cypriot kingdoms independent
600–475	**CYPRO-ARCHAIC II**
c. 569	Amasis of Egypt takes control of Cyprus
c. 569–545	Egyptian rule
560–525	Reign of Euelthon of Salamis
c. 545	Cypriot kings transfer allegiance to Cyrus the Great, king of Persia; beginning of Persian domination
c. 521	Included in the fifth satrapy of the Persian Empire under Darius
499	Outbreak of Ionian revolt against Persian rule; participation of all Cypriot cities except for Amathus, at the instigation of Onesilos, King of Salamis
498	Reduction of Cypriot cities
480	Battle of Salamis; Cyprus contributes 150 ships to the Persian fleet
475–400	**CYPRO—CLASSICAL I**
450–449	Cimon's expedition to liberate Cyprus from Persia
448	Peace of Callias; Cyprus left firmly under Persian control
411	Evagoras I becomes king of Salamis
400–325	**CYPRO-CLASSICAL II**
by 391	Evagoras I master of the whole of Cyprus
386	Peace of Antalcidas; Athens recognises Persian sovereignty over Cyprus
c. 381	Siege of Salamis by the Persians
380–379	Evagoras I loses control over Cypriot cities other than Salamis under a peace concluded with Persia
374/3	Murder of Evagoras I
351	Cypriot kings join Egypt and Phoenicia in revolt against Persia; siege of Salamis, revolt suppressed.
c. 335	Birth of Zeno, founder of Stoic school of philosophy, at Kition
c. 333	End of Persian domination; Cypriot kings support Alexander the

	Great after his victory over the Persian forces at the battle of Issus
332	Cypriot ships take part in Alexander's naval siege of Tyre
331	Nicocreon becomes king of Salamis

325–150   HELLENISTIC I

323	Death of Alexander the Great; Cyprus becomes involved in struggles among his generals over the division of his empire
312	Certain Cypriot kings object to the rule of the general Ptolemy and are imprisoned or executed; Marion razed to the ground
310	Nicocreon, last king of Salamis, forced by Ptolemy to commit suicide. End of other city kingdoms
c. 310	Zeno founds school of Stoic philosophy in Athens
305	Ptolemy proclaimed Ptolemy I Soter, king of Egypt
294	Annexation of Cyprus by Ptolemy I; Cyprus becomes part of the Hellenistic state of Egypt
c. 264	Death of Zeno
168	Attack on Cyprus by Antiochus IV Epiphanes of Syria; withdrawal on intervention of Rome

150–30   HELLENISTIC II

c. 106/5–88	Cyprus ruled as an independent kingdom by Lathyrus (Ptolemy IX Soter II) after his expulsion from Egypt
88	Lathyrus restored as king of Egypt
88–80	Cyprus returned to Egyptian rule
80	Death of Lathyrus. Ptolemies partly withdraw from Cyprus
80–58	Reign of Ptolemaios in Cyprus (brother of Ptolemy XII Auletes of Egypt).
58	Cyprus reduced to the state of a Roman province; suicide of Ptolemaios
c. 47	Cyprus returned to Egyptian rule by Julius Caesar
30	Suicide of Cleopatra VII of Egypt; Cyprus finally becomes part of the Roman Empire

30–A.D. 330   THE ROMAN PERIOD

30BC	Cyprus annexed by Augustus; forms part of province of Syria
22BC	Cyprus a separate province under a proconsul
15BC	Paphos almost completely destroyed by earthquake
45AD	Missionary journey of SS Paul and Barnabas
47	Second missionary journey by SS Barnabas and Mark

76/77	Serious earthquake damage throughout Cyprus
116	Jewish insurrection
164	Heavy loss of life from plague
269	Raid by Goths
313	Edict of Milan grants freedom of worship to Christians
325	Cypriot bishops attend the council of Nicaea

330–1191 THE BYZANTINE PERIOD

330	Inauguration of Constantinople as capital of the Roman Empire
c. 330	Empress Helena said to have visited Cyprus. Foundation of Stavrovouni Monastery
332	Paphos ruined by an earthquake
342	Salamis ruined by an earthquake and a tidal wave. Rebuilt as Constantia
431	Council of Ephesus. Cypriot Church given conditional autonomy
488	Discovery of relics of St. Barnabas. Emperor Zeno gives Cypriot archbishop full autonomy and privileges
c. 550	Establishment of silk industry in Cyprus
649	Arabs invade island under Muawiya. Death there of the lady Umm-Haram, cousin of the Prophet
653-4	Second Arab invasion. Arab garrison placed in Cyprus
688	Treaty between Emperor Justinian II and Caliph al-Malik neutralising Cyprus
689	Numbers of Christian Cypriots moved to Bithynia
698	Cypriots in Bithynia return to Cyprus
723	English pilgrim Willibald visits the island
743	Arabs complain of breach of Treaty and raid Cyprus
806	Raid on Cyprus ordered by Caliph Harun ar-Rashid
c. 870–877	Temporary Byzantine occupation of the island
910	Byzantine admiral Himerius lands on island. His sailors molest Moslem villagers
912	Emir Damian of Tarsus raids island as a reprisal
965	Byzantines re-occupy Cyprus under Emperor Nicephorus Phocas. It becomes a province of the Empire
1043	Unsuccessful revolt of Theophilus Eroticus, governor of the island
1993	Revolt of Cypriot governor Rhapsomates, put down by John Ducas and Butumites
1094	Monastery of Kykko founded by monk Isaias, under Butumites' patronage
c.1093–1100	Philocales Eustathius governs the island
c.1100–1105	Constantine Euphorbenus Catacalon, governor. Church at Asinou decorated under his patronage
1105–1112	Philocales Eustathius' second governorate

1099	Pisan fleet attempts unsuccessfully to raid the island
1157	Severe earthquake in Cyprus
1158	Egyptian fleet raids island
c.1170	St. Neophytus founds monastery at Enkleistra
1185–1191	Isaac Ducas Comnenus takes over the government of the island and declares himself independent

1191–1192   RICHARD I (the Lionheart) AND TEMPLARS

1191	King Richard I of England defeats Isaac Comnenus and takes possession of Cyprus. He sells it to the Templars for 100,000 dinars. Richard marries Berengaria of Navarre in Limassol, where she is crowned queen of England.
1192	The Templars resell Cyprus to King Richard, who transfers it at the same price to Guy de Lusignan

1192–1571 THE FRANKISH PERIOD

1192–1489   THE LUSIGNAN DYNASTY

1192–1194	Guy de Lusignan, Lord of Cyprus
1194–1205	Aimery, brother of Guy, succeeds; he later obtains royal title from Emperor Henry VI
1197	Coronation of Aimery
1205–1218	Hugh I
1209	Foundation of Cathedral of Ayia Sophia in Nicosia
1217	Hugh I takes part in Fifth Crusade
1218–1253	Henry I
1220	Orthodox Archbishop and Bishops replaced by Latins
1228	Emperor Frederick II in Cyprus; he is recognised as suzerain
1229	Frederick II returns to West; rising of Cypriot barons against his deputies
1232	Battle of Aghirda. Imperialists defeated
1233	Imperialist garrison of Kyrenia capitulates
1249	Henry I takes part in Seventh Crusade
1253–1267	Hugh II. Plaisance of Antioch acts as Regent until 1261
1260	Orthodox Church in Cyprus subordinated to Latin Church by Papal Bull (Bulla Cypria)
1261	Hugh of Antioch Regent; becomes king on death of Hugh II
1267–1284	Hugh III
1284–1285	John I
1285–1324	Henry II
1291	Fall of Acre and extinction of Latin rule in Syria
1306	Henry II's brother Amaury ursurps power
1310	Henry II exiled to Cilicia; returns after murder of Amaury

1324–1358	Hugh IV
1350	Consecration of Orthodox Church of Phaneromeni
1359–1369	Peter I
1361	Capture of Adalia
1362–1365	Peter I travels in West to obtain support for new Crusade
1365	Sack of Alexandria
1369–1382	Peter II
1372	Rioting between Venetians and Genoese in Famagusta
1373–1374	War with Genoa. Cyprus agrees to large indemnity and cession of Famagusta
1382–1398	James I (prisoner in Genoa at accession)
1385	James I released by Genoese and crowned in Nicosia
1393	Assumes title of King of Armenia
1398–1432	Janus
1426	Invasion of Cyprus by Egyptians. Janus defeated and taken prisoner at battle of Khirokitia
1427	Janus ransomed and returns to Cyprus
1432–1458	John II
1441	John II marries Helena Palaeologina, daughter of Despot of the Morea
1458–1460	Charlotte, Queen of Cyprus
1460–1473	James II
1464	James expels Genoese from Famagusta
1472	James marries Catherine Cornaro (married by proxy in 1468)
1473–1474	James III, posthumous child of James II and Catherine
1474–1489	Catherine Cornaro Queen of Cyprus
1479	Conspiracy against Catherine in favour of King of Naples suppressed
1489	Catherine cedes Cyprus to the Venetian state

1489–1571   THE VENETIAN PERIOD

1510	Death of Catherine
1517	Ottoman Sultan, having conquered Egypt, becomes Suzerain of Cyprus
1562	Conspiracy of Greek Cypriots against Venetian rule
1566	Accession of Sultan Selim
1570	Turkish invasion force lands. Capture of Nicosia. Siege of Famagusta begins
1571	Famagusta capitulates to Turkish commander Lala Mustafa. Breach of capitulation by Turks. Cyprus annexed to Ottoman Empire

1571–1878   THE TURKISH PERIOD

1572	Expulsion of Latin hierarchy and restoration of Orthodox

1578	Mutinous Turkish troops kill the governor Arab Ahmet Pasha
1641	Suppression of Pashaliks of Paphos and Famagusta
1670	Cyprus downgraded from Pashalik and put under Kapudan Pasha
1673	Rebellion of Mehmed Agha Boyajioglou
1680	Boyajioglou executed
1703	Cyprus transferred to direct jurisdiction of Grand Vizier
1745	Cyprus removed from Grand Vizier and created an independent Pashalik again
1746–1748	Abu Bekr Pasha, only well-regarded governor
1751	Cyprus returned to direct jurisdiction of Grand Vizier
1754	Archbishop and Orthodox hierarchy made responsible for collecting taxes
1764	Chil Osman Agha appointed governor. After more than doubling taxes he is killed in revolt
1765–1766	Revolt of Khalil Agha, Commandant of Kyrenia
1777–1783	Haji Baki Agha governor
1820–1822	Küchük Mehmed governor
1821	Execution of Archbishop Kyprianos and three bishops
1833	Insurrection of Ibrahim of Paphos, known as Giaur Imam
1849	Cyprus included in Pashalik of Archipelago
1856	Government takes over collection of taxes from Archbishop
1861	Cyprus an independent province
1868–1871	Cyprus put under vilayet of Dardanelles
1871	Cyprus put under vilayet of Archipelago

1878–1960   THE BRITISH PERIOD

1878	Under the Cyprus Convention Britain assumes administration of the island which remains formally part of Ottoman Empire. Sir Garnet Wolseley first High Commissioner
1880	Greek established as medium of education (Turkish in Turkish schools)
1881	Administrative supervision transferred from Foreign Office to Colonial Office
1883	First meeting of elected advisory Council
1908	Riots in Nicosia over election of Archbishop
1914	Cyprus annexed by Britain in consequence of outbreak of war with Turkey
1924	Under Treaty of Lausanne Turkey renounces claim to Cyprus in favour of Britain
1931	Greek elected members resign from the Legislative Council; pro-Enosis riots in Nicosia; Government House is burned down; Constitution suspended
1941	Prohibition on political parties rescinded
1947	Lord Winster appointed Governor; his proposals, including an

	elected legislature, rejected
1948	Elections for a consultative Assembly are boycotted
1949	Ethnarchic Council created under Archbishop Makarios II. All parties represented on it
1950	Plebiscite of Greek Cypriots, organised by Archbishop, shows 96% in favour of Enosis; election as Archbishop of Makarios III
1954	Further British proposal for a legislative Council is rejected; frustration of first appeal to U.N. by Greece leads to strikes in Cyprus
1955	(April 1) Campaign in favour of Enosis started by EOKA under Grivas, code-name 'Dighenis'; a state of emergency is declared; tripartite conference in London
1955–1957	Sir John Harding (later Lord Harding of Petherton) Governor
1956	Archbishop Makarios exiled to the Seychelles
1957	Radcliffe proposals rejected; Turkish-Cypriots declare for Federation or partition; Makarios released from the Seychelles but banned from Cyprus
1957–1960	Sir Hugh Foot (later Lord Caradon) Governor
1958	Zurich Agreement between Greece and Turkey
1959	(January) London Conference (Greece, Turkey, U.K., Greek-Cypriots, Turkish-Cypriots) agrees on Independence of Cyprus; (March) Makarios returns to Cyprus; (December) Makarios elected President and Dr Fazil Küchük Vice-President
1960	**INDEPENDENT REPUBLIC**
1960	(July) General elections to House of Representatives; (16th August) Cyprus becomes an independent republic
1961	Agreement on British Sovereign Bases signed
1963	(December) Outbreak of intercommunal fighting; "Green Line" dividing communities in Nicosia established
1964	(January) Announcement by Dr Küchük in favour of partition; - (March) Security Council resolution in support of Cyprus sovereignty denounces threat or use of force; arrival of UNFICYP; (May) conscription is introduced; (June) Grivas returns and assumes command of Cyprus National Guard
1965	(March) Galo Plaza, U.N. Mediator, publishes report and proposals; rejected by Turkish Government
1966	(February) Joint Communiqué signed by the Governments of Cyprus and Greece that any solution excluding Enosis would be unacceptable
1967	(April) Military coup in Greece; (Nov.) fighting between National Guard under Grivas and Turkish-Cypriots in Kophinou area leads to Turkish ultimatum; accepted by Greek junta which withdraws troops, and Grivas, from Cyprus; (Dec.) Turkish-

	Cypriots announce formation of "Provisional Cyprus-Turkish Administration"
1971	Grivas returns secretly to Cyprus; start of renewed campaign for Enosis by EOKA-B
1974	(January) Death of Grivas; (July) Makarios demands withdrawal of Greek officers; (15th July) Conspiracy against Makarios inspired by Greek junta; Presidential Palace destroyed; Nikos Sampson declared President; (20th July) start of Turkish invasion; (23rd July) Glafkos Clerides Acting President; (7th December) Makarios returns
1975	Start of inter-communal talks, in first place in Vienna
1977	(January) Meeting between Makarios and Denktash; (3rd August) death of Makarios; succeeded as President by Spyros Kyprianou, as Archbishop by Chrysostomos, Bishop of Paphos
1978	(January) President Kyprianou returned unopposed for five-year term
1981	Elections for House of Representatives under new electoral system (reinforced representational)
1982	Greek Prime Minister, Andreas Papandreou, pays official visit to Cyprus

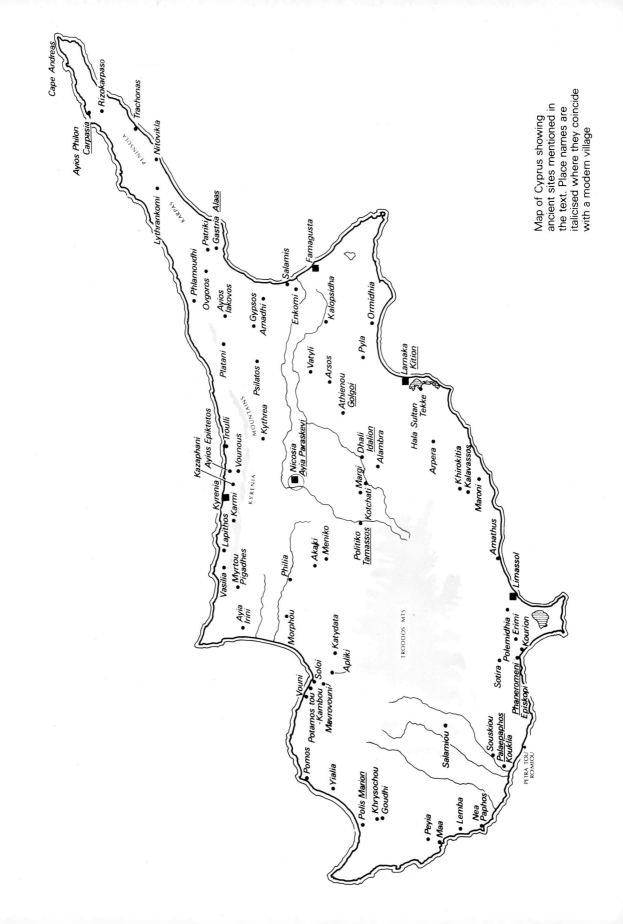

Map of Cyprus showing ancient sites mentioned in the text. Place names are italicised where they coincide with a modern village

Cape Andreas

Rizokarpaso

Ayios Philon
Carpasia

Trachonas

Nitovikla

KARPAS PENINSULA

Lythrankomi

Patriki
Gastria *Alaas*

Phlamoudhi

Ovgoros

Ayios Iakovos

Gypsos
Arnadhi

Famagusta

Salamis

Enkomi

Kazaphani
Ayios Epiktetos

Troulli

Platani

Psilatos

Kythrea

Vatyli

Kalopsidha

Pyla

Ormidhia

Kyrenia Vounous

Lapithos *Karmi*

KYRENIA MOUNTAINS

Arsos

Athienou
Golgoi

Larnaka
Kition

Vasilia

Myrtou
Pigadhes

Nicosia
Ayia Paraskevi

Dhali
Idalion

Alambra

Hala Sultan
Tekke

Ayia
Irini

Philia

Margi
Kotchati

Politiko
Tamassos

Arpera

Khirokitia

Kalavassos

Morphou

Akaki

Meniko

Maroni

Katydata

Amathus

Apliki

TROODOS MTS.

Limassol

Vouni
Soloi

Potamos tou
-Kambou
Mavrovouni

Salamiou

Sotira
Polemidhia
Erimi

Pomos

Yialia

Souskiou

Kourion
Phaneromeni
Episkopi

PETRA TOU
ROMIOU

Polis Marion

Khrysochou
Goudhi

Palaepaphos
Kouklia

Peyia
Maa

Lemba

Nea
Paphos

Greek

Turkish

Map showing the pre-1974 distribution of Greek and Turkish villages over the island

Famagusta

Larnaca

Kyrenia

Nicosia

Limassol

Paphos

Modern Cyprus, showing the delimitation line of Turkish occupation (The Attila line)

A Satellite photograph shows the central plain of Mesaoria between the Pentadaktylos range to the north and Troodos to the south

BIBLIOGRAPHY

This is a short list of selected books referred to by the contributors or recommended for further reading.

ALASTOS, Doros: Cyprus in History (London) 1976
BROWN, A and CATLING H. W.: Ancient Cyprus (Oxford) 1975
CATLING H. W.: Cypriot Bronzework in the Mycenaean World (Oxford) 1964
CATLING H. W: Cyprus in the Late Bronze Age, CAH (3rd ed.) Vol II part 2 (Cambridge) 1975
CHRISTODOULOU, D: The Evolution of the Rural Land Use Pattern in Cyprus (World Land Use Survey 2) (London) 1959
COBHAM, C. B: Excerpta Cypria (Cambridge) 1908, repr. 1969
CONSTANTINE PORPHYROGENITOS: De Administrando Imperio, Commentary (London) 1962
COOK, B. F (Ed.): Cypriote Art in the British Museum (London) 1979
CROISET, François: Le Conflit de Chypre (Brussels) 1973
DIKAIOS, P: A Guide to the Cyprus Museum (3rd ed.) (Nicosia) 1961
DIKAIOS, P: Enkomi Excavations 1948–1958 (Mainz) 1969
EKDOTIKE ATHENON SA. (Publishers): *Istoria tou Ellinikou Ethnous* (16 Vols, two in English) Athens
FOLEY, CHARLES: Island in Revolt (London) 1962
FOOT, SIR HUGH: A Start in Freedom (London) 1964
GJERSTAD, E: Swedish Cyprus Expedition Vol. IV part 2 (Stockholm) 1948
HACKETT, J: History of the Orthodox Church in Cyprus (London) 1901
HARBOTTLE, Brigadier M: The Impartial Soldier (Oxford) 1970
HILL, Sir George: A History of Cyprus (4 Vols) (Cambridge) 1940–1952
JENKINS, R. J. H.: Studies on Byzantine History of the 9th and 10th Centuries (London) 1970
KARAGEORGHIS, V.: Salamis (London) 1969
KARAGEORGHIS, V. and des GAGNIERS, J: La Céramique Cypriote de Style Figuré (Rome) 1974
KARAGEORGHIS, V: The Civilization of Prehistoric Cyprus (Athens) 1976
KARAGEORGHIS, V: Kition, Mycenaean and Phoenician Discoveries in Cyprus (London) 1976
KYPRIANOS: Chronological History of the Island of Cyprus (Venice) 1788
LUKE, Sir Harry: Cyprus Under the Turks — 1571–1878 (London) 1921 repr. 1969
MARITI, Giovanni (trans. Cobham): Travels in the Island of Cyprus (London) 1971
MAIER, F. G: Cyprus — from Earliest Times to the Present Day (London) 1968
MICHAELIDOU-NICOLAOU, I: Prosopography of Ptolemaic Cyprus (Studies in Mediterranean Archaeology Vol. XLIV (Gotenburg) 1976
MYERS, J. L: Handbook of the Cesnola Collection, Metropolitan Museum of Art (New York) 1914
MUSEUM OF FINE ARTS — Boston: Art of Ancient Cyprus (Boston) 1972
ORR, Capt. C. W. J.: Cyprus Under British Rule (London) 1971
PELTENBURG, E. J.: Recent Developments in the Later Prehistory of Cyprus. (Studies in Mediterranean Archaeology Pocketbook 16 (Gotenburg) 1982
POLYVIOU, P. G.: Cyprus — The Tragedy and the Challenge (London) 1975
POLYVIOU, P. G.: Conflict and Negotiation 1960–1980 (London) 1980
PRICE, Stanley: Early Prehistoric Settlement in Cyprus (British Archaeological Reports International Series 65) (Oxford) 1979
PURCELL, H. D.: Cyprus (London) 1969

ROBERTSON, Ian: Benn's Blue Guide to Cyprus (London) 1981

SAKELLARIOS, A. A.: *Cypriaka,* The Geography, History and Language of the Island of Cyprus (Athens) 1891

SJOQVIST, E.: Problems of the Late Cypriote Bronze Age (Stockholm) 1940

STANLEY-PRICE, N.: Early Prehistoric Settlement in Cyprus (British Archaeological Reports International Series 65 (Oxford) 1979

STYLIANOU, A. and J.: The Painted Churches of Cyprus (Nicosia) 1964 (now being reprinted in very extended form)

STYLIANOU, A and J.: History of the Cartography of Cyprus (Nicosia) 1980

TATTON-BROWN, V.: Cyprus B.C. 7,000 Years of History (Exhibition Catalogue) (London) 1979

THUBRON, Colin: Journey into Cyprus (London) 1975

VANEZIS, P. N.: Makarios: Faith and Power (London) 1971

VANEZIS, P. M.: Makarios — Life and Leadership (London) 1979

VERMEULE, C.: Greek and Roman Cyprus (Boston) 1976

VESSBERG, O.: Swedish Cyprus Expedition Vol. IV part 3 (Stockholm) 1956

XYDIS, Stephen A.: Cyprus, Reluctant Republic (The Hague) 1973

INDEX

296